EUROPE IN CRISIS

This book analyzes the European Great Recession of 2008–12, its economic and social causes, its historical roots, and the policies adopted by the European Union to find a way out of it. It contains explicit debates with several economists and analysts on some of the most controversial questions about the causes of the crisis and the policies applied by the European Union.

It presents the cases of Iceland, Greece, and Ireland, the countries that first declined into crisis in Europe, each of them in a different way. Iceland is a case study for reckless banking practices, Greece of reckless public spending, and Ireland of reckless household indebtedness. At least seven other countries, mostly from the peripheries of Europe, had similarly reckless banking and spending practices.

In the center of the book are the economic and social causes of the crisis. Contemporary advanced capitalism became financialized, de-industrialized, and globalized and got rid of the "straitjacket" of regulations. Solid banking was replaced by high-risk, "casino-type" activity. The European common currency also had a structural problem—monetary unification without a federal state and fiscal unification. The other side of the same coin is European hyper-consumerism. A new lifestyle emerged during two super-prosperous periods in the 1950s to 1960s, and during the 1990s to 2006. Trying to find an exit policy, the European Union turned to strict austerity measures to curb the budget deficit and indebtedness. This book critically analyzes the debate around austerity policy.

The creation of important supranational institutions, and of a financial supervisory authority and stability mechanisms, strengthens integration. The correction of the euro's structural mistake by creating a quasi-fiscal unification is even more important. The introduction of mandatory fiscal rules and their enforcement promises a long-term solution for a well-functioning common currency. These measures, meanwhile, create a two-tier European Union with a fast-track core. This book suggests that the European Union will emerge stronger from the crisis.

This book will be of particular interest to students and researchers of economics, history, political science, and international finance, but will also prove profitable reading for practitioners and the interested public.

Ivan T. Berend is Distinguished Professor in the Department of History at the University of California, Los Angeles, USA.

EUROPE IN CRISIS

Bolt from the blue?

Ivan T. Berend

Routledge
Taylor & Francis Group

NEW YORK AND LONDON

First published 2013
by Routledge
711 Third Avenue, New York, NY 10017

Simultaneously published in the UK
by Routledge
2 Park Square, Milton Park, Abingdon, Oxon OX14 4RN

Routledge is an imprint of the Taylor & Francis Group, an informa business

© 2013 Ivan T. Berend

British Library Cataloguing in Publication Data
A catalogue record for this book is available from the British Library

Library of Congress Cataloging in Publication Data
Berend, T. Ivan (Tibor Iván), 1930–
    Europe in crisis : bolt from the blue? / by Ivan T. Berend.
        p. cm.
    Includes bibliographical references and index.
    1. Recessions—Europe—History—21st century. 2. Europe—Economic policy. I. Title.
HB3782.B47 2012
330.94—dc23   2012016014

ISBN: 978-0-415-63722-0 (hbk)
ISBN: 978-0-415-63724-4 (pbk)
ISBN: 978-0-203-08470-0 (ebk)

Typeset in Bembo
by Keystroke, Station Road, Codsall, Wolverhampton

MIX
Paper from
responsible sources
FSC
www.fsc.org   FSC® C004839   Printed and bound in Great Britain by the MPG Books Group

CONTENTS

TABLES

PREFACE

The shock that the European Union is endangered inspired me to write this book. I belong to those generations that had dramatic and bitter personal experiences during World War II. I found personal happiness in the foundation and development of the EU, since it has been based on solidarity and eliminated the most dangerous conflicts within the continent. I considered the integration of Europe one of the greatest achievements in the entire history of the continent.

In recent years, politicians, economists, and journalists have made dramatic critical remarks about the inner cohesion of the EU and proposals for a lasting solution that would save the common currency and the Union. The solution strongly depends on a deep understanding of the roots and causes of the European crisis. This book, evidently with several other similar works, wants to serve this goal. I am in debate with many other analysts on the topic and convinced that the confrontation of views helps create a better understanding. There are very few world problems today that attract more public interest, and generate more questions and emotions than this crisis. This book also offers a complex description and analysis for the interested public.

The crisis is not ended yet and I finished the manuscript in early 2012. During the technical preparation of the publication in the summer of 2012, I was able to add only a few sentences to the text. I still hope, however, that the analysis and conclusions of this work that are based on the lessons of long historical developments are well-founded and will stand the test of time.

I am in debt to the History Department of the University of California Los Angeles. My Department organized two panel debates on the European crisis. As a member of these panels, I profited from the preparations and debates and got further incentive to write this book.

I am most grateful to the only reader of the manuscript, my wife Kati, who, as always, contributed a lot to the final version of this work through her questions and critical remarks. Lastly, I should like to thank Routledge, and personally the Editor, Robert Langham, and the Copy-editor, Ian Critchley, for their excellent work that made possible the exceptionally fast publication of this book.

Ivan T. Berend
June 1, 2012

INTRODUCTION

"Unprecedented freedom from cyclical instability"

The half-century after World War II exhibited cyclical trends in Europe. Beginning in the reconstruction years, Western and Southern Europe experienced history's most exuberant boom until the late 1960s–early 1970s. This was based on a new technological revolution, imported from the United States, signaled by atomic energy and the opening of the age of computer, transistor, and chips. Troubles started gathering from the late 1960s, with increasing inflation and slowing down. Two oil crises and a marked structural crisis generated the new phenomenon of stagflation and an economic downturn until the mid–late 1980s. Since that time, the communication revolution, signaled by the start of the personal computer age and followed by an endless wave of electronic inventions and innovations, generated a new boom period that lasted for an additional quarter-century.

This last period became the age of globalization, characterized by an exceptional increase of three-and-a-half times in trade from $1.7 trillion to $5.8 trillion between 1970 and 2000, and a unique financial and credit expansion. Foreign Direct Investments totaled $2.5 trillion by 2004, and daily financial transactions jumped from $15 billion to $1.3 trillion in the quarter-century after 1973.[1] Deregulations changed "the rules of the game" and the characteristics of the capitalist market economy. The morals of solid banking, together with trust in institutions, were lost. Gambling replaced a solid business attitude and increased both gains and risks. The boom culminated in the first years of the twenty-first century. The Gross Domestic Product of the most advanced EU-15 countries increased by nearly 58% between 1992 and

2005, while the per capita income grew by more than 60%. The six decades before 2008 exhibited an almost perfect Kondratiev long-wave model, with 25–30 years of upward trend, rapid growth, followed by 25–30 years of stagnation, or very slow growth. As Joseph Schumpeter explained the causes of the long economic cycles, it was indeed generated by a technological-communication revolution that made the old sectors obsolete and declining, while new sectors, based on the new technology, gradually emerged. This structural change or crisis may take 20–25 years.

However, the cycle was unusual in many ways, as well. The postwar upward trend was unique in its scale and unheard-of rapidity of growth, nearly 4% per annum for a quarter of a century. The new upward period at the turn of the millennium was peppered with regional financial crises and burst bubbles here and there. Michael Krätke speaks about a "short term erratic cycle of financial bubbles,"[2] with one major financial crisis every three years somewhere in the world economy: the American savings and loan crisis in the early 1990s, the Japanese banking and real estate crisis in the entire 1990s, the Mexican financial crisis in 1994–5, the Asian and Russian crisis in 1997–8, the Argentine crisis in 2001, and the 'dot.com bubble' in 2000–2.

The economies of the most advanced countries became strongly "financialized." The FIRE (finance, insurance, real estate) sector became more important than manufacturing. Households behaved like banks, banks behaved like hedge funds and they created profits without creating values. Technology was in permanent change and renewal. The age of personal computers was followed by an endless electronic revolution: mobile phones, smart phones, computer tablets, iPods, iPads, and several others. All these phenomena became signs of new major changes.

The economists, the new 'witch-doctors' of the age, developed the strong belief that they can monitor, control, and guide the economy. By monetary measures, increasing or decreasing interest rates, and pumping money or not into the economy, they thought they could guarantee sustained economic growth and eliminate crises. They thought and triumphantly declared that economic cycles belonged to history. Classical economics since Adam Smith already had the strong belief in the genuine harmony of the market, if it is not disturbed from outside. The market regulates itself and does not need outside intervention. If a crisis erupted, it must have been caused by exogenous factors. Transitory, mild recession may deepen into a depression only if incorrect outside intervention disturbs the market mechanism. Milton Friedman explained the cause of the Great Depression by blaming incorrect outside interventions that deepened what was otherwise a recession into a depression.

These ideas started flourishing during the unique postwar prosperity. As R.A. Gordon euphorically described: in the time of "unprecedented freedom from cyclical instability, some forty economists from Japan, North America, and Europe converged in London in 1967 to debate the question: 'Is the business cycle obsolete'?" Their conclusion was striking: modern economy has only "cycles of acceleration and retardation in the rates of growth," or "growth recession."[3] In other words, a recession-free economy in permanent growth sometimes accelerates and sometimes slows down the rate of growth.

These views, in spite of various economic turbulences since the late 1960s, remained dominant even in the early twenty-first century. One of the most influential economists of the Western world, Chicago School of Economics' Robert E. Lucas, Jr., who was the Nobel laureate in economics in 1995, started his presidential address at the annual meeting of the American Economic Association in 2003 with the following sentences: "Macro-economics was born as a distinct field in the 1940s as part of the intellectual response to the Great Depression. The term then referred to the body of knowledge and expertise that . . . would prevent the recurrence of that economic disaster. My thesis is . . . that macroeconomics . . . has succeeded: *Its central problem of depression-prevention has been solved,* for all practical purposes."[4] Government attempts to manage the economy are unnecessary and counterproductive. A new way of thinking became dominant in economics. "Economic theory is mathematical analysis. Everything else is just . . . talk," Lucas stated with high self-confidence in 1980.[5] A blind belief in market equilibrium, that troubles may come only from external shocks, and that even if imbalances happen, the market jumps back into equilibrium at the next period, became entrenched. Except for temporary imbalances, in Lucas' model "there was no place for stupidity, ignorance, or herd behavior. Economic slumps and mass joblessness were ruled out by assumption."[6] In his lecture of February 20, 2004, which carried the title "The Great Moderation," Ben Bernanke, Princeton economist and later United States' Federal Reserve Chairman, discussed in detail "why macroeconomic volatility declined?" He said he found the answer in "improvements in monetary policy."[7]

The OECD—the organization established in 1961 by 20 advanced countries to create an institution and forum for its members "to contribute to sound economic expansion" and "offer development assistance" (as the founding convention phrased it)—suggested in 1974: "The output of goods and services in the OECD area . . . nearly doubled in the past decade and a half . . . There is a strong presumption that the GDP of the OECD area may again double in the next decade and half . . . Governments, therefore, need to frame their policies on the assumption that the forces making for rapid economic growth are likely to continue and that potential GDP . . . might quadruple between now and the end of the century."[8] Limitless optimism and an almost religious belief in the free market system took strong root with the assumption that the wealth of nations can double in every one-and-half decades.

"The dominant theoretical model," argued eight economists in a joint study on the systemic failure of academic economics, "excludes many of the aspects of the economy that will likely lead to crisis. . . . The most recent literature provides us with examples of blindness against the upcoming storm." Meanwhile, "the mathematical rigor and numerical precision of . . . [the] tools has a tendency to conceal the weaknesses of the model." Economists generated an illusion of solid control and direction, although they "have an ethical responsibility to communicate the limitations of their models and the potential misuses of their research." The eight economists conclude that "a systemic failure of the economics profession" also contributed to the eruption and rapid spread of the crisis.[9]

The chief economist, Alan Greenspan, directed the American economy as the Federal Reserve's Chairman for about two decades. He was the main advocate of deregulation before the economic crisis. When the devastating Great Recession erupted, Greenspan was "shocked," and said during his Congressional hearing that he "still [did] not fully understand why [the financial-economic crisis] happened." "I do have an ideology," he stated. "My judgment is that free, competitive markets are far the unrivaled way to organize economies. . . . I made a mistake in presuming that the self-interests of organizations, specifically banks and others were such that they were best capable of protecting their own shareholders and their equity in the firms. . . . Indeed, a critical pillar to market competition and free markets did break down."[10]

During the quarter of a century of postwar prosperity—and then again in the good years of the 1990s—the advanced world lived in a myth, fueled by the ideologically motivated economics profession. In his article, "How did economists get it so wrong?", Nobel laureate Princeton economist Paul Krugman speaks about the "profession's blindness to the very possibility of catastrophic failure in the market economy. . . . Hard won knowledge has been forgotten . . . [because] economists, as a group, mistook beauty, clad in impressive looking mathematics, for truth . . . [because] economists fell back in love with the old idealized vision of an economy in which rational individuals interact in perfect markets."[11]

Indeed, hard-learned knowledge was denied or forgotten. The previously dominant Keynesian crisis management theory that was broadly applied and worked during the 1930s and after, but did not work in the price explosion that was politically generated in the 1970s–1980s, became disqualified by the triumphant neo-liberal school. As Lucas noted: "one cannot find good, under-forty economists who identify themselves . . . as Keynesian. . . . People don't take Keynesian theorizing seriously anymore."[12] Francis Bator, Harvard economist in the 1950s–1960s, was also forgotten. He gave a punctual analysis on "The Anatomy of Market Failure," listing imperfect information, inertia to change, and several other factors.[13] Neo-liberal economics eliminated the past.

As the Commission of the European Union stated in its analytical report on the crisis in 2009, "Before the crisis there was a strong belief that macro-economic instability had been eradicated. Low and stable inflation with sustained economic growth (the Great Moderation) were deemed to be lasting features of the developed economies." Moreover, the report added, "It was also widely believed that the European economy, unlike the United States economy, would be largely immune to the financial turbulence."[14]

In this intellectual environment, economists and governments did not recognize the clear signs of a coming crisis. To mention only one element, huge household expenditures in several countries, based on borrowed money, should have been a warning. Joseph Schumpeter in his monumental analysis of the economic cycles clearly stated: "Consumer's borrowing is one of the most conspicuous danger points in . . . prosperity, and consumer's debts are among the most conspicuous weak spots in recession and depression."[15] Huge public debts that in some cases reached and even surpassed the entire value of given countries' GDP, should have made us fearful. The enormous real estate bubbles that ballooned in several countries should have made us wary. A gigantic self-confidence, however, blinded the experts.

The clouds of a coming new thunderstorm already started gathering around the turn of the millennium, but the boom was still culminating in those years. The summer of 2007 became the turning point. In April, New Century Financial, an American subprime mortgage specialist, filed for bankruptcy. In June, two Bear Stearns-run hedge funds suffered huge losses and failed. In August, one of the largest American home loan providers, the American Home Mortgage, became bankrupt, followed in three days by three investment funds run by the French company BNP Paribas. In the same month, the German Sachsen Landesbank avoided bankruptcy only because it was rescued by the Baden-Württemberg Landesbank. The European Central Bank, to ease the liquidity crisis, was running to provide €156 billion to the eurozone banks in two consecutive steps. Similar steps were taken in the United States and Japan. In mid-August, the European Central Bank pumped another €47.7 billion into the money market.

Nevertheless, the real estate crash became unstoppable. Its first milestone was the collapse of the largest British mortgage bank, Northern Rock, in September 2007, and its nationalization that followed. In those years, over-expanded banking and crediting of the deregulated financial sector, reckless government and private spending beyond their means, and a growing real estate bubble paved the way toward the collapse. This did not become manifest, however, until the American financial crisis erupted and changed the entire financial market.[16]

The opening of the downward half of the long cycle might be symbolically connected with the collapse of Lehman Brothers in the United States in September 2008.[17] The company, which was highly involved in the subprime mortgage business, started sliding, and it lost 73% of its stocks value in the first half of 2008. On September 9, shares plunged by 45% to less than $8, and on September 15, 2008, the company filed for bankruptcy. On September 15, and then September 29, the New York Stock exchange suffered dual 500-point losses of −4.4% and −7.0%, respectively. Compared to the October 9, 2007 peak, the Dow Jones dropped from 14,164 to 6,469 point, a 54% decline. This reminded many people of the infamous "Black Thursday" in 1929. Prosperity ended with an international financial crisis.

1

VARIATIONS ON A THEME: ICELAND, GREECE, AND IRELAND'S ROAD TOWARD THE CRISIS

In September 2008, an international financial crisis exploded in the United States. In November of that year, Joseph Stiglitz, the Nobel laureate American economist, stated that "the financial crisis with a 'made in USA' label on it" flooded the globe.[1] Europe was not an exception. The continent declined into a crisis that was extremely deep in the peripheries of the South and parts of the East, but hardly missed any of the major countries of the continent. The crisis was universal, but differed country by country in scope and depth. This was the deepest economic shock since the Great Depression of the 1930s, but rather different in many ways. "Each [crisis] is a historical individual and never like any other," noted Joseph Schumpeter in his monumental work on the business cycle.[2] This is true and valid for 2008 as well. And how very clear it was that the financial crisis might also have the label, "made in Europe," on it. How surprising, however, that the roads toward the crisis varied tremendously. In this chapter I am going to present three totally different roads into the same universal and all-European economic crisis.

Variation no. 1: Iceland

Iceland's crisis was in many ways the most unique, the deepest, and also the very first in Europe. This small Scandinavian island with 320,000 inhabitants was not really on the map of the modern European economy for very long. Until the late twentieth century, the leading business of the country was fishing, which produced 40% of their exports and nearly 12% of the country's

GDP until the mid-1990s. Industry provided another 20%. The interior of the black volcano stone-covered country is mostly empty. Cultivable soil, as well as woods or vivid vegetation, hardly exists. About 92% of the population lived in mostly seashore urban settlements. The abundant geothermal energy resources, however, made Iceland a world leader in the role of renewable energy supply. Compared to the OECD, or to the European Union countries' roughly 6% share of renewable energy in their energy supply, Iceland had 73% in 2001.[3]

Iceland, which became independent from Denmark in 1944, had a strongly state-run economy with large state ownership, including the bulk of the financial sector. The government set the exchange rate, prices for agricultural products, the maximum rate of return for retail businesses, controlled imports, and influenced the allocation of foreign exchange. The country was rich: its per capita GDP surpassed the well-to-do Scandinavian average in the early 1990s. According to the United Nations Human Development Index,[4] Iceland was the 17th most developed country of the world in the early twenty-first century. Similarly to the other Scandinavian countries, the government built up a developed welfare system.

From 1990 on, Iceland broke with its natural isolation and state control, liberalized the economy, made capital movement free, and became integrated into the globalized world economy. In 1991, a privatization program introduced by a coalition of the Independence Party and the Progressive Party included the coastal shipping line, the printing industry, insurance business, fertilizer, Internet, and pharmaceutical companies, and most of all the big banks. By 2000, privatization was accomplished, and the state withdrew from several areas while deregulating the financial sector. The government gave up the fixed exchange rate system and turned to a floating rate. The Prime Minister pushed the Central Bank to lower interest rates.

As a Parliamentary investigation later concluded,[5] "the restraints in the fiscal policy were almost nonexistent. . . . The freedom of credit institutions to make riskier investments was greatly increased . . . inter alia with the authorization of investment banking in conjunction with the traditional activities of commercial banks."[6] As a consequence of privatization, the value of stocks at the Stock Exchange— established in the 1980s—increased by nine times. Compared to 1998, stock values had further increased by 329% by July 2007, which was unprecedented in an advanced country.

The first years of the twenty-first century became the scene of an unprecedented, radical transformation of Iceland. The main actors of this process were the three, now already private banks, the Kaupthing, Landsbanki, and Glitnir banks. In the five years after privatization, they went from being almost entirely domestic lenders to becoming major investment banks and international intermediaries. They opened branches in Britain and the Netherlands and offered 50% higher interest rates than local banks to attract deposits. While two-thirds of their financing came from domestic sources in 2000, by 2005 the role of domestic sources dropped to one-third, and foreign capital became the dominant factor. "Access to international financial markets was, for the banks, the principal premise for the growth. This was especially the case in the years 2004 to 2006."[7] The assets of the three banks totaled Icelandic krona (ISK) 1,451 billion in 2003, but increased to ISK 14,437 billion, roughly ten-times more, by 2008. Loans increased so breathtakingly that by 2007, they totaled 430% of the country's GDP. As an example of their international business, the three banks "fetched around 14 billion euro in foreign debt securities markets" in 2001, doubling their foreign securities. This action itself surpassed the country's domestic product for the year.[8]

This increase was so spectacular that, in less than a decade, the assets of these banks reached ten times the total GDP of the country. The three leading banks rose to the ranks of the world's 300 biggest banks. The share of banking in the production of the nation's income doubled and reached 9%, while fishing's role halved to 4% in those years.

The combined debts of the three banks, mostly from abroad, surpassed the country's GDP by six times. The leading three Icelandic banks started buying foreign assets, Danish and Norwegian banks, British companies, and retail chains.[9] Strangely enough, increased foreign lending received a special incentive when the international financial market started declining and getting loans became more difficult. Several banks turned to Icelandic banks after having failed to get credit elsewhere. Lending to foreign parties recklessly increased by 120% in the first six months of 2007, "magnifying the refinancing risk."[10] Meanwhile, the Icelandic banks turned to extremely risky short-term loans in order to be able to continue their expansion. In 2008, the banks became "unable to redeem" their investments from short-term credits "to meet their obligations."[11] Interest payment to foreign countries increased from 6% of the country's GDP in 2005, to 23% by 2008.

Icelanders, like most Scandinavians, well knew the name of Ivar Kreuger, the Swedish "Match King" who built a huge business empire on American loans in the 1920s. Kreuger owned match companies in 33 countries and had monopolies for producing matches in several others. He controlled two-thirds of the world's match production, owned mines, pulp and paper factories, banks, and iron ore mines, altogether about 200 companies, and the world's third largest gold deposit. In 1930, 64% of the entire trade on the Stockholm stock exchange was related to Kreuger's empire. He was a creditor of several governments, and provided a total of $350 million in loans to a dozen European countries, among others Germany, Hungary, and Yugoslavia. He combined reckless borrowing with reckless lending and investing. Kreuger became a multi-billionaire in a decade. When the American stock market collapsed in 1929, and borrowing new money became impossible, especially after the banking crisis in 1931, he was unable to get new money and repay old debts. On July 13, 1931, as the greatest sensation of the Great Depression, and also a symbol of it, Kreuger committed suicide. Ivar Kreuger's name is in Scandinavian text books, but the lessons of his type of business activity were seemingly forgotten—at least in Iceland.

The Icelandic banking industry followed in his footsteps. The dramatic, borrowing-based overexpansion of the three leading banks led to the dangerous relative decrease in the strength of the Central Bank of Iceland. "By the end of 2007 the nation's short-term debts were fifteen times larger than the foreign exchange reserves of the Central Bank of Iceland."[12] Additionally, several loans were made in foreign currencies, the British pound and euro, which made the "banking network as a whole highly vulnerable to external setback, such as sudden decline in credit lines to the country."[13] Nevertheless, the big banks flourished. The Kaupthing Bank alone had 150,000 British depositors, and it became the biggest lender for some of the biggest entrepreneurs in Britain. By 2007, the share of foreign deposits rose to 50%. The bank's liabilities were several times bigger than Iceland's GDP. The three big banks doubled their debts in one single year in 2005.

Iceland's credit rating was excellent, partly inherited from the previous years when the state stood behind the banks. Moody's Investor Service gave its 4th highest rating to the Icelandic banks even in 2007. They could sell securities on the international market, especially because—in spite of their good credit rating—they paid higher interests than their rivals.

The growth of the financial sector was extremely fast and lacked experienced experts and well-established state control activities. Although mostly legal in the deregulated environment, bank activities often touched the border of criminal actions. The owners of the banks were their biggest borrowers and they also appointed the board members. Small wonder that they enjoyed "abnormally favourable deals."[14] "The Icelandic banking system has been based . . . [on the principle of] financing of owners' equity. . . . They maximized the interests of the larger shareholders, who managed the banks, rather than running solid banks."[15] As Peter Gumbel put it, "Iceland: The Country that became a Hedge Fund."[16] This parallel was well based. The country's banking industry worked and made business with others' money. Compared to the assets and debts of the private banks, the Central Bank became unable to play the role of "lender of last resort." Its assets were not sufficient for that anymore.

The extreme growth of international financing activity fueled the Icelandic economy in the first few years of the 2000s. After 2001, when the stock market slid, savings moved into the real estate market. This tendency was helped by the government, which, seeking reelection,[17] rearranged the housing policy and allowed a maximum loan of 90% of the estates' value, increased the maximum mortgage loan from ISK 9 to ISK 15.4 million, and decreased the down-payment from 30% to 10% in 2003. Interest rates decreased from 5.1% to 4.15% in 2004–5—all contributing to the overextension of the banks.

International financing generated high prosperity. Growth rates were very high: from the last years of the 1990s, they reached between 4% and 5.5% per annum, often twice as much as the OECD average. In 2004 and 2005, growth rates rose to nearly 8% per year. Taxes were extremely low in comparison to the rest of Europe and especially Scandinavia: 25.7% of income (compared to the Swedish 48.6%). In the middle years of the first decade of the new century, wages increased by 7% per year, and unemployment was virtually non-existent (1%). Although house prices doubled in a couple of years, more homes were built between 2004 and 2008 than in the previous decade altogether. Interest rate and mortgage policy definitely contributed to the huge increase of household debts: from ISK 200 billion in 1992, they jumped to ISK 800 billion by 2004, and then to ISK 1,900 billion, more than nine times greater, by 2008. Stock market values increased by nine times between 2001 and 2007. Income levels surpassed the United States by 60%. Overexpansion characterized the entire economy of the island-state.

In 2006, the first frightening signs of an impending crisis appeared, and the need for government action became manifest. The bubble increased to "perilous proportions," as the Parliamentary report later stated, but the government remained passive. The country's credit rating from Fitch declined for the first time in early 2006, and other negative assessments from Merrill Lynch and the Danske Bank also became public. The Danish report, "Iceland: geyser crisis" clearly signaled the problems on March 21, 2006.[18] The OECD and IMF also "pointed out repeatedly that in recent years fiscal policy was not restrictive enough during the economic upswing."[19]

Interest rates started increasing for Iceland to borrow money. In order to limit the decline in the price of their shares, the big banks started taking loans and buying their own shares. By 2008, they bought 44% of their own shares for ISK 100 billion, and soon—by 2008—ISK 175 billion. The three big banks' debt at that time reached the extreme level of $200,000 per inhabitant of the country. On top of that, in the second half of 2007, the banks significantly increased their foreign lending, increasing it in six months by 120%. The Board of Governors of the Central Bank reported the danger to the government. Between February and May, the Board of Governors met with the Prime Minister and other members of the government five times, but actions did not happen and records were not even made of the meetings. The catalyst for the collapse was the 2008 international financial crisis that emerged from the United States. The milestone of the event was the Lehman Brothers bankruptcy. The international financial market was shocked and became immediately frozen. The Icelandic banks were unable to get fresh credit. Since their entire business was based on foreign credits, including the repayment of the old ones, they lost their liquidity and the ability to repay old loans in the fall of the year.

In this environment, Glitmir Bank's debt securities were maturing in October 2008, but the bank was unable to get new credit to repay. They also failed to sell assets. In September Bayerische Landesbank refused to extend their two loans. But in October, another €1.4 billion was coming due to pay. Deposits started flowing out from all the three big banks. Landsbanki did not allow its 300,000 British depositors to withdraw their money in early October. The British government declared financial war and froze the assets of Landsbanki in Britain, claiming 50% of the remaining GDP of Iceland as compensation.

The government provided €600 million for 75% of the bank's shares. The Central Bank sacrificed one-quarter of its hard currency reserves in a single action to rescue Glitmir, and then it was unable to assist Landsbanki. The latter closed its London branch on October 6. All three banks collapsed that month. Their assets dropped to 40% of their booked value, and ISK 7,000 billion disappeared. The government rushed to enact an Emergency Act, and it took control of all of the big banks on October 8. By November 2008, the krona lost 58% of its value, and the following year inflation increased to 19%, GDP declined by 7%, and unemployment increased to nearly 7%.

On February 1, 2009, Iceland's Geir Haarde government collapsed after 14 weeks of anti-government protests. President Ólufa Ragnar Grinsson appointed the new coalition government of the Social Democratic and Left-Green Movement, under the Premiership of Johanna Sigurdardottir. On April 9, 2009, new elections provided a majority to this coalition, which started consolidating the economy. The three big banks were split into old and new entities. The old deposits were transferred to the new state-owned banks. The government did not burden the taxpayers with the banks' losses, and the creditors had to swallow them. Moreover, the government eased the debt burden of the population by a huge amount, equal to 13% of the GDP. Meanwhile, uniquely in the advanced world, the government investigated about 200 protagonists in the bank crisis, including politicians, indicting about 90 of them. The former CEOs of Glitnir and Landesbanki, and several chief executives of the three biggest banks, are facing criminal charges.[20] The country filed the application for membership to the European Union. Reconstruction and recovery gradually started. After the 6.7% decline in GDP in 2009, in 2011 economic growth of 2.9% signaled a healthy recovery.

Variation no. 2: Greece

Greece emerged on a different road toward the same end. A characteristic episode explains a great deal about the proud sailing toward the crisis. In 1996, Athens lost its bid to hold the Olympic Games to Atlanta, United States. The application was sloppy and somewhat arrogant. Greece, where the ancient Games started, the application argued, had the right to organize the 1996 centennial Games. The Olympic Commission rejected the Greek application, maintaining that the country's infrastructure was not developed enough and that its pollution was too high for the Games. The over-commercialized Atlanta Olympics changed the atmosphere, and a new, much better prepared Greek application was successful in 1997.

In spite of the euphoric reception of the decision in Greece, Athens did not start preparations until almost 2000. To cope with the three-year delay, a new organization committee was formed, headed by Gianna Angelopoulos, and construction works started that year. An understandable but expensive rush of constructions and preparations started. This led to the bravura of being ready with everything, just one–two weeks before the opening of the Olympics. 150,000 staff members helped smooth operations during the Games. Against a possible terrorist attack, 50,000 policemen were mobilized. "Athens had to spend record sums on security."[21] On August 13, 2004, the XXVIII Olympics were opened with the participation of nearly 11,000 athletes from 201 countries.

This was a gigantic accomplishment. Athens built a new main Olympic Stadium with a retractable glass roof, an Olympic Sport Complex, and several sport complexes outside the capital city in Faliro and Helliniko. The old Athens airport was transformed into a sport center for fencing, volleyball, and basketball competitions, and a brand new modern airport, the Eleftherios Venizalos International Airport, was built. The city's transportation systems were dramatically modernized, with a 40-kilometer light-train system, connecting the suburbs to the center, and a 25-kilometer tram system connecting the sport centers and the port city of Pireus—where the sailing events were held—with the city. A new subway system modernized the obsolete transport facilities. An upgraded "Attiki Odos" toll-motorway encircled the city and connected to the neighboring settlements with new expressways. In the city center and traditional tourist locations, streets were transformed into pedestrian walkways. An Olympic village was built with nearly 2,300 apartments. A "nerve center" was established with 11,000 computers, 23,000 fixed telephone lines, and 16,000 TV and video devices with 6,000 kilometers of cabling. The original budget for the preparations was €2.5 billion, but soon it was increased to €4.6 billion. Outside the Olympic budget, €1.3 billion covered the transportation investments and €600 million went toward building the Olympic village. The government, however, lost control of the expenses, which, in the end, neared €10 billion—much above the planned amount—and consumed 4% of the country's GDP. The main trouble, however, was not just the accelerated expenses, but the fact that it was mostly *covered from foreign loans.* "The legacy of the Games is a public sector debt likely to hit 100% of GDP this year and the budget deficit forecast to reach 4%, well beyond the euro-zone 3% limit."[22] Indeed, the national debt, which totaled €168 billion in 2004, jumped to €262 billion.

The rebuilding and modernizing of Athens for the Olympic Games meant great progress for Greece. The British newspaper, *The Guardian*, predicted in 2001 that the country would flourish when it joined the euro-zone: "The historic achievement will put Greece at the heart of Europe and guarantees stability and prosperity."[23] Or, was just the opposite true? Greece, the poor Balkan country, exhibited the characteristic attitude of modernization-seeking backward nations. What John Kenneth Galbraith noted much earlier in his "Economics, Peace, and Laughter," looked liked it was tailored to Greece: "In the less developed lands the simple goal of an expanding production . . . is not a satisfactory guide. . . . Leaders have always known the importance of the concrete and visible expressions of national being. . . . There are certain things the modern state must have. These include a decently glittering airport, suitably impressive buildings of state, one or more multi-lane highways." Galbraith called this kind of policy "symbolic modernization."[24] A modernized Athens and the spectacle of the Olympics were to show, indeed, that "we are going to be at the heart of Europe."

In reality, ten billion euros, mostly borrowed, would have served investment projects to modernize the Greek economy much better, and with much higher return. The comparative figures of foreign trade in 2004 express a lot: while the EU-15 (most advanced) countries imports and exports total 32%

and 34% of their GDP, i.e. with some surplus, the Greek imports amount to 25% of GDP, but its exports only 8%. Greece is unique in this respect in Europe. The EU-27 countries' exports amount to 37% of their aggregate GDP. The Greek 8% reflects the total lack of competitive exports.[25] An Olympic Games is rarely profitable. The advanced and well-organized Canada suffered such a tremendous financial disaster by organizing the Games in 1976 that extra taxes were kept until 2005 to finance the losses.

The 2004 Athens Olympics, however, was only one of the characteristic episodes. This event expressed well the deeply rooted cultural problems of Greece. The European Union rushed to accept Greece in 1981 when the military dictatorship collapsed. The non-industrialized Balkan country with deeply rooted Balkan traditions of corruption and cronyism, a country that reached only 64% of Western Europe's average income level, was accepted by what was then called the European Economic Community, later to be known as the European Union. During the Cold War decades, Greece (and Turkey) were adopted by the Western Alliance as part and honorary members of the West. In reality, they were ages away from that status.

As foreign credits covered the huge expenses of the Olympic Games, credits fueled other elements of modernization as well. This country did not have a welfare system during the postwar dictatorship, and it started building it up mostly from the second half of the 1980s on, and during the 1990s. Greece at the time of the military junta was a poor country with a high poverty level, and only some groups loyal to the dictatorial governments, e.g., the police force and the army, had sufficient welfare institutions. Gro Hagermann calls this "cliental corporatism."[26] Otherwise, the extended families and local communities organized mutual help.

Social demands indeed accumulated, and the democratic governments had to cope with them. The country rushed to join "Social Europe" and built up the welfare institutions it had previously mostly lacked. Retirement age became 58 years for a great part of the labor force, but in certain categories was only 45 years (!). After 35 years of service—instead of after 40 years, as in most European countries—full pensions were paid. Public pension payments consumed 11.5% of the country's GDP. Wages that reached 5% of GDP in 1960, increased to 13% of it. "It is a paradox," as John Ifantopoulos noted, "that when the rest of the Western European countries started rolling back their welfare states under the pressure of the economic crisis of the early 1980s . . . Greece's shift of political environment impelled an opposite trend."[27]

Indeed, in 1980, Greece was far, far behind the West with regard to its social expenditures, which totaled only 10.2% of GDP, while in the EU-15 group as an average they reached 24% of GDP, but 28% in Norway and Denmark, and 31% in Sweden.[28] In 1983, the National Health Service was established. Hospitals were modernized and 180 primary health centers established. Healthcare expenditures increased from €4,000 million to €14,377 million between 1990 and 2006. By 1985, they represented 16% of GDP and 23% by 2005, thus elevating the country near the average EU-15 level. Healthcare was, nevertheless, only the second largest element of the increased welfare expenditures. Pension schemes consumed 66% of the social expenditure and 12% of GDP. Similarly to the expenditure for the Olympics, "social expenditures," maintains Manos Matsaganis, "were [also] allowed to spiral out of control."[29]

How could Greece swim against the stream and finance the building of an expensive welfare system? The increasing social expenditures were partly (roughly 20%) supported by the budget, i.e., through government borrowing, and mostly from employers' and employees' contributions, which also came partly from credits. That was possible since about $414 billion in credit flooded the country.

The economy started growing rapidly, about 4% per year, fueled by consumer spending. Wages increased twice as much as in the European Union, by an annual 5% since the country joined the EU. As a thorough analysis of the American Congressional Research Service disclosed, the engine of higher consumption was "largely fueled by easier access to credit," and the government's public investments. Between 2000 and 2008, government expenditures increased by 87%, while revenues increased only 31%. The total lack of fiscal discipline, along with corruption, and a non-taxable black economy—which, according to various calculations, represented 25–30% of the country's GDP—ruined the state household. According to some calculations, tax evasion costs the country $20 billion per year. About 30% of the Value Added Tax is never paid, and, according to Stergios Babanassis, tax evasion consumes 5–6% of the country's GDP. Corruption in Greece is much more widespread and higher than in other European countries. Among the world's 185 countries Greece's corruption index puts the country in 80th place.[30]

The deeply rooted Balkan culture, developed during the roughly 500 years of Ottoman rule, considers the state alien, hostile, an institution not to trust, but to cheat in any way possible. From 1981 onwards, as Greece was incorporated into the "West," contemporary Western consumerism was merged with the old habits. This generated a new cultural behavior that characterized governments and population alike: to spend and consume non-earned, non-existent incomes, thus spending from credits, i.e. assumed future income. The odd couple, made up of a population that was not paying taxes and over-spending governments, became ruinous for state financing and, in the long run, for the entire population of the country. In 2009, government expenditures reached 50% of GDP. Three-quarters of public spending covered wages and social benefits. This was a tragic and irresponsible practice since Greece became member of the European Union. This happened in spite of the fact that in 1997, the European Union's Stability and Growth Pact introduced rules to control and enforce the principles, adopted by the Maastricht Treaty in 1992, regarding the member countries' public finances. The so called "convergence criteria" required budget deficits no higher than 3% of GDP, and public debts not higher than 60% of the GDP of a given country. However, sanctions and penalties have never been used to enforce the regulations, and 25 of 27 countries in the Union, including Germany and France, at least during certain periods of time, did not respect these limits.

Greece was not eligible to join the common currency at its introduction in January 1999 because the country did not fulfill the required prerequisites. However, in his televised New Year's message, Prime Minister Costas Simitis announced on January 1, 2001: "Greece is already experiencing euro conditions. . . . Our inclusion ensures us greater stability and opens up new horizons."[31] When the euro banknotes were issued in 2001, Greece, indeed, was accepted and became a member of the euro zone.

In reality, Greece did not fulfill the requirements for joining. The government *falsified* the budgetary figures. As *The Guardian* reported the sensational news on November 15, 2004, the Greek government admitted that "it has not actually met the qualifying standard to join the euro zone at all. Revised budget data show that the Greek budget deficit has never been below 3% since 1999 as European Union rules demand."[32] The European Union investigations between 2004 and 2007 discovered that Greece had violated the rules since 2000 and falsified the statistical figures. Nevertheless, sanctions were still not introduced. The European Union accepted the government's promise to cut the deficit to 2.4% by 2007.[33]

Greece did not go far enough toward the Western economic, social, and cultural behavioral standards to be a solid and strong member of the community. Such a transformation may take generations. Its premature acceptance into the euro-zone did not bring greater stability to Greece; instead, in a decade, it brought greater instability to the euro. It is impossible not to recall Joseph Schumpeter's warning: From "recession, depression may easily develop. Whether it occurs or not . . . depends on accidental circumstances, such as the *mentality and temper* of the business community and the public, the prevalence of the *get-rich-quick morals*, the way . . . in which credit is handled in prosperity."[34]

While irresponsible borrowing and spending worked during years of prosperity, the American financial crisis of September 2008 stopped the cash flow and created an international liquidity crisis. All of a sudden, getting fresh money and credit became extremely difficult. Banks, companies, and governments lost their liquidity. The Greek crisis, however, did not come to the surface yet. This exploded only in 2009, as the consequence of a tremendous scandal after the elections in October, when the PASOK party of George Papandreu took office. One month after the elections, "he discovered the full extent of the deficit. . . . Mr. Papandreu shocked investors and politicians across Europe when he announced in December 2009 that his predecessor had disguised the size of the country's ballooning deficit."[35] The real figures, as he made them public, were 12.7% budgetary deficit and a €300 billion public debt, 110% of GDP. These figures surpassed the previous, falsified official statistics by more than *twice*. In April 2010, the European Union Statistical Office further revised the deficit and revealed that it was 13.6%.

Standard & Poor's had already downgraded the Greek credit rating to A- in January 2009. In December, Fitch Rating, for the first time in a decade, gave only a BBB+ rating for Greece, followed by Standard & Poor's BBB- rating a few days later. By April 2011, Greece's debt rating declined to "junk rate" level. Lower ratings made borrowing more expensive because creditors developed doubts about the borrowers' capacity to repay. The increased risk led to higher interest rates. In January 2010, the interest rate on Greek two-year government bonds were 3.47%, by July it had increased to 9.37%, in another half year to 12.27%, and by July 2011 to an unheard of 26.65%. As Papandreu confessed in April 2010, the "Greek economy is a sinking ship." The new Prime Minister openly recognized that "Greece was riddled with corruption, which he claimed was the main reason for its economic woes." His Minister of Finance added: "tax collection . . . collapsed almost totally" because of corruption.[36]

Indeed, Greece had to borrow €50 billion to pay its annual bill that year, but the country was unable to do it. A series of more and more severe austerity measures were forced on the country as a prerequisite for assistance and a bailout. Violent public demonstrations flooded Athens. The significantly—from 19% to 23%—increased sales taxes (VAT) and the newly introduced taxes on real estate, alcohol, higher salaries and pensions, together with the reduced level of tax-free income (from €12,000 to €5,000) augmented consumer prices by nearly one-quarter and reduced income seriously. Wages in the state sector were cut in some cases by 15%, and in others by as much as 40%, and in the private sector by 14% during 2010 and 2011. The 13th and 14th month salaries, whereby the state, in certain public sector offices, paid an additional 1–2 months salary, were eliminated. For every five employees who retired, only one was employed. High pensions were cut by 35% and the pension age increased.[37] Until 2015, 150,000 people have to be dismissed from the public sector's 750,000 employees. People, virtually from one day to the next, lost what they had gained in the previous decades. The government became paralyzed and a deep political crisis emerged. Small and relatively far-away Greece shocked the entire European Union and the common currency.

To avoid bankruptcy, the European Union and the International Monetary Fund put together a bailout fund, created a $1.4 trillion fund to help out Greece and some other, mostly Mediterranean euro-zone states in financial trouble. Greece, with its 11 million inhabitants out of the 500 million citizens of the European Union, and representing only 2.6% of the aggregate GDP of the euro-zone of 17 countries, endangered the Western economies. The euro, the common currency of the European Union, an economic superpower, was devaluated by the market from €1=$1.5 to €1=$1.2.

The European Union was strong enough to solve the problem by one single financial action, but it would have transferred billions in German and French taxpayers' money to countries showing irresponsible fiscal behavior. Because of the huge political risk within the strong countries, this drastic action was rejected.

History matters. Greece has a bad record regarding indebtedness and repayment. It defaulted on the repayment of loans quite a few times in the nineteenth century: in 1843, 1860 and 1893. Greece reached only 44% and 38% of Western income levels in 1913 and 1950, respectively. Education was backward, industry hardly existed. By 2008, after three decades of EU membership, the manufacturing industry produced only somewhat more than 9% of the country's income, and 18% of its exports. The country did not produce durable goods, so these needed to be imported. True, the country increased its GDP by 4.5-fold between 1950 and 1980, but modern, competitive industry did not emerge. Moreover, in the common European market without protective tariffs, a de-industrialization followed from the 1980s on. Characteristically enough, foreign direct investments (FDI) did not rush to Greece.

Greece, based on old traditions, developed a one-sided service economy. Two service branches, tourism and shipping, produce nearly 80% of the country's income. The on average 16 million tourists that visit Greece annually produced more than 18% of the Greek GDP in 2008 and created jobs for 840,000 people, 19% of the labor force. Shipping is the main industry, with more than three-thousand vessels, with 163.4 million tons of deadweight capacity representing 18% of world shipping capacity. Greece ranks number one in the world in its tanker and bulk carrier fleets, number four in container ships, and altogether fourth in merchant shipping. From the mid-1980s, when prosperity returned to the world economy, income increased from both sectors.

Economic modernization in other sectors, however, hardly progressed. The fixed capital formation that reached 32% of GDP in 1979, declined to 21% in a few years after the country joined the EU. Postwar Greece was a backward country. In 1958, its per capita GDP reached only 42% of the just established European Economic Community's average level. Growth, however, became rather rapid between 1950 and 1970: 6.5% per annum, and 4.9% during the 1970s. At the time of the country's acceptance into the European Union in 1981, its income level amounted to 64.4% of the EU-9 countries' average. After slow growth during the 1980s (1.6% per annum), an annual 4% followed between 1994 and 2007. As a consequence, by 2008, the country's per capita income level totaled 94.8% of the EU-27 average.[38]

In May 2010, *The Economist* reported that "the unprecedented prosperity enjoyed by most Greeks during the past decade . . . reflected the windfall of cheap euro interest rates, which stoked an exuberant consumer market, complete with smart cars, foreign travel and personal trainers."[39] By 2004, there were 368 cars for every 1,000 inhabitants in the country, virtually the same level as that of the West, whose per capita income was nearly twice as high. Mentioning "most Greeks" was certainly an exaggeration since the poverty level was relatively high, especially among the older generations and pensioners. About 22% of them have incomes below the poverty level. This share is 28% for those who are older than 75. Nevertheless, consumption increased, and in a country with half of the United States' per capita income, the cost of living reached 84% of the expensive New York level by 2008.

Budget deficits and public debt rapidly increased. Before joining the EU, the budget deficit was only 2% of GDP, but by 1990, it had reached 16%. Public debt increased from 22% of GDP to more than 100% between 1979 and the 1990s. Public debt in "its main part was financed through increased government borrowing. . . . Increase in 'non-productive' Greek public consumption and personnel expenditure are not followed by increase in Greek GDP. . . . The major fiscal expansion undertaken by Greece between 1975 and 1990 . . . was mainly directed to personnel and 'non-productive' public consumption purpose . . . [thus] the expansion . . . has contributed . . . to the prolonged economic stagnation."[40]

When the international financial crisis hit the world economy in the fall of 2008 and new borrowing became extremely difficult and much more expensive, when tourist and shipping incomes decreased significantly—in 2009 by 15%—the boat of the over-spending, over-consuming, debt-ridden Greece started sinking. In 2010, building activities decreased by 73%, retail sales by 9%, and the unemployment rate jumped to 36% at the end of 2010. The tragedy was unstoppable, but it would have been multiplied without outside intervention and the sacrifice of other countries' taxpayers' money. The euro-zone countries ran to help, though not without hesitation, and in 2011 they agreed to three comprehensive packages, first to fill the gap and then to assure that Greek repayments happened on time. The third package, signed on October 27, 2011, increased the European rescue fund, the European Financial Stability Facility, to €1 trillion ($1.4 trillion) to save financially troubled member countries, and "the most notable achievement was to forge an agreement to write down the Greek debt held by the private sector by 50%."[41]

The Greek tragedy, however, was not yet at its end. The self-devastating idea of having a referendum on the life-saving Brussels bailout agreement, followed by the withdrawal of the agreement, the resignation of Prime Minister Papandreu, and then domestic political blackmailing, maneuvering, and bargaining, caused a few days of political drama (or farce) that ended with the formation of a transitory national unity government led by Lucas Papademos, the former Governor of the Bank of Greece, and later Vice-President of the European Central Bank between 2001 and 2010. Although the government is backed by three of the four political parties, the task is tremendous, and a decades-long crisis, with Greece dropping out of the euro-zone, is still among the possibilities.

In January 2012, roughly two months before a huge new repayment was due, and in a situation where the country's debt totaled roughly 160% of GDP, Greece, practically bankrupt, was unable to repay the matured securities without a new €30 billion ($38 billion) IMF and EU bailout. Although the debtors were already forced to accept the loss of about 70% of their investments, it became clear that in the best case, it may decrease the burden of the Greek debt payments by €100 billion, but lower the indebtedness level to a still unacceptable 120–130% of GDP by 2020. Meanwhile, until 2014, the country still needs about €200 billion of outside help for repayment.[42] The country is in a deep recession and its GDP during the last quarter of 2011 declined by 7%, and the forecast of the European Commission for 2012 is still more than 4% decline. Before a new major Greek deadline to pay $19 billion in March, in mid-February 2012, the finance ministers of the EU decided to provide a second huge bailout and pay $40 billion from the planned $171 billion.[43] Two dramatic elections and a new EU intervention saved the day in the spring of 2012. The sword of Damocles, the possibility of default, still hangs above the country with the prospect of dropping out from the euro-zone and the EU.

Variation no. 3: Ireland

The Icelandic crisis was caused by overextended and hazardous bank activities, based on reckless international borrowing and extensive lending of the borrowed money. The Greek crisis was the outcome of a recklessly spending state, based on increased borrowing. Ireland represents a third type of road toward the crisis. The Irish crash was caused by reckless private borrowing and spending, the ballooning and then bursting of an oversized real estate bubble.

Ireland was the most successful economic performer in the European Union. When accepted by the Union in 1973, Ireland was a relatively backward country, dependent on Britain, with one-sided economic ties. The European Union introduced its cohesion policy and started to pump aid into backward regions, including all of Ireland. From the mid-1990s, the Irish economy grew by a robust 6%–12% per annum.

Foreign direct investment rushed to Ireland, and its stocks totaled more than $217,000 million. Compared to the country's GDP, it was the highest in the entire Organization for Economic Co-operation and Development (OECD) group of 34 countries (except Luxembourg), reaching 140% of its average. Huge capital inflow, low interest rates, and then a 50% tax cut pumped investments into the economy.

In 1973, when Ireland joined the European Union, its per capita GDP of $7,023 was only 37% of the (later) euro-zone countries' average of $19,192. By 2005, the per capita GDP of Ireland had increased by seven times (!). Meanwhile the euro-zone's income level grew only by 67%; consequently, the Irish per capita GDP ($49,220) surpassed the euro-zone's average ($32,130) by 53%.[44] Ireland became one of the richest European countries. Between 1996 and 2006, the increase in the real disposable income of the Irish population was more than twice the average European Union-15 level.

During the first quarter-century after joining the European Union, export-led growth, spurred by huge multinational direct investments in the most modern sectors of the economy, was the engine of growth. From the last years of the 1990s, however, domestic demand of the enriched population took over and pushed the economy ahead. The psychological impact of this unparalleled transformation on the Irish population was tremendous. A couple of generations before, the country was poor. In the mid-nineteenth century, one million people died of starvation and another million emigrated, and the country's population decreased by roughly one-quarter. That was the greatest population tragedy in nineteenth-century Europe. The poor and dependent neighbor of rich England, incorporated into the United Kingdom, and serving as its labor source until World War I, became richer than England in three generations. This generated a historic euphoria. People wanted to enjoy and exploit this great historical luck, and they started consuming and buying in a way that generations of Irish people had only dreamed about.

They sought, first of all, to move into their own houses, and the housing business started flourishing. The unlimited bank lending to property developers created a huge building boom, and as always in such a boom, speculators wanted to make fortunes and contributed to extreme house price increases. The rising boom was helped by the government policy of eliminating real estate taxes and making mortgage loans tax-deductible, which—together with low interest rates—attracted investments in housing. As a special factor, the European Union's monetary policy also contributed to the Irish real estate boom. The EU's uniform interest rate served the large economies well and was slightly restrictive in Germany and France, but it became too loose for smaller countries such as Ireland. Compared to the so-called Taylor Rule,[45] the gap between the real and ideal interest rates was −0.46 in France and −0.87 in Germany, but +3.38 in Spain and +5.17 in Ireland. The interest rates were too low for Ireland, and according to certain calculations assuming "ideal" interest rates, house prices would have increased only by 57%, a small portion of the increase that really happened.[46]

The redevelopment of Dublin, especially its 4th district, signaled an unprecedented real estate boom. University College Dublin sold two pieces of its landed estates, the veterinary surgeon site in 2005 and another area in 2006, for €85 million and €95 million per acre (€212 million and €240 million per hectare), respectively. As one extreme example, the property tycoon Sean Quinn paid €379 million for seven acres of land in an exclusive part of Dublin to destroy hotels and build fashionable shopping malls, luxury shops, and apartments. That was the highest amount paid for land in Europe to date. Similar to the seventeenth-century Dutch tulip speculators,[47] the Irish developers also believed in an unending price increase. Banks, too, held to this belief. The Anglo-Irish Bank, for example, increased its market capitalization ten-fold after 2000, basing its success mostly on its property-loan portfolio.

Major suburban developments started in Wicklow, Kildare, Meath, Louth, and Carlow. Between 1980 and the 1990s, 23,000 houses were completed per year, but between 2000 and 2006, when the boom culminated, 75,000 units were built annually. In 2006 alone, 93,000 units were completed. From 1993, house prices started increasing, but in the few years between 2000 and 2006, house prices jumped by 300% in constant prices, and in Dublin—certainly unprecedented in history—by 500%. Houses became highly overvalued: according to some calculations, by 20% to 40% by 2006. Residential mortgage lending grew by an annual 25% in the early 2000s, and increased between 2003 and 2007 from 40% to 65% of GDP.

The Anglo-Irish Bank, the Bank of Ireland, and the Allied Irish Bank took short, three-month interbank loans to provide more and more long-term mortgage loans. Financing long-term investments by short-term loans is the most reckless business behavior. Profit from long-term investments comes much later than the deadline for repayment of the short-term credit. In such a situation, repayment is made through fresh loans. In spite of the high risk, this system worked because low-rate loans flooded the country and its population. An unprecedented 60% of bank lending was concentrated on property.

The newly enriched population became intoxicated by the new possibilities and started spending recklessly. Household indebtedness jumped from 60% to 160% of GDP, with 80% of personal credits secured by property. All these are shocking and unique figures. Ireland realized the so-called "American dream" better than the United States: 75% of all households were living in owner-occupied houses, compared to 67% in the US in 2009. A great part of construction, nevertheless, served investment purposes. About 115,000 units were holiday houses, and 230,000 units could not find buyers and remained vacant in 2006.

The housing boom elevated Ireland's economy. The share of housing in employing the population almost doubled and increased to 20–30% of the work force, 12% directly in construction. These are figures that usually represent the entire industrial population in advanced countries. While in 1996 the construction sector represented 5% of GDP, by 2006 it was already 10% of it. Residential construction consumed 80% of the total growth in the value of investments in the early 2000s.

When housing prices run amok, the income level of the population cannot follow suit at a certain point. This happens in every bubble. That point arrived in Ireland in 2006. There was not sufficient demand any longer for the extremely expensive houses. The skyrocketing house prices stopped increasing further, and because of the decreasing demand, even dropped by 18%. In 2007, existing house prices—which had increased three times during the boom period—started declining faster than new house prices. By July 2008, house prices declined in real terms by more than 9% in a year. After 2002, disposable income no longer followed the rise of prices and interests. The bubble started dangerously shrinking, but it did not burst yet.

When the American financial crisis hit Europe hard, and new credits were no longer available, Irish house prices dropped by half and bank shares by 90% in the fall of 2008. The Irish banks were overextended. Their liabilities were equal to 304% of the country's entire GDP, the third highest in Europe. When liquidity was lost, repayment of such an amount became impossible. Approved mortgage loans decreased by 73%. In June 2009, 40% of the rise in house price from 2001 to 2007 was already lost. The Irish Stock Exchange dropped by more than 80% from April 2007 to February 2009, from the 10,000 point to 1,987 point. From super-prosperity, Ireland fell into severe crisis. The recklessly lending banks lost their liquidity and suffered tremendous losses. The value of their shares had halved by May 2008. In 2009, national income declined by 7.1%, and unemployment reached 13% and later 15%. GDP per head dropped by nearly 20% from €43,000 to €35,000.

As a symbol of the changed destiny of the country, the one-time richest man in Ireland, Sean Quinn, filed for bankruptcy in January 2012. Emerging from a farmer's family, he started his business in 1975 by borrowing 100 Irish pounds. During the high-flying prosperity years, Quinn built up an international empire. The Quinn Group, a holding company, owned 70 companies in 14 countries, employing 6,000 people. He used a private jet and helicopter. Everything was built on borrowed money, which he used for gambling on derivatives, speculation with "contacts for difference," or asset price changes. As he said in an interview in 2005, "I was never happy with what we had, and I was always looking for new opportunities." In 2008, *Forbes Magazine* estimated his personal wealth at $6 billion. The financial crisis, however, burst the "Quinn bubble." He "gambled away his fortune," probably losing everything (except some hidden assets). The nationalized Anglo-Irish Bank tried to regain €2.8 billion from him. "Mr. Quinn personified Ireland's boom. Now, he has come to personify its bust."[48]

People were traumatized. As reported in the spring of 2011, "treatments at suicide prevention centers increased by a third last year."[49] Two dramatic bank runs de-capitalized the Irish banking system. In 2008, a three-week run led to the withdrawal of €4 billion in deposits, but a second run in late 2010 caused a deposit loss of €67 billion. The top six Irish banks lost more than €90 billion after the crisis erupted. Ireland had to bail out its banks with €64 billion and a European and IMF rescue package of €85 billion. The government bought €2 billion in shares from the Bank of Ireland and the Allied Irish Bank, and €1.5 billion from the Anglo Irish Bank. The total funding of the six largest banks of the country by the European Central Bank and the government totaled about €150 billion. That was still not enough, and another €24 billion was needed to remain solvent.[50] With drastic austerity measures, the budget deficit was strongly cut and a very modest, slow recovery started in 2012. In a gloomy mockery of market capitalism, while the banks' gains were privatized, the losses became socialized.

In different ways and forms, Iceland, Greece, and Ireland followed suicidal fiscal and economic policies, with irresponsible borrowing and lending. They dug the huge hole of depression for themselves. Although they were among the very first to fall into that hole, they were not alone. Most of Europe soon followed.

2

THE FALL—OF 2008: FROM THE FINANCIAL CRISIS TO THE CRISIS OF THE EURO

The exploding financial crisis

After the collapse of Lehman Brothers in the United States in September 2008, panic, liquidity, and financial crisis spread like wild fire throughout the globe. It is hard to understand that about 2.5% of American financial assets, such a marginal amount of money absorbed by the American subprime mortgage failure, had the potential to destroy the entire financial system of the world. How could it shock the European Union and the euro-zone countries? Even in the deep crisis of 2011, six members of the 17 euro-zone countries—France, Germany, Austria, the Netherlands, Finland, and Luxembourg—still had the best AAA credit ratings, (although France and Austria lost theirs in January 2012). These six countries, with their combined $5,486.5 billion GDP, represented nearly half of the euro-zone's $11,818.5 billion aggregate GDP. Their government debts are between 60% and 80% of their GDP, and three of them have budget deficits as low as 1% and 2% of their respective GDPs, while two others have less than 4%. Germany has a current account surplus that "rivals China's and the Netherlands and Austria also exhibit surpluses."[1] The core of the euro-zone was thus still economically stable and healthy in the middle of the deep crisis.[2] How and why did the financial crisis flood Europe and the euro-zone?

Digging deeper into the facts regarding Europe, the first thing one finds is that not only Iceland, Greece, and Ireland marched fast and steadily from the turn of the century on toward a self-inflicted economic crisis, but several other countries did as well. The crisis was not "made in the USA" alone, but in several countries in Europe. A year before the collapse of Lehman Brothers, on September 17, 2007, thousands of agitated people were queuing in front of the various branches of the British Northern Rock Bank wanting to withdraw their deposits. The Bank of England rushed to extend a $4.4 billion credit line. The bank rush stopped only two days later when the Bank of England guaranteed 100% coverage for deposits.[3] Housing bubbles had grown huge in Spain and Latvia. When a housing bubble bursts, it generates an indebtedness crisis. In this respect Ireland's example is instructive: in 2007, the country had an outstanding record on government debt, which totaled only 25% of GDP. However, when the housing market collapsed, several banks lost huge amounts of money, and the government had to run to save them. This action cost 42% of the national output. As a consequence, the debt burden rose dramatically to 112% of GDP by 2011.

Indebtedness became dangerously high in Italy and Portugal, as well as in some of the most successful transition countries in Central and Eastern Europe, such as Hungary and Latvia. Based on huge capital inflows, the latter countries accumulated tremendous amounts of debts, including household debts. Countries, such as some of the peripheral countries of the South and the so-called transition countries of the East, which all of a sudden became consumer societies with a significantly increasing well-to-do layer of society, hungry to buy durables, cars, and new homes, and to make exotic foreign tours used credits excessively to spend. Credit was virtually unlimited and cheap, and it was difficult to resist the temptation. The introduction of the common currency contributed significantly to the credit boom in the early 2000s. The cost and risk of transferring capital decreased, and in several countries, such as Ireland and Spain, the interest rates decreased as well.

A series of European Union and euro-zone countries experienced a similar economic crisis to Iceland, Greece and Ireland. It is remarkable that most of the countries that were hit by the crisis first were located on the Southern or Eastern peripheries of Europe. All of the sudden, Greece and Ireland were not alone in trouble, but together with a group of other countries. The world started calling them PIIGS, a sardonic acronym for Portugal, Ireland, Italy, Greece, and Spain, the "sick men" of the European Union and the euro-zone. At first glance, they were stable members of the European Union. Italy belonged to the founding six, Ireland joined in 1973, Greece in 1981, Spain and Portugal in 1986. Most of all, these countries were considered to be part of the rich "Western world," and in 2006 their combined per capita GDP amounted to 94% of the level of the so-called EU-15, the 15 richest West European Union countries.[4]

Why did the entire Southern or Mediterranean Europe decline into crisis? Searching for an answer, we have to turn first to history. History matters. The crisis-ridden PIIGS countries had one conspicuous similarity: as peripheral countries, they were all latecomers to industrialization and economic modernization. Their income levels reflected characteristic peripheral backwardness. Instead of 94% of the West European core's level, as in 2006, their combined per capita GDP amounted to only 57% of the West European average before World War I, roughly a century before the 2008 crisis. Greece and Portugal had only 44% and 37% of the West European average at that time. Their position even somewhat declined by 1950, but then a rapid catching-up process emerged from the 1970s–1980s on.

As Table 2.1 shows, the Mediterranean periphery was rather backward until the mid-twentieth century, or even until the last third of it. Peripheral backwardness in the not too distant past had an impact on today's already more advanced countries. Their economies were less stable than the established advanced core countries' of Europe. Economic growth was often generated by foreign investments to subsidiaries, while the more traditional domestic sectors of their economies were weak. The features or elements of a kind of so-called "dual economy" were often present and made for certain instability.

Peripheral backwardness is a complex phenomenon and is always combined with institutional weaknesses. Modern institutions were definitely introduced within the European Union, but their strength and practice were often weakened by social and behavioral traditions. Clientalism and corruption always accompany backwardness. Avoiding tax payments is considered to be a virtue because, in most cases, the state in peripheral countries was considered to be an enemy, not a protector. This problem was painfully present in today's Greece, where tax collection, as discussed in Chapter 1,

TABLE 2.1 GDP/capita in the South European periphery—compared to Western Europe, 1913–2006[5]

Year	Portugal	Ireland	Italy	Greece	Spain	Western Europe	PIIGS as % of West
1913	1,354	2,733	2,506	1,621	2,255	3,704	57
1950	2,069	3,446	3,502	1,915	2,397	5,013	53
1973	7,343	6,867	10,643	7,655	8,739	12,159	68
1998	2,929	18,183	17,799	11,268	14,227	18,183	82
2006	19,889	38,850	28,094	29,518	27,400	30,438	94

virtually collapsed. In January 2012, the Greek government published a list with more than four thousand names of leading tax evaders, financiers such as Tolis Voskopoulos and Pavlos Psomiadis, who had stolen $19 billion from the state. In Italy "it's absurd that only 0.17% of taxpayers (76,000 people) declare an income over €200,000 when about 210,000 luxury cars are sold in Italy every year."[6] The multi-billionaire Prime Minister Berlusconi was long admired for his skill in tax evasion. Social networking remains a strong substitute for efficient institutions. Citizens' discipline and a smoothly working civil service bureaucracy are almost always weak. Offices are packed with unnecessary employees of clients and friends. Non-taxable "black economy" represents about 25–28% of the Greek, and 22–26% of the Italian economy. Tax evasion in Greece totals about €13 billion per year, 7–8% of the GDP. About 30% and 22% of the VAT tax is not paid in Greece and Italy, respectively. These two countries, respectively, are placed 80th and 69th among 185 countries regarding the corruption index.[7]

Thrift and the central value of work, the so-called Protestant ethic, are not characteristic. In several places, the former hidalgo-noble attitude—that is, a mentality among the gentry inherited from the feudal society—preserved the habits of careless spending based on borrowed money. Behavioral habits and deeply rooted values change much more slowly than the economy and the living standard.

Most of all, former peripheral countries that became rich in the recent few decades have created a huge hunger for lavish consumption. A strong attempt to catch up with the traditionally advanced countries' living standard became characteristic (as discussed in Chapter 4). In other words, the peripheral past is in many ways present in countries that have already caught up with the most advanced ones.

The PIIGS group as a whole is much more significant and dangerous for the entire European stability than the "pioneering" bankrupts such as Iceland, Greece and Ireland. The mere facts are rather telling: Iceland (320,000 inhabitants), Greece (11,319,000), Ireland (4,481,000), even together with Portugal (10,563,000) are relatively small countries with limited economies. Their combined GDP totaled $710.1 billion before the crisis. Spain, however, has 41.1 million inhabitants, and a GDP of $838.7 billion. Italy, with 60,483,000 inhabitants, has the third largest economy in the euro-zone, and the eighth largest economy in the world. Italy's GDP of $1,644.3 billion amounted to one-fifth of the euro-zone aggregate GDP, and it was bigger than the other PIIGS countries' GDP combined. A crisis in the Mediterranean endangers the entire Union.

What exactly happened on the Mediterranean periphery?

Portugal

In spite of the 2,580-kilometer (1,600-mile) distance between them, Greece at the eastern end of Southern Europe, and Portugal at the western end, exhibited certain similarities. In the case of Portugal, the economy was genuinely weak. In 1986, when the country was accepted into the European Union, its $8,904 per capita GDP level was only 57% of the West European average. By 2000, it increased to 65%, but economic growth slowed down in the early 2000s to an average 0.7% per annum. Unemployment rose to 10% in 2009. In 2005–7, Portugal had the 6th lowest purchasing power and the 5th lowest quality of work in the EU-27 group. Its global competitiveness index was only 43rd among 134 countries in the world, worse than the bulk of European countries.

As an interviewee said, "Two, three, five years ago, you can buy a car, you can buy a house, you can buy everything, because the banks give you money." [8] During the slow growth period, as reported, people bought on credit and the government spent from loans: private and public debts accumulated in Portugal "to finance its western life style."[9] For years, during which the clouds of economic trouble gathered, and for years of galloping budget deficits that reached 9.4% of the GDP in the summer of 2010, the governments always maintained that "we are not Greece."[10] Prime Minister José Socrates claimed that the country did not need outside financial help and could solve its problems alone. When his austerity plan was rejected by the Parliament, he resigned. Meanwhile, debt levels totaled 76% of GDP in 2009, by 2010–11 surpassed 100% of GDP, and in 2012, it amounts to as much as 112%. The economy spiraled out of control. The economy declined by 2.7% in 2009, but, unlike Greece, achieved some growth in the following years. In November 2011, it was forecast that public and private debt would reach 360% of GDP in 2012, much worse than in Greece. Bond yields of 5.8% increased to 8.54% in a few months, and then Portuguese government bonds were rated at a junk bond level. Consequently, for new loans, 13%, and in some short periods even 17%, interest had to be paid, the second highest in Europe.

In early 2011, the country was on the verge of bankruptcy, and in the spring Portugal became the third euro-zone country, after Greece and Ireland, to be bailed out by the IMF and the European Union, to the tune of €80 billion. In November 2011, as a historical freak, the new Prime Minister, Pedro Passos Coelho, made an official visit to Angola, the poor former Portuguese colony where two-thirds of the population lives on less than $2 per day. However, Angola became an oil-producing country with large reserves. Coelho stated: "we should take advantage of the moment of financial and economic crisis to strengthen our bilateral relations." He added, in a more open way, "Angolan capital is very welcome." President José dos Santos of Angola answered with satisfaction: "Angola is open and available to help Portugal face this crisis."[11]

Italy

The country—a peripheral, relatively backward and freshly unified country in the late nineteenth century—during the postwar economic miracle became one of the founders of the European Union, and one of the richest that joined the core of the Union.

Italy's previously rapid growth, however, slowed down by almost half during the 14 years around the turn of the century. The years between 1992 and 2005 were characterized by stagnation. Regional differences, a long unsolved problem from the nineteenth century and before, still remained huge: while the North grew by 3%, the South—where 40% of the youth were unemployed—declined by 2%. Meanwhile, private consumption and the net capital formation of the country increased faster, by 1.3% and 1.5% per annum, respectively.

Public debt successively accumulated and accompanied Italy's development. In the mid-1990s, it already totaled 120% of GDP, twice as high as the European Union's requirement norm for public debts. At the end of 2008, it transitorily declined to 106%. Nevertheless, Italy had the world's third-largest public debt level. Finance Minister Giulio Tremonti successfully kept the budget deficit at bay. In 2008, its level was only 2.8% of GDP, and during the years of the European financial crisis it increased relatively moderately. In 2010, it reached 4.6%, still below the targeted 5%, and it dropped to 3.9% by November 2011. The most dangerous financial whirlpool, the deficit-debt spiral—when accumulating budget deficits increase debts and push the country's finances down—was skillfully avoided by cutting the budget deficit. The country's credit rating consequently did not decline like Ireland's and Greece's for quite a while. For years, Italy had no problem selling their 10-year sovereign government bonds on the financial markets for not much higher yield than that of Germany, and paying low interest on the new debt to repay the old.

The debt situation of Italy, however, was a ticking time bomb. The populist Berlusconi government denied the depth of the debt problem, postponed unpopular actions, and paid empty lip-service to the need for intervention, while the country was pushed to the brink of a sovereign debt crisis.[12] Already in December 2008, *The Economist* raised the question about the future of the Italian bonds, stating that, "the government may end up paying more in interest, and that increases the risk of the budget deficit getting out of hand." This forecast was well-founded. In the same article, the journal reported that the gap between the German and Italian 10-year bonds increased from 38 base points in May to 144 base points by December of 2008.[13] In November 2011, the debt level increased to 121.5% of GDP. The debt reached an extraordinary amount, $2.758 trillion, which even the entire European Union would be unable to swallow. It is true that more than half of this debt is held by Italians within the country, but $1.191 trillion is held abroad, representing a tremendous financial risk. Towering Italian debt overshadowed the euro-zone. Its amount was more than five times bigger than the Greek and alone became nearly three times higher than the Icelandic, Greek, and Irish debts combined.

The unsolved problems renewed the troubles of the European financial markets and, as reported in August 2011, "Europe's money markets are undoubtedly starting to freeze up." Banks again refused to lend, and this situation pushed the yields of Italian government bonds up to 6.20%, which meant that the government had to pay significantly more to get fresh money.[14] The increase in the yield was a dramatic 1.5% compared to the summer of the same year. Paying higher interest for the bonds added $4.1 billion in interest payments annually. The more than 6% interest rate was already dangerously high and rising. If it reached 7%, as one expert said, it "would be the point of no return."[15] This actually happened in a couple of days: on November 8, the news reported that the rates jumped to a record 6.63% level, but the very next day it surpassed the dangerous 7% level. The news generated a shock-wave on the financial markets. Even the American Stock Exchange suffered a dramatic loss. Insurance against default (credit default swaps) also increased dramatically. The annual cost to insure $10,000,000 debt was $145,000 in the summer of 2011, but it rose to $300,000 in September and $511,000 in early November. This was a frightening sign just before the issuing of new Italian bonds in the latter part of November and then again in December, when the country had to raise €53 billion for the repayment of debts.[16]

The price of loans increased in general. European interbank loans also became more expensive. In June 2011, the rate was 20 basis points (a basis point is one-hundredth of a percentage point) and it jumped to 100 points by November. Giulio Tremonti used a frightening parallel: "it is like the Titanic." And in a warning to the political elite, he added, "not even the first class passengers get saved."[17]

This development, as in several other countries, generated a political crisis and led to the resignation of Silvio Berlusconi, the leading political figure in Italy for 17 years and a three-term prime minister between 1994 and 2011. Berlusconi, a media tycoon, the third richest man in Italy and the 47th richest in the world, had a political career colored by permanent scandals. As he once complained, 789 prosecutors and magistrates had investigated him, the police visited his home 577 times, 2,500 hearings and several trials were held for bribing, lying in court, false accounting, and numberless sex scandals. Berlusconi survived all of these, was acquitted, the statute of limitations expired, or his Parliamentary majority rushed to change the law. He was, however, unable to survive the financial crisis.

A renowned economist, Mario Monti, a former European Commissioner and the President of the famous Bocconi University, formed the new Italian government to put the fiscal household in order and regain trust. Government change had an immediate positive impact but the interest rates started increasing again in 2012. The austerity measures made economic revival difficult and from the last quarter of 2011 on, Italy declined into recession again and the government initiated a new stimulus program.

Spain

The causes of the emerging crisis in Spain had rather different origins than in Italy, and were more similar to Ireland. The Spanish state was in good order, public debts were less than 40% of GDP in 2007, and even by 2010 they increased only to an acceptable 53% of it. Spain's banks were better regulated and solvent. Nevertheless, the 17 regions of the country have significant autonomy and half of the Spanish banking industry consists of *cajas* or local savings banks. This sector was not as safe as the big banks and required major reorganization and recapitalization. Their number decreased from 45 to 18 and they became joint stock companies in order to be able to raise money. However, each autonomous region is responsible for its own healthcare, social services, and education. Thus, the regional budgets are significant and produced huge deficits. Besides, regional politicians, as in Greece, often spend for symbolic modernization. One of the outstanding examples was the building of a modern airport for jumbo jets in Castilla-La Mancha, an agricultural region near Madrid. The airport has had to be closed because no one wanted to use it. Municipalities followed a similar policy, as the example of Alcorcón shows: they built an expensive cultural center ten miles from Madrid. In September 2010, regional debts totaled $144 billion, and in one year increased by 22% to $176 billion.[18]

However, Dean Baker flatly denied that Spain had a financial crisis at all. "The real story," he noted, "was the rise and demise of the housing bubble."[19] Construction of houses, indeed, reached an unheard-of level. In 2004 and 2005, 1,370,000 units were built. Home prices skyrocketed: in the single decade between 1996 and 2006, prices in some years increased by 17–18% annually, and at the end nearly trebled.

People felt enriched by the dynamic development of Spain. Per capita GDP trebled between 1973 and 2005, while the euro-zone's growth reached only 67%. Spain's income level rose from roughly half to 81% of the average level of the euro-zone countries.[20] The suddenly enriched people rushed into buying houses: 80% of the population became homeowners, a much higher percentage than in the United States (67%). This development was strongly initiated by the housing policy. Banks offered 40- and 50-year loans—though 97% of the mortgages were at variable rates—and 15% of mortgage payments were deductible from taxable personal income. Construction loans almost doubled between 2005 and 2009. Families bought houses with loans. Mortgage debt jumped by 25% per year (!) between 2001 and 2005, and reached the incredible heights of €651,168,000,000 by mid-2005. Family indebtedness increased by 115% in a decade around the turn of the century.

Speculation that pushed house prices up had the lion's share of responsibility for this development. The real estate boom transformed the construction industry into one of the leading sectors of the economy. In advanced countries, construction's contribution to GDP is about 6%. In Spain, its share increased from 8% at the end of the 1990s to 12.3% by 2007. In a broader sense, nearly 20% of GDP was related to real estate and construction, and that sector employed one-sixth of the work force. "The rapid rate of construction led to enormous overbuilding, which means that a collapse was inevitable."[21] Overbuilding, indeed, became evident from the fact that every fourth newly built unit remained vacant between 2001 and 2007.

When the bubble suddenly burst, 1.5 million unfinished and unsold units remained behind, and 1.4 million units were on sale. Between the summer of 2007 and the summer of 2008, sales dropped by more than one quarter, but in Catalonia the figure was more than 42%. As a sad symbol of the bubble, the just-finished 420-foot Torre Lugano in eastern Valencia remained one-third empty. "It is the hangover after an epic fiesta, a period Spaniards now refer to as 'cuando pensábamos que éramos ricos,' when we thought we were rich."[22] Banks owned most of the vacant units and are now trying to sell them. Prices, of course, sharply declined. Newspapers reported that a 200-square-meter frontline golf villa was offered for €1.3 million but sold for €601,000; in Santa Maria village, the modest "Elviria" was offered for €269,000 and sold for €188,400. The construction industry collapsed. In one year between the fall of 2007 and the fall of 2008, unemployment increased by 37% and reached 17.4% of the labor force. Although these figures are dramatic themselves, the most burning social problem is the tragic 45% unemployment rate among the young generation under the age of 25. The movement of the *los indignatos,* the protesting youth, has gained general social sympathy and backing. The country's GDP declined by 4% in 2009. Savings halved. Gross capital formation that had increased by about 4% per annum during the boom years, declined by −4.8, −16.0, and −7.6% in 2008, 2009, and 2010, respectively.[23]

Spain and Italy together accumulated a $3.3 trillion debt burden by the end of 2011. In the first half of 2012, the more expensive debt service in the two countries amounted to $426 billion more than the $400 billion the IMF has to lend worldwide.[24] In the summer of 2012, the EU had to bail out the Spanish banks again.

Do the "transition" Eastern peripheries have a special crisis?

The former Soviet Bloc countries, which were in transition from a state socialist, non-market system to market capitalism for more than one-and-half decades when the crisis erupted, were evidently vulnerable. Their market institutions were new and relatively weak, they were strongly dependent on the advanced economies of Europe, and they did not have an independent banking sector because, as an average, 87% of their banking capital was in the hands of Western banks. This share was much higher in some of the countries that virtually lacked their own banking sector at all: in 2005–8, 88% of Romania's, 96% of Slovakia's and 99% of Estonia's banks' assets were foreign-owned.[25] Most of all, they did not have experience in how to run a market economy, and they also carried their old cultural habits and behavioral patterns.

Those countries belonged historically to the Central and Eastern European peripheries, and they were non-industrialized peasant countries until the middle of the twentieth century, in most cases with a deeply rooted noble (or as it was called in Poland, "szlachta") anti-capitalist tradition where spending was elegant and thrift was looked-down upon. The peasant societies of the Balkans carried a strong collectivist anti-capitalist legacy. Traditionally, the Eastern periphery was, and still is, in a backward peripheral situation. History matters.

TABLE 2.2 GDP/capita in Central and
Eastern Europe as % of the West[26]

Year	East as % of West
1820	59
1870	51
1913	46
1950	51
1973	47
1989	40
1995	39
2005	46

As the calculations in Table 2.2 show, the Eastern peripheries were and remained continuously backward for nearly two centuries, fluctuating at around half of the West European income level. Ten of those countries, however, had already become members of the European Union in 2004 and 2007, and three of them joined the euro-zone before or during the crisis. Almost the entire region was strongly integrated into the European single market and especially into the financial markets. The economies of most of those countries, especially from the mid-1990s, were in the midst of an impressive expansion, financed by foreign direct investments and borrowing. After 2000, a credit-fueled, demand-generated economic boom pushed forward a catching-up process with the West. Lending growth, as Matthias Person called to our attention, has been well into double digits for several years in Central and Eastern Europe.[27] Nearly half of the 12 years between 1996 and 2007 were credit-boom years in the transition countries, especially after 2002 when a credit boom became the norm in that region.[28]

The previously mostly poor population that had experienced shortages for generations, all of a sudden enjoyed the huge offerings of the market, and new financial-technical possibilities to buy on credit. The entire region, or at least that one-third to one-half of its population which belonged to its winners, turned to passionate consumerism. In this respect, one can speak about some similarities with Ireland and Spain, but also with Greece and Portugal. The former Soviet Bloc countries could easily be the weak and highly susceptible part of Europe, exposed more to the crisis than established market systems in the West.

In reality, however, it was not the case in the region as a whole. In a very surprising way, they were less homogenous than the former Southern

European peripheries. The Mediterranean countries declined into a deep crisis almost in unison. The Central and Eastern European countries exhibited a great deal of differences regarding the spread and deepness of the crisis. Some of them, such as Hungary, Latvia, Estonia, Lithuania, Bulgaria, Romania, Serbia, Ukraine and Russia, were especially hard hit. In 2009, five countries of the region had a double-digit decline in GDP, while the region's average decline was 6%. The sharpest decline in GDP in 2009 was experienced by Lithuania (17.4%), Ukraine (14.8%), Estonia (14.3%), Slovenia (8.1%), and Russia (7.8%). In 2010, however, only Croatia and Romania had negative growth, and all the others started recovering. Slovakia, Russia, and Ukraine already had 4% growth again. Until the end of 2011, among the transition countries, only Hungary, Latvia, and Romania had to have outside assistance to avoid collapse and were bailed out by the IMF.

Surprisingly enough, a great part of the former Soviet Bloc countries do not belong to the most troubled areas of the European Union. Poland, the Czech Republic, Slovakia, and Slovenia had a somewhat slower and export-driven economic development during the boom period and avoided a deep or long recession. This is highly surprising in the case of a transforming country that only recently started integrating into the European economy and experienced a difficult transition to the market system.

Slovakia, Slovenia, and the Czech Republic, however, exhibited relative financial order and a strong recovery. In those countries, current account deficits were nearly balanced by foreign investments. Most of the transition countries were eager to join the euro-zone and, unlike those countries that were already members of the zone, they took seriously the Maastricht requirements of keeping budget deficits and indebtedness levels below the European Union's requirements of 3% and 60% of GDP, respectively. From a high deficit rate at the end of the twentieth century, they put their financial households in good order. Slovenia, Slovakia, the Czech Republic, and Poland fulfilled the EU requirements between 2002 and 2007, just in time before the financial crisis erupted. That was probably the most important defense against the financial crisis, or at least, a great advantage in coping with it and recovering relatively quickly.

The Central and Eastern European transforming countries, however, had a special situation. Their banking system, as noted before—87% of bank capital—was in the hands of the big Western banks, and, at least transitorily, there was a possibility that they would stop financing the region. In several East European countries, a direct impact of the financial panic was a paralyzed banking system. As the *Telegraph* reported on October 16, 2008, "German banks that had very active subsidiaries in Eastern Europe have given orders not to lend foreign currency in East European countries already totally exposed to massive debts."[29]

On the other hand, after the first shock, a foreign-owned banking system turned to be a great advantage. In Estonia, for example, the Swedish-owned banking system soon guaranteed normal crediting since the Swedish banks remained solvent and rich. Estonia did not have to recapitalize its banking industry by increasing government debts. Foreign-owned banking in the Baltic countries helped the return to impressive growth in two years. The European Union was very cautious to defend the new member countries. In March 2009, EU institutions, the IMF and the World Bank, the European Bank for Reconstruction and Development and about 40 banks involved in cross-border operations met in Vienna and made an agreement to keep lending to the region. This Vienna Initiative saved the region from a collapse in banking and crediting.

In the last quarter of 2011, however, in the depth of the European crisis, lending to the new member countries was cut by $35 billion (according to other calculations, probably $80 billion) and EU-based banks started selling their assets in Central and Eastern Europe. To stop this process, on January 2012, the EU and the international financial institutions called for a Vienna Initiative II. The Brussels meeting targets an agreement with the European regulators not to push banks, among them Austrian banks with a huge involvement in the region, to withdraw from risky business in the new member countries. As one of the top officials of the Austrian Raiffeisen Bank International stated: "We welcome the agreement reached in Brussels as a further important step to supporting the stability of Central and Eastern Europe's financial sector."[30]

As a consequence, none of the banking subsidiaries were closed or liquidated in Eastern Europe. As the European Bank for Reconstruction and Development concluded, "foreign bank ownership is a highly significant predictor of smaller net outflows . . . a 10 percentage point increase in foreign ownership reducing the net outflow of cross-border loans by 1.4 percentage points." [31]

In a quite miraculous way, one of the transforming countries, Poland, became the *only* country in Europe that was able to avoid any crisis. Bank lending was on a low level in this country, the mortgage market was small, a housing bubble did not emerge, and the government introduced mortgage restrictions in 2006. Foreign capital inflow was not dramatically broken. In 2011, the country ranked fourth in the amount of capital raised. At the Warsaw Stock Exchange, 38 new companies were listed and Poland ranked behind only China regarding the number of initial public offerings in the third quarter of the year. New ring roads and public transportation facilities are under construction in Warsaw. As the head of the Polish branch of the Austrian Raiffeisen International Bank noted, "I have never seen such a tremendous scale of investments."[32] The relatively large Polish domestic market of 38 million people created a strong domestic demand—retail sales increased by 7% in 2009—and the country did not rely one-sidedly on exports, which accounted for only 40% of GDP, half the percentage of the Czech Republic or Slovakia.

The cohesion policy of the European Union that assisted the backward regions—including Poland as a whole—pumped about €80,000 billion aid into Central and Eastern Europe between 2000 and 2006, of which about one-quarter went to Poland. Moreover, during the European Union's funding period between 2007 and 2013, the Union allocated more than one-third of its budget for assisting backward regions. Assistance from the Common Agricultural Policy added a further amount of aid money: these subsidies doubled the income level of the Polish farmers. Among the new member countries, the largest amount from the European Union budget was transferred to Poland, and it had a significant impact: "It is reported that the transfer from the Union made it possible for the Polish government to minimize effects of the crisis of 2008–10."[33] Altogether, in 2011, Poland had an annual 4% economic growth and the forecast for 2012 is still 2.5%.

In the case of Slovakia, after the first shock, the country was even able to join the euro-zone with its solid fiscal situation. The small country of 5.5 million inhabitants is virtually attached to the German economy. In journalistic writing it was often called "Volkswagen Land" or "Detroit in the East," because German—and some others, including Asian—companies' investments and huge subsidiaries there created a large and advanced car industry. Slovakia produced 630,000 cars in 2010, thus becoming number one in the world in car production per inhabitant. The connection with the strongest and most solid European economy stabilized Slovakia's economic situation as well. The Baltic countries, in spite of their sharpest decline in 2009, already returned to rapid growth from 2010 on, mostly because of their close ties to healthy Scandinavia. The foremost advantage of the majority of the transition countries was their low level of indebtedness compared to their GDP. For 12 transition countries, the average debt level totaled 30.2% of GDP, half the level that the European Union required.[34] Low wages and a well-educated labor force in proximity to rich markets, as the Baltic countries exhibit more than elsewhere, may lead to continued growth.

On the other hand, some of the forerunners and most successful countries of transformation, including Hungary and the three Baltic "Tigers," declined into deep recession and even depression. In the three Baltic countries, Hungary, and Romania, current account deficits were not covered by direct investments that contributed to their severe crisis. Three transition countries, Hungary, Latvia, and Romania, declined into the deepest economic crisis. The indebtedness of Hungary, Estonia, Latvia, and Bulgaria surpassed the amount of their GDP. Their crisis did not challenge the European Union much, though, because the combined GDP of the three hardest-hit countries amounted to only about 2% of the Union's total GDP, and was roughly equal to Greece's share. However, their troubles contributed to others and represented some danger for European financial markets.

The Baltic region belonged to the Soviet Union until 1991, and it became a late starter, but super-performer, at transformation. Hungary was the pioneer and model country for market transformation from the very beginning. While a few of the transition countries enjoyed a healthy fiscal situation and low public debts, some others "prepared" their own crisis for years before 2008. Some of the most successful transforming countries had impressive structural change and rapid growth, fueled by foreign capital inflows from the mid–late 1990s on. Capital inflow to private borrowers in the transition region reached its zenith in 2007 with $93 billion. Several of them had overheated economies already from the turn of the century on. This was clearly signaled by double-digit inflation in all three Baltic countries and Bulgaria.

The three Baltic states reached the highest—in some years even double-digit—growth rates, and, as an average, grew by 7% annually between 2000 and 2008. The "extreme credit booms had peaked and began to reverse even before the onset of the global crisis."[35] The two EU-member Balkan countries, Romania and Bulgaria, had nearly 6% yearly growth in those years, while the Central European countries also experienced 4.4% growth in the early years of the twenty-first century.[36]

If financial integration was the engine of transformation and growth, it also became the source of accumulating debt troubles and contributed to the crisis. In some cases, capital inflow stopped all of a sudden, and was replaced by capital outflow. That was the case in Estonia, Latvia, Ukraine, and Russia. The latter country suffered a capital outflow of $136 billion immediately in the fourth quarter of 2008. Most of the other countries, however, did not suffer from significant capital outflow since that remained generally mild, only 1% of GDP in the most crisis-ridden half-year around the turn of 2008–9.

After the collapse of Lehman Brothers, a global liquidity crisis dried up the capital flow. The leading global credit lenders turned more inward and increased their lending in their home countries from 29% to 34%, but in real terms halved their crediting in their home countries. For the so-called emerging countries, crediting declined from 8% to 4%, and the real volume of credits dropped by 75%. Some transition countries, such as Ukraine, were shut out from the international capital market.[37]

More important was the impact of declining export possibilities. The labor-seeking foreign companies built up a modern export industry in most of the region's countries, based on the cheap and well-trained labor force. Export was a leading factor of growth. The volume of foreign trade in the Central European and Baltic countries, as an average, surpassed the value of GDP. Export possibilities, however, sharply declined. Global trade volume declined by roughly 12% in 2009, but in the transition countries, in the fourth quarter of 2008, by 5–15%, and in the first quarter of 2009, by 10–25%, compared to the same period of the previous year. "Export and financial shocks magnified the reversal of credit booms that had already been under way in many countries before the September shock." [38] Two countries deserve special attention.

Hungary and Latvia: lost in transition?

Hungary's market transformation started the earliest in Eastern Europe, already during the 1980s, and thus before the collapse of communism. Foreign direct investment in Central Europe and the Baltic countries totaled $161,255 million between 1989 and 2004. In the first 5–7 years, Hungary received half of the foreign capital inflow in the region, and altogether until 2004, $36,189 million, more than 22% of it. On a per capita basis, it reached $3,719, 61% more than the region's average.[39] Hungary belonged to those countries of the region that recovered from the severe collapse of the early 1990s with record speed and reached 150% of the pre-1989 level by the end of the twentieth century. At first glance, rapid development continued between 2001 and 2006 with an annual 4.2% growth rate in GDP, more than twice as high as the European Union's average in those years. The yearly 6.4% industrial growth was several times faster than the 1.3% European Union average. The country impressively progressed, and a significant catching-up process elevated its per capita GDP from about half of the EU-15[40] level to 63% of it by 2006.

Behind the remarkable growth, however, imbalances and negative economic trends also gained ground, especially after the turn of the millennium. What happened? As in several other former communist countries, the economy became overheated. Anders Åslund maintained that, before the crisis, ten Central and East European countries had "multiple preconditions of crisis . . . Excessive current account deficit, large foreign debts, small currency reserves . . . huge credit expansion, sharp real estate price rises, and rising inflation."[41]

Nevertheless, Hungary made more devastating mistakes than many of the others. In a heated political competition, the rival Center-Left and Center-Right parties both realized a populist policy by outbidding each other's promises. Surprisingly enough, these parties, when in power, even fulfilled the promised increase in the living standard and in social benefits. Consequently, Hungary was the only country in the region that never cut its budgetary deficit back to the Maastricht requirements of 3% of GDP, and by 2006, it reached 9.3% of it. It was also the only one whose public debts surpassed the 60% European Union ceiling when compared to GDP. "Hungary stood out," concluded the same author, "because of its patently weak public finances . . . and it fell like ripe fruit in the global financial storm."[42]

In the 1990s, export-led growth, fueled by foreign investments and demands, was the engine of economic development in Hungary as well as in other transforming countries of Eastern Europe. From the turn of the century, domestic consumption became the prime mover. Hungarian governments turned toward demand-stimulating measures of wage and pension increases, also granting 13th-month salaries and pensions. Population income increased much faster and higher than productivity and national income did—and augmented government expenditures. Monetary policy, trying to control the inflationary consequences of the increase in wages and state expenditures—similarly to most other countries—one-sidedly concentrated on anti-inflationary measures by raising interest rates and overvaluing the currency. This policy turned out to be counterproductive because the virtually unlimited and cheap credits, available in Swiss francs and other currencies, still made borrowing easy.

Government expenditure and investments increased faster (4.7% per annum) than GDP. Foreign trade, meanwhile, had a permanent deficit. The current account deficit, €1,921,000 in 2000, had jumped to €5,835,000 by 2006. Hungary's indebtedness, which remained below the European Union norm in 2000 (54.3% of GDP), had increased sharply to 78.7% by 2009.

From 2006, political chaos flooded the country. The vehemently attacking opposition party of Viktor Orbán's FIDESz successfully exploited the secretly recorded words of the socialist Prime Minister Ferenc Gyurcsány, when he told to his cabinet that before the elections they lied about the financial situation of the country in order to be reelected. He wanted to put the financial household in order, and indeed, the government started cutting and decreasing the deficit. FIDESz, however, successfully mobilized its constituency and violent prolonged demonstrations followed each other. An openly neo-fascist party also gained ground.

Before the international financial crisis became manifest in 2008, Hungary had already declined into a severe economic and political crisis. The high share of foreign direct investments in the country, $74,037 million in 2006 (3.2-times more than in 2000), was followed by a significant withdrawal of profits beginning mid-decade because of the political turmoil in Hungary.

Austerity and corrective measures were especially successfully carried out after the resignation of Ferenc Gyurcsány, when a transitory technocratic Gordon Bajnai government (the first of this type in Europe during the crisis) took over. Hungary turned to the IMF for a huge loan. As the IMF Survey Magazine reported on October 28, 2008, "The IMF, the European Union, and the World Bank announced a joint financing package for Hungary, totaling $26.1 billion . . . ."[43] The stabilization program and the lack of counter-cyclical resources led to a recession. In 2007 and 2008, economic growth slowed and then declined. After the slow 1% and 0.6% growth in 2006 and 2007, respectively, industrial output declined by 17.4% and GDP by 6.7% in 2009. In 2010, GDP declined 2.5%, and unemployment increased from 7.8% in 2008 to 9.6%. The successful austerity measures, together with the IMF loan, prevented financial collapse by drastically slowing down and changing the direction of the economy.

The new Viktor Orbán government declared with nationalist fervor that the IMF may not dictate to an independent Hungary, and it left the IMF stewardship in 2010. In a speech on the national holiday, Orbán proudly stated: "We fought for our country in the European Union, when dishonest and lying attacks were launched against our nation. . . . We do not allow to anybody to dictate to us from Brussels or anywhere else. . . . It is clear that we will be free only if we are ourselves."[44]

"Hungary could [still] be the most vulnerable," reported *The Economist* in the summer of 2011, "thanks to a combination of indebtedness and political unpredictability. Foreign currency borrowing, 95% of it in Swiss francs, accounts for two-thirds of total lending."[45] This forecast became reality in three months. The country's public debts increased to 81% of GDP, and two-thirds of debts are in foreign currencies. Because of the devalued Hungarian currency, paying back the household loans, taken in Swiss francs, has more than doubled the repayment burden on the population. It caused a nearly unsolvable problem. The Orbán government offered a solution: it allows repayment in three years at a fixed rate, much lower than the official exchange rate. The difference between the official and lowered rates had to be absorbed by the mortgage lenders. "Transferring all foreign-currency debt into local currency," calculates the Hungarian National Bank, still "could cost 7% of the GDP" of Hungary.[46] The government had to go to Canossa, and turned again to the IMF in late November 2011. The credit rating of Hungary, however, dropped below the junk level, thus below investment grade. The country had to pay nearly 10% interest on their bonds, the third highest in Europe after Greece and Portugal. The Hungarian government, in a typical East-European style, characterized the downgrading as "the latest in a string of financial attacks against Hungary."[47] By January 2012, the country was at the edge of the abyss: there were no buyers for one-quarter of government bonds, and the European Union required the withdrawal of certain laws that were against European Union rules, among them the subordination of the Hungarian National Bank to the government, stripping it of independence. The alienation of the European Commission and the IMF in a situation when only outside assistance could save the country from freefall created an immense danger of state insolvency. In January 2012, the government announced the withdrawal of the laws that were against the European Union's rules. Nevertheless, in February 2012, for the first time in EU history, the European Council suspended the payment of €495 million cohesion fund money for Hungary in 2013 if the government did not cut the budget deficit to the required level.[48]

High performing Latvia, with 6–8% annual economic growth for a decade (11.9% in 2006), achieved a unique and internationally admired catching-up process: in 2000, the former Soviet republic reached only 31.1% of the per capita GDP level of the euro-zone, but by 2008 it had already achieved more than 50% of it. However, that the country's economy was overheated was clearly signaled by high inflation and indebtedness. In 2007, the inflation rate hit 10% and the national account deficit reached 22% of GDP. The rapid enrichment also led to a huge real estate bubble.

In 2008, high prosperity was disrupted by a "hard lending." In 2008, Latvia's GDP dropped by 3.3%, and in 2009 by a dramatic 18%, the sharpest decline in Europe. The following year the decline slowed down to 0.3%, but unemployment rose to nearly 20% of the work force, more than twice the euro-zone average of 9.1%. Austerity measures were immediately introduced in December 2008 that reduced wages in the public sector by 20%, and increased value added tax by 3% to 21%, aiming for 7% of GDP. In June 2009, a second austerity package cut a further 4% of GDP through a second 20% wage decrease and a slimming of the public administration by 20%. Pensions were curbed by 10%, and one of the most painful cuts hit the healthcare and educational systems. The healthcare budget lost 30%, 24 out of 49 hospitals were closed, and teachers' salaries were reduced by one-third. The harsh measures stopped the decline and had seemingly stabilized the economy by 2011 and a quite robust 4% growth returned. This was almost three times greater than the euro-zone average 1.5% growth rate.

The entire Mediterranean, and part of the Central and East European peripheries thus declined into deep crisis. Six former peripheral countries— Ireland, two South European countries, and three East European countries— had to be bailed out, some of them twice. Their crisis unavoidably penetrated all the others and the contagion generated an all-round European crisis.

The all-European crisis

The European Union and the euro-zone countries were all infected. Some advanced core countries, nevertheless, made similar policy mistakes and suffered from the same troubles as their peripheral neighbors. They also caused the same self-inflicted recession as did the peripheral countries. Housing bubbles, besides those in Ireland, Spain, Italy, Russia, Ukraine, Romania, and the three Baltic states, also expanded in several advanced European countries, such as Britain, France, Norway, Sweden, and Finland. House prices increased by 80–82% in Sweden, Norway, and Denmark between 2000 and 2007, and by 100% in Ireland, 108% in France, 128% in Britain, and 135% in Spain in the same period. Germany and the Netherlands did not follow that pattern with 18% and 38% house price increases, respectively.[49] *The Economist*, in an article on "The Global Housing Boom," warned in June 2005: "The world wide rise in house prices is the biggest bubble in history."[50]

As a clear sign of an overheated economy, Reuters reported in February 2008 that "global inflation [between 10% and 20%] climbs to historic levels."[51] Solid Western countries such as Sweden, Belgium, and Austria also had quite reckless lending practices: Belgium and Sweden—the main patrons of the Baltic transformation—provided a huge number of loans for transforming countries that amounted to 30% of their respective GDPs. Austria, a major patron of the neighboring former communist Central European countries, had lent 30% of its banking assets, which totaled 70% of the country's GDP.[52] When the former Soviet Bloc countries declined into deep crisis, the lender banks had to be bailed out by the state.

In this environment, the explosion of the American financial crisis spread to the European core instantaneously. Beside the rippling domestic crisis in several European countries, the impact of the American financial turmoil itself had a dramatic effect.[53] Psychological factors are crucial in all economic turmoil. If people believe that banks may go down, this may become a self-fulfilling belief because people start withdrawing their deposits from banks and selling their stocks trying to escape, putting their money into assumed "safe havens," such as real estate and gold. This really happened in the fall of 2008 in Europe. *Trust* oils the machine of the market economy: you buy because you have trust in the seller; you invest because you trust in return; you buy stocks because you trust in the profitability of companies; you put money into a bank account because you trust that it is safe in the bank; you lend money because you trust in the borrower to repay.

Trust, however, was the first victim of the financial panic. In 2007–11, distrust became widespread in Europe. People lost their trust in institutions, governments, and even in each other.[54] *Der Spiegel* reported in November, 2008: "Because trust has been essentially destroyed in the financial and credit markets, banks, companies and consumers are hoarding their money instead of lending or spending it."[55] The European Commission retrospectively noted in 2009 that the crisis began to feed on itself.

The write-down of the British banks was estimated at $300 billion, and those of banks in the entire euro-zone amounted to $500–$800 billion, which reached 10% of their aggregate GDP. In April 2009, the IMF estimated losses originating in the euro-zone and Britain at $1.2 trillion.[56] Interbank loans dried up, because banks did not believe in each other any longer. Because of panic selling on European stock markets, the drop in financial wealth in the euro-zone was one-half of the value of the European stocks. On September 17, the Russian stock market had to be closed down to avoid a total landslide of stock values. On October 10, the biggest British companies lost £100 billion from the value of their stock. In a week, the French savings bank, Caisse d'Epargne, lost €600 million.

Extensive foreign direct investments (FDI) were one of the prime movers of previous European prosperity. In the globalized world economy—with Europe as one of its pillars—financial transactions multiplied. In 2007, FDI inflow totaled $0.85 trillion in Europe, but it declined by nearly 34% by 2008, while in the entire advanced world it dropped from $1.25 trillion to $0.84 trillion, a fall of nearly 33%.[57]

In September 2008, Germany, without a real estate bubble, with solid banking, and a massive export industry, looked like the island of stability. On October 2, however, *The Guardian* reported the "end of optimism" in Germany, since a severe liquidity crisis emerged from the lack of trust. The second biggest German commercial property lender, Hypo Real Estate, declined to the edge of bankruptcy. "At the end of the day, Germany is in the same boat as the rest of Europe."[58] *Der Spiegel* presented graphic evidence with a seemingly marginal, but in reality very typical example. One hundred and twenty three congregations in north Germany wanted to get higher returns from their savings than they got from the government bonds they traditionally invested in. Thus, the Oldenburg State Church invested €4.3 million with the American Lehman Brothers. "In the end, even prayers didn't help. The . . . [money] had simply gone up in smoke." The magazine also listed examples of withdrawn machine orders—from Koenig and Braun, a printing machine company—because of a lack of credit and confidence. "Fear of the future is already shaping the behavior of citizens . . . those who could buy goods are no longer interested in doing so." Retail sales, as a consequence, had declined by 3% and Germany's exports by 2.5% by August 2008.[59]

The crisis, because of the close interrelations of the financial systems, crossed borders rapidly and easily. In the same month as Lehman Brothers collapsed, the crisis became manifest in Europe. To keep the banking system alive, the British government guaranteed bank deposits up to £50,000, and the Russian Central Bank pledged 500 billion roubles to finance the banking sector. The Netherlands, Belgium, and Luxembourg rescued the banking and insurance giant Forbis with €11.2 billion and partly nationalized the company. Two days later they bailed out Dexia with €6.4 billion. The next day Britain nationalized the Bradford & Bingley mortgage lender with £50 billion. The Royal Bank of Scotland lost 20% of its shares' value on the same day. All these events happened within two weeks of the collapse of Lehman Brothers. This was still in September 2008.

After October, the avalanche of collapses and bailouts became unstoppable. News on bailouts, huge bank losses, and the freefall of stock exchanges became everyday phenomena.[60] The European Union's Paris meeting on October 12 agreed to prepare a coordinated plan to prevent the meltdown of the banking system. On November 26, the European Commission announced a €200 billion recovery plan. As reported in December 2008, the European Economic Recovery Plan pumped funds equal to 5% of the European Union's aggregate GDP into the economy, including the so-called automatic stabilizers.[61] Britain, France, Germany, and several other countries initiated stimulus packages to revitalize the ailing economy (as will be discussed in Chapter 5).[62]

As a consequence, the European Commission proudly announced in 2009 that "large-scale bank runs have been avoided, monetary policy has been eased aggressively, and governments have released substantial fiscal stimulus."[63] Nevertheless, the banking crisis still was hanging over the Union. In November 2011, the Financial Stability Board of the Group of 20 (or G-20, the world's 20 leading economies), named 29 major banks worldwide needing more recapitalization and close control because of their fragile financial situation. Among the endangered banks, they listed several major European banks such as the Banque Populaire, Barclays, BNP Paribas, Commerzbank, Crédit Agricole, Credit Suisse, Deutsche Bank, Dexia, Royal Bank of Scotland, and Société Générale.[64] Several of them already had to write off huge amounts of their loans and suffered significant losses.

Banks play a central role by "lubricating" the machine of the capitalist economy. Credit creation is essential for a capitalist market system. In Joseph Schumpeter's definition, "capitalism is that form of private property economy in which innovations are carried out by means of borrowed money, which in general . . . implies credit creation. . . . We shall date capitalism as far back as the elements of credit creation."[65] If banks are unable or unwilling to extend credits to companies and the population, the so-called real economy, industry, trade and the entire economic system stop working.

The decline of the real economy

Because the "mother of all financial crises"—as *The Economist* dubbed the 2008 panic—paralyzed the banking sector, recession, i.e. decline in the entire economy, became unavoidable. The European Commission report also noted that "the transmission of financial distress to the real economy evolved at record speed."[66] The facts signal the close connection between the financial market and the so-called real economy. Lack of credit, the dramatic loss of stock values, and lost confidence and trust slowed down the European economy.

The financial crisis spread into the real economy of the euro-zone in the third quarter of 2008. Banks curbed crediting, including to each other and the population. Mortgage credit was hardly available. The lack of money limited economic activities including investments and consumer spending. The member countries of the euro-zone declined into recession in the second and third quarters of the year when they had an average 0.2% decline in GDP. In February 2009, the euro-zone's GDP dropped by 1.5%, while the group's industrial output declined by 3.5% in a year.

The official definition of a recession is two consecutive quarters of decline in GDP, and that was already happening in Europe from the fall of 2008. The British Office for National Statistics reported zero growth in the second quarter of 2008, and the first decline in 16 years during the third quarter of the year. British GDP declined by 6.15% for six consecutive quarters until January 2010. That was not the worst by far. Italy had seven quarters of 6.76% decline, and Ireland a 12.24% decrease that lasted 13 quarters. However, no other country suffered as big a decline as the previously super-performer "Baltic Tigers." Their economies were overheated, and the global recession curbed their GDP drastically: Estonia had a 20.33% decline for seven quarters, Latvia a 25.14% decline for eight quarters, and Lithuania a 16.95% drop for six quarters. However, even France and Germany were no exceptions. Both had four-quarter declines of 3.87% and 6.62%, respectively. The prosperous and solid Nordic countries and Switzerland followed: Sweden's GDP dropped by 7.43% for seven quarters, Finland's fell by 9.93% for four quarters, Denmark lost 8.06% for six quarters, Norway shed 3.44% for eleven quarters, and Switzerland's GDP shrank by 3.25% for four quarters.[67]

Europe declined into a major economic recession in 2008–9. As early as April 8, 2008, the IMF forecast $1 trillion losses.[68] The global equity market lost more than half of its value in one year. The European car industry dropped into a deep hole: Russian passenger-car production dropped from 1.5 million units to 597,000 between 2008 and 2009. Jaguar-Land Rover in Britain and Volvo and Saab in Sweden were bailed out with billions. Compared to 2007, the profits of the French Renault decreased by 78%. About $14.5 trillion of the value of global companies was erased. In 2009, the euro-zone's aggregate GDP declined by 4.2%, and in 2010 by 0.7%, and the unemployment rate reached 9.1% of the labor force. In April, 20 million people became unemployed in the European Union. The debt level of the member countries, which reached 61–62% of the aggregate GDP of the Union in the early 2000s—i.e. about the level that the Maastricht Agreement required—rose to 74.4% in 2009, and then to 82.3% by 2011. The debt level of the 17 members of the euro-zone already reached 70% of GDP in 2008 and 88% by 2011.[69]

However, the recession and, in some countries, even depression[70] did not expand for several years. According to the Economist Intelligence Unit, after the general decline in GDP, the first signs of recovery became visible in 2009. Between the end of the second quarter of 2010 and the second quarter of 2011, the euro-zone countries had a small, 0.6% increase in their aggregate GDP and a 5.3% increase in industrial output. Unemployment, however, remained high at 16.5 million people, 10.4%, in the euro-zone, and 23.8 million, 9.9%, in the EU-27 countries in December 2011. The most tragic and dangerous phenomenon, however, is the extremely high young unemployment rate. In the EU-27 group, 5.5 million young people, under the age of 25, are unemployed, representing 22% of that age group. In some countries such as Slovakia (36%), Greece (47%), and Spain (49%) the figures of youth unemployment are frightening.[71] The 2011 output figures reflected a solid recovery in the euro-zone with 1.4% GDP growth, but in the last quarter of the year, five countries declined back into recession.[72]

TABLE 2.3 Main economic parameters of the European Union[73]

	1992– 1996*	1997– 2001*	2002– 2006*	2007	2008	2009	2010
GDP**	1.3	2.9	2.1	3.0	0.5	−4.2	1.8
GDP/capita**	1.1	2.7	1.6	2.5	0.1	−4.6	1.5
Investment**	2.4	4.3	2.6	5.8	−0.8	−12.0	−0.7
Private consumption**	2.5	2.5	2.1	2.5	3.0	0.3	2.2
Unemployment as % of workforce	10.1***	8.8	8.8	7.2	7.1	9.0	9.6
Government expenditures as % of GDP	50.1***	46.7	46.7	46.3	46.9	50.8	50.3

*5 year average; ** % change to previous year; *** the euro-zone countries

While some European countries have a double-dip recession, others have sluggish growth (Britain 0.9%, Italy 0.5%, Spain 0.6%, Norway 0.8%), but for some it is already quite robust: Austria 2.9%, Poland 3.8%, Sweden 4.3%, and Russia 4.0%. Greece represents a special case: during 2009 to 2011, and according to the 2012 forecasts, the country's GDP declined for four years by 2.0, 4.5, 6.0, and 2.8% respectively.[74] Several other countries in the core of Europe had a solid fiscal situation and modest economic growth in 2011. The euro-zone current account deficit was only 0.5% of the aggregate GDP of the region, and the combined budget deficit was 4.1%.

Some of the least affected economies are undergoing an impressive recovery and return to the pre-crisis growth pattern. Surprisingly enough, the three Baltic countries recovered from their most severe decline, and healthy growth already returned to Estonia in 2010, then to Lithuania, and then to all three of them. In 2011, Estonia already had 6.5% economic growth, Lithuania 6.3%, and Latvia 4.0%.[75] The fast recovery of Estonia and Latvia was closely connected to their extremely close economic ties with the Nordic countries, the healthy economy of Finland, and especially with Sweden, whose banks own the small Baltic countries' banking industry. Slovakia had somewhat similar pulsation: 4.2% decline in 2009, but 4.2% growth by 2010. All these figures clearly show that the real economy of Europe was rapidly climbing out of the recession of 2008–9. This was an international trend. In the first quarter of 2009, out of the 42 countries that are monitored by the

Economist Intelligence Unit, 28 countries had declining GDP figures, but in August 2010, only nine declined, and in 2011, only two.

The Statistical Office of the European Union, Eurostat, also reports the rapid recovery of Europe. The European Union-27 countries had an average 2.4% annual growth between 2005 and 2008, but they slowed down to 0.5% growth in 2008, suffered 4.3% declines in 2009, but by 2010 achieved 1.8% growth again, and 1.5% growth in 2011. In 2010, six countries in Europe still had further GDP decline: Iceland 4.0%, Greece 3.5%, Romania 1.9%, Croatia 1.2%, and Ireland 0.4%; in 2011, only one country, Greece, suffered a further decline. However, in the last quarter of the year, already five countries reported recession. All of these countries were located on the peripheries and, except Italy, represented only a small segment of European economic power. Their situation, theoretically speaking, should not have negatively influenced the European recovery.[76] But it did. In early 2012, however, the European Council revised its November 2011 forecast for 2012. According to the new calculations, nine countries will decline into a mild recession again and the entire euro-zone will suffer a 0.3% decline. This situation generated the crisis of the common currency.

The crisis of the euro

The 2010 figures for output and domestic production, though somewhat uneven, could signal a healthy and fast recovery. The storm, however, returned with multiplied strength by transforming from a financial and banking crisis into a *sovereign debt crisis*. It exploded in the spring of 2010. Public indebtedness elevated to dangerous levels in 2010: 137% of GDP in Greece, 119% in Italy, 85% in Portugal, and 79% in Britain, far above the European Union norm of 60%.[77] The total debts of the ten most developed countries of Europe—counting government, financial institutions, and households—reached 200% of GDP in 1995, but rose to 300% by 2008.It totaled 466% of GDP in Britain in 2009, 366% in Spain, 323% in France, 315% in Italy, 313% in Switzerland, and 285% in Germany. Between 2000 and 2008, only Germany, Switzerland, and Russia did not have a debt increase.[78]

The debt crisis significantly deepened in 2011, especially in its last quarter. The media and the financial markets reacted in a hysterical way. Newspapers did not exclude the possibility of the collapse of the common European currency within a few weeks. "Eighteen months into a sovereign debt crisis," forecasted *The New York Times* on November 28, 2011, "the endgame appears to be fast approaching for Europe."[79] On the cover page of *The Economist*, in one of the November issues of that year, appeared a euro coin, depicted as a comet plunging to its annihilation. "Is it the end?" A similar financial-economic crisis did not undermine the American dollar. How did it destabilize the euro? The 16-country euro-zone was an economic superpower in 2008. The bloc of more than 320 million people has a $13.6 trillion GDP,[80] 22% of the world's total and nearly equal with the USA's $14.1 trillion. The euro-zone has a 29% share in the world's exports and received 23% of the world's foreign direct investments.[81] The short, one-decade-long history of the euro was a success story. After a very short period of decline after its introduction, its value increased by 50% compared to the US dollar. Moreover, the euro rose to be a second international reserve currency, and one-quarter of international transactions used it. That has never happened in such a short time with any of the world's currencies.

Why was the euro endangered? The recurrence of economic ills and the endangering of the common currency had two major sources. One was the harsh austerity policy, introduced in most of the countries to cope with huge indebtedness and deficit. Banks also became overcautious with their crediting. These measures—cutting state expenditures, the income of the population, and the general credit supply of the economy—not only strictly limited but even curbed demand for investment and consumer goods. In the most crisis-ridden countries, such as Ireland, investments declined by 34%, in Britain they declined by 20% and in Spain by 12% by the last quarter of 2008. Private consumption decreased by 34% in Ireland, 21% in Spain, and 15% in Britain.[82] Because of the austerity measures, "we're going straight into a wall with this kind of policy. It's sheer madness," maintained an economist of the Graduate Institute of Geneva.[83] Italy's Prime Minister, Mario Monti, at his meeting with Angela Merkel on January 11, 2012, tried convincing the German Chancellor that "austerity alone was not the answer to Europe's sovereign debt crisis. . . . I cannot have success with my policies if the EU's policies don't change."[84] Indeed, Italy's new government in December 2011 introduced a $40 billion austerity program by reforming the pension system and increasing taxes. Its consequences on the negative side, however, will be a new recession of 1.5–2.2% decline in 2012. On January 20, 2012, Mario Monti announced the introduction of a new $7.1 billion stimulus package for infrastructural investments to "avoid an austerity trap." The new government of Spain cut spending by $11.3 billion and increased taxes by $8 billion. Austerity measures, while a cure for the debt crisis, are meanwhile decreasing demand in the domestic market and building barriers for economic growth. The harsh decline of investments and consumption slowed down the recovery and frightened itself with a double-dip crisis. This is coming to be realized in 2012. Cutting demand in the middle of a still-existing economic slump when demand is already decreased—as history illustrates[85]—may easily stop a nascent recovery and push the economy back into a second wave of recession.

Curbing the deficit and debt, although unavoidable, was slowing down economic growth, and thus an increase in the income of the population and the state. This situation expanded the indebtedness crisis and the crisis of trust in the repayment of debts. The financial markets started doubting the solvency of some of the euro-zone countries and turning away from the euro. The "austerity crisis" thus made the unsolved indebtedness crisis more dangerous in some of the euro-zone countries, including Italy. The international financial markets rapidly lost confidence in repayments and started considering possible defaults. Buying government bonds, once one of the safest forms of investment, lost its attraction, and the bond market went from being a buyer's market to a seller's market. Moreover, it became an immense danger that investors wanted to get rid of European bonds. *The Economist* reported in mid-November 2011: "The immediate risk is that banks which might have held Italian bonds as part of their liquidity reserves . . . are dumping them for safer bets. . . . Among the large European banks that are dumping Italian bonds are BNP Paribas and Commerzbank. 'It is what the market is asking us to do'. . . . Now that a run on bond markets has started, it may well keep feeding on itself."[86] Indeed, in early 2012, investors were ready to suffer some losses to be able to keep their money safe: for the first time German bonds sold with negative interest rates.

The debt crisis, the huge accumulation of government, and private, indebtedness, mostly in peripheral countries, at that point generated a bank crisis in the core of Europe as well, since the leading banks of Germany, France, Britain, and other strong core countries were buyers of bonds and lenders of credits. German, but especially French, banks own huge parts of the Greek, Italian, and Spanish debts, and they have had to write off significant parts of them. Between the second quarter of 2007 and the third quarter of 2009, Greek, Irish, Italian, Portuguese, and Spanish bond purchases by European banks increased by roughly one-quarter. By December 2010, French banks owned about €650 billion debts of the PIIGS countries; Germany's share was more than €500 billion, Britain's €350 billion, and the Netherlands' and Belgium's combined about €250 billion. Very few banks were not involved. Even small transformation countries were not exceptions. The Czech Komercni Bank—with its majority owner, the French Société Générale—invested in Greek bonds and had to write off about $200 million.[87] This nearly €1.8 trillion of poisonous bonds in the portfolios of banks of the stable core countries of Europe are the contagious virus of the ills that might contaminate healthy economies.

The European banks had to be recapitalized and the European Central Bank pumped €489 billion in cheap, long-term credits into the system on December 21, 2011. The European Banking Authorities required the increase of the banks' core reserve capital to 9% of their assets. Financial institutions have to raise a combined $145 billion by June 2012. This measure definitely decreases the risk of banking, but causes major problems for several banks. UniCredit, the largest Italian bank, for example, made its major stock offerings in January, planning to sell stocks for €1.943/share, but it suffered a "freefall" as investors have neglected buying. Most recently, shares sold for 47 euro-cents. The shares of the bank lost nearly one-quarter of their value. "Banks have been saying for some time that it's impossible for them to raise money collectively in this market." The leading Grupo Santander bank of Spain, however, easily raised $19 billion, the amount required to increase its reserves, six months before the deadline. Nevertheless, it will be a huge problem for the euro-zone banks and governments to raise the roughly €1.9 trillion ($2.43 trillion) that are needed for financing in 2012.[88] Several banks are trying to find a tricky exit by decreasing their capital and selling shares to avoid raising new capital.

The psychological factors, I have to stress again, are the most decisive at this movement. Italy's indebtedness was more or less on the same high level for at least 5–6 years, but the interest rates it had to pay on its bonds were not dramatically higher than for most of the countries with solid fiscal order. Paul Krugman noted this phenomenon: there was a general confidence in European Union countries regardless of their real economic strength. "Fiscal fears vanished" in the middle of the 2000s. "Greek bonds, Irish bonds, Spanish bonds, Portuguese bonds—they all traded as if they were as safe as German bonds. The aura of confidence extended even to countries that weren't in the euro yet but were expected to join in the near future."[89]

Domestic economic strength was mostly missing, and, because of the lack of a radical solution to the Greek crisis and of a safety net for highly indebted euro-zone countries, e.g., "a fire wall" around Italy and Spain, the financial market reacted in a hysterical way. The usual panic effect started working with renewed strength.

Less demand in the real economy and the new wave of panic on the financial markets made the selling of government bonds—the main weapon to finance governments' expenditures, including the repayment of old debts—increasingly difficult. The irresponsible financing practice of several countries, not staying within the limits of their budgetary constraints, making public debts and then servicing existing debts by issuing additional debts to cover the repayment of interests and principle in an endless vicious circle, was reminiscent of a Ponzi scheme.[90] This practice and the difficulties of repayment pushed interest rates up to dangerous heights, thus making the loans extremely expensive for the debtor countries. The declining bond market—higher cost of credit—and the increased possibility of default generated a frightening downward spiral toward the failure of the highly indebted governments. One may add to this trend that endangered governments try to cut their expenditures further, thus further decreasing domestic and consequently euro-zone demand.

The downward movement on the indebtedness spiral gained deadly strength in the last quarter of 2011. In November, when the Italian crisis significantly deepened, contagion became frightening for France because of the $100 billion worth of Italian bonds in the French banks. Consequently, the rate of the ten-year French government bonds also rose to 140 basis points.[91] Because the French banks have a huge chunk of peripheral bonds, the French government and its opposition, and even a great part of the public, are ready to assist the troubled peripheral countries.[92] France's AAA credit rating started to be questioned. If it was downgraded, the euro-zone as a whole would be severely endangered and the entire rescue operation would need an urgent reorientation. And downgrading was what happened in January 2012.

"The borrowing cost of nations at the heart of Europe jumped sharply on Tuesday. . .," reported *The New York Times* in November, 2011, "they also continued to increase in France, Spain and Belgium. The latter country's credit rating was already downgraded. Borrowing costs also moved upward in Finland, Austria, and the Netherlands, which have relatively strong underlying financial positions and until recently had mostly been spared the full effect of the financial crisis.. . . The ubiquitous nature of the increase of the yields suggests that the problem is spreading well beyond the troubled peripheral countries."[93] This movement was no longer a danger just for some national economies. The most seriously alarming possibility was the collapse of the common currency.

"The euro is endangered!" cried several experts and the international media in unison.[94] Some pundits already question the entire "artificial" construction of the European Union, "to build an economic and legal superstructure without linguistic, cultural, historic and civic base. . . . But now the inherent flaws are undermining the project. . . ."[95]

The "inherent flaws" were partly policy mistakes. The heart of the matter was the unsolved Greek debt crisis and the huge delay in stabilizing Italy and Spain, two solvent but troubled large countries which had also entered a dangerous stage of their own debt and bank crises. The possibility for default in two or three euro-zone countries endangered the common European currency, the euro. Several of the crisis-ridden countries, in particular Greece, Ireland, Italy, and Spain, use the euro. Their huge debt crises and the possibility of their default challenge the market value of the common currency, and have a bad impact on all the countries of the currency group. The crisis of the euro opened a new chapter in the entire European financial system.

The European Union was hesitant to act. No doubt, support for the banking sector helped curb the spread of the crisis: nine countries supported the banks with upfront payments and guarantee measures of $4,979 billion (nearly half this amount was paid in Britain alone). Bank rescue amounts rose to 82% of GDP in Britain, 70% in Sweden, 40% in the Netherlands, 35% in Austria, and 31% in Belgium.[96] Except liquidity-creating steps, hardly any other major steps were taken for nearly two years after the crisis erupted. Instead of taking the single large step of bailing out the banks and guaranteeing repayment of debts through radical structural changes to the euro-zone's financial mechanisms, only small steps were taken to provide the amount of money required at the moment when some government bonds matured and required repayment. The several small steps did not solve the debt problem and, at the end of the day, fueled its continuation and the deepening of the financial crisis.

"At every stage of this crisis Europe's leaders have reacted late and inadequately," commented *The Economist*.[97] Experts and the media blamed Germany and Chancellor Angela Merkel personally for the lack of radical actions. "At the center of it all sits Germany, leading the bloc of Northern European countries. . . . Any proposals to share the burden with the heavily indebted countries by collectivizing European debts . . . are rejected out of hand, largely for fear of a political backlash. . . . When Germany's council of independent economic advisers proposed to Chancellor Angela Merkel last week a way to share European debt to protect Italy and Spain, she dismissed the idea."[98] The powerful leaders did not recognize in time that the "north Europeans (and Mrs. Merkel's thrifty Germans in particular) will end up footing a good part of the bill, either by transferring money to the south or by bailing out their own banks."[99] Pundits complain about the lack of political leadership. "The European Union has a particularly acute version of leaders-who-will-not-lead." The author of another article saw a characteristic sign in the fact that in two countries of Europe "politicians accountable to the people must give way to unelected experts. . . . Leaders shape polls. They don't just read polls . . . [but] today, across the globe . . . leaders are in dangerously short supply."[100]

In principle the accusations are partly right because the damage caused by a potential collapse would definitely be much bigger, and the expenses much higher for all of the euro-zone countries, including Germany, than the sacrifices needed to solve problems. Charismatic leaders are, indeed, missing. However, Angela Merkel and the German government definitely had a strategy that they consistently followed. Instead of immediate financial help to solve the problems they actually forced the troubled countries to accept new rules of the game, a major step toward fiscal unification at the December 2011 Brussels meeting. In the long run, this step toward even closer integration and solving the mistaken monetary unification without fiscal unification is of the greatest importance. Without the refusal to transfer the required money immediately to the insolvent or near-insolvent countries, this agreement would probably have never been accepted. True, the short-term problems were not solved and require several further steps to avoid the collapse that was always just an arm's length away for a few countries.

However, in the democratic, parliamentary system, with the complicated European Union decision-making process, decisive action often hit the hard wall of public and political dissatisfaction and resistance, and the barrier of slow and complicated institutional mechanisms. One should not forget that during these few crisis years between 2008 and 2012, a dozen governments and leading European politicians lost power in, among others, Iceland, Ireland, Italy, Hungary, Finland, Denmark, Greece, Slovakia, France, Romania and Spain. This fact influenced government decisions elsewhere.

For months, France and other euro-zone countries urged Germany to accept the issuing of euro-bonds that would save Italy, Spain, and others from overpaying for their new debts. Germany consistently resisted doing so. It is easy to understand why. The German bonds (dubbed "bunds") were effortlessly sold on the financial market at the lowest rates. The crisis increased the comparative strength of, and the demand for, German bonds. Their interest rates consequently decreased from 4.7% in the summer of 2008, to 2% by late 2011, and even fell to negative interest rates in early 2012, a two-century low. As a Brussels research institute calculated, Germany saved $26.7 billion in borrowing costs between 2009 and 2011. Dutch savings neared $10 billion in those years. Germany and the Netherlands gained from the debt crisis since investors turned from the peripheral countries' bonds to the stable German and other bonds.[101] The euro-bond, since it would represent the entire euro-zone, would have higher rates than the German ones, thus Germany ought to pay more for their "Europeanized" bonds than for their own. The population of solid countries did not feel the crisis yet, and they even gained from it. Even if it is short-sighted, it is still understandable that the politicians of strong countries are hesitant to act, to sacrifice the advantages of their countries, and to endanger their own political careers.

The lack of efficient actions to save euro-zone countries from nearing bankruptcy, and instead giving only the relatively small amounts required to avoid an immediate crash when interest payments were due, generated an increasing financial panic. In the last months of 2011, the financial markets started considering the collapse of the euro. The possibility that some euro-zone countries would financially collapse started to generate an attempt to escape from the euro. The panic was fueled by frantic forecasts. "The euro-zone financial crisis has entered a far more dangerous phase," analysts stated, "a euro breakup now appears probable rather than possible."[102] Regulators in other countries, including the United States, were pushing their banks to reduce their exposure to European banks. The market was getting hesitant to buy European bonds at all, and in the last week of November, for the first time, one-third of the German bonds offered for sale was not sold. If only one euro-zone country defaulted, its impact on the financial markets would be magnified and endanger the entire bloc. As "first aid," six national banks, led by the American Federal Reserve and joined by Japan as well, offered cheap credits to bridge the gap until radical European decisions could be made. In the summer of 2012, even the Chinese National Bank decided to contribute.

Why did the euro become endangered? Was it only the consequence of policy mistakes, hesitation, and inefficient help to the crisis-ridden member countries of the euro-zone? Or was it an unavoidable phenomenon that originated from deeper structural problems? To answer these questions, one has to dig into deeper layers of the causes of the crisis.

3

THE ECONOMIC CAUSES: CONTEMPORARY EUROPEAN CAPITALISM

The financialized, deregulated market system in the globalized world economy and partially integrated Europe

What caused the 2008 European financial crisis? Using Günter Grass' metaphor,[1] we have to "peel the onion," disclosing several layers of the crisis *below* the irresponsible government and private spending, ballooning housing bubbles, and accumulating debts that planted a whole field of mines in Europe that were ignited by, and exploded after, the international liquidity crisis. Although the economic turbulence is not over yet, several studies and books have already been published,[2] partly on the American crisis phenomenon. The American and European crises, however, are not only closely related but in fact basically the outcome of the same development.

In *What Caused the Financial Crisis,* edited by Jeffrey Friedman, 22 economists discuss various aspects of the causes of the crisis. The editor, in his introduction on "Capitalism and the Crisis," stated that "this was a crisis of regulated capitalism, but the pressing question is whether it was the capitalism or the regulations that were primarily responsible." His answer to the question "whether it was . . . a crisis that can be attributed to capitalism," is negative, noting that the crisis "took place within the economy . . . but [as the contributors of the book agree] this was a crisis of politics, not economics." Economists, including the authors of that volume, do not agree about the causes: "some of our authors," the editor noted, "blame the crisis on government action while others blame it on government inaction." Since both action and inaction are government policy, the crisis was thus "the result of government policy," or a "policy failure."

If some of the readers are surprised to read that it was a crisis of "regulated capitalism," it is important to add that according to Friedman even laissez-faire, deregulated capitalism is a "system of laws – that is, of regulations." [3] He is right, of course, that both regulation and deregulation are policy decisions. However, the set of regulations or the laws of deregulation are based on totally different political philosophies and economic theories. To put both systems under the same umbrella of "regulated capitalism" is more than confusing.

One, what is commonly called a "self-regulated" or laissez-faire, market system is based on the ideology of and belief in a perfect, harmonious market automatism, a market that successfully regulates itself. It is also based on the experience that some deregulations improve economic efficiency. In its most extreme form, the representatives of this ideology also argue that the market is the best regulator of and solution for social problems as well. Outside intervention, i.e., government regulations, according to this concept, are harmful since they destroy the smooth work of market automatism.

The other system, commonly called a regulated market economy, is based on the experience that the market is not perfect and in several situations unable to successfully regulate itself. It is also based on the ideology and belief that mankind is able to understand society and economy, and therefore people (governments) are able to implement regulations that improve the economy and defend society from the negative side effects of the market. The representatives of this concept stress that markets do not solve but, rather, create social problems such as huge income inequalities that endanger both the social fabric of the society and balanced growth. The operation of market mechanisms thus requires a policy to counterbalance its negative social consequences. Government interventions and regulations are, therefore, needed.

Dr. Friedman's formulation confuses these two main historical types of market capitalism, the *regulated market system*, and the *self-regulating market economy*, as Karl Polanyi differentiates them.[4] It is the wrong question to ask whether capitalism or regulation policy is responsible for the crisis. The real question is *which type of capitalist market system is responsible*? My answer to this question, as discussed below, is that "contemporary capitalism," i.e., *the globalized deregulated or self-regulating, financialized market system is responsible for the crisis.*

Several economists blame the banking system. "I would argue," Nobel laureate Joseph Stiglitz said, "that blame should be centrally placed on the banks (and the financial sector more broadly) and the investors. The banks were supposed to be the expert of risk management. They not only didn't manage risk, they created it."[5] Gary Gorton agrees: "The current crisis has its roots in the transformation of the banking system. . . . The banking system metamorphosed in the last 25 to 30 years, and this transformation re-created the conditions for a [banking] panic."[6] A similar view was expressed by Jeremy Atack: "In the past three decades, the world has witnessed dramatic changes in the organization and operations of financial intermediaries and markets . . . [since] successive waves of financial deregulation spread around the world beginning around 1980—a process often referred to in each country as the big bang."[7] The author describes pre-1980 traditional banking as a procedure where banks derived loanable funds from depositors and lent it to creditworthy customers. Until full repayment, a relationship developed between lender and borrower. Nowadays banking depends upon impersonal capital markets. "They increasingly repackage and resell their loans to third parties. . . . This behavior changes their incentives from concern about the long-term outcome to immediate cash income."[8]

What was the essence of the transformation of the financial system? First, the birth of "shadow banking" outside any kind of banking regulations. However, shadow banks, including insurance companies, hedge funds, pension funds, and several other institutions, acted and operated as real banks. Second, several financial "innovations" transformed banking activities by creating a derivative securities business that totaled an astronomical amount of money and used it to gamble at extremely high risk. As several economists agree, all these were closely connected with the deregulation of the financial system.

Recessions and depressions, short, medium, and long economic waves are regular parts of economic development, which is never linear but exhibits some pulsation, the so-called business cycle.[9] The 2008 crisis, however, was not just a usual cyclic phenomenon. It was not even a usual "bubble" that also goes together with the market economy. Friedman notes on the first page of his edited volume that "no contributor argues that the Great Recession was just a normal business-cycle downturn or even a normal popped asset bubble."[10] Schumpeter is thus right when he states: "each [crisis] is a historical individual and never like any other."[11]

The main peculiarities of the 2008 European crisis are the consequences of the transformed contemporary market capitalist system. From the 1970s– 1980s on, a new chapter was opened in the history of capitalism and Europe. Industrial capitalism turned to be a highly financialized, drastically deregulated, speculative market system in a closely interrelated, globalized world economy. All these factors worked in a partially integrated Europe where a non-federalized, but economically integrated group of independent countries established a monetary union without fiscal unification. This system has been designed and realized by neo-liberal economists, neo-conservative or new-centrist politicians, and central bankers. They kept interest rates irresponsibly low. Bankers and hedge fund managers took high risks for extra-high profits and implemented an irresponsible crediting policy. Several governments and a huge part of the population of consumer societies relied on equally irresponsible borrowing practices. In the case of Europe, the mistaken arrangement of monetary unification without fiscal unification, and a one-size-fits-all policy in the highly diverse Union, also played a major role in the crisis.

In this chapter, I am going to present all of these special features of European capitalism in the last three–four decades and show how their impact led to the crisis.

The financialized capitalist system

Sixty years ago the famous British economist Joan Robinson noted: "where enterprise leads, finance follows."[12] This is not the case any longer. As one of Europe's leading bank experts, the German Jürgen Stark, former member of the executive board of the European Central Bank, stated in November 2011: "the financial sector stepped out of its role of serving the real economy . . . the financial sector had grown too large and became too self-referential." Stark illustrated his statement by shocking facts. As a typical trend in the OECD countries, *mutatis mutandis*, the financial sector has grown six-times faster than the nominal GDP of the United States. The value of shares, bonds, and loans to the private sector is more than three times (315%) the GDP in the United States, more than four times (430%) the GDP in Britain, and—as an average—nearly three times (262%) the GDP in the euro-zone.[13] It is also characteristic that European direct investments in other European countries skyrocketed. After 1985, its amount doubled in every two years. Two-thirds of them were channeled into the service sector, and within it, finance and insurance received the lion's share. Manufacturing's share was only one-third.[14] George Soros is right to say that "the system is very favorable to financial capital which is free to pick and choose where to go. . . . It can be envisaged as a gigantic circulatory system. . . . Financial capital [was put] into the driver's seat."[15]

What is the connection between the financialization of the economy and the 2008 crisis? A financial panic always has a negative impact on the entire economy. However, if it is not finance, but the so-called "real economy," and most of all industry that is dominant within the economic system, a financial panic is only a transitory blow to the real economy. If the financial sector plays the dominant role, a panic may lead to the collapse of the leading sector of the economy. In such a situation, the state has to run to bail out the banking sector to save the economy and consumers merely because of the size of the financial sector. One can use for the entire financial sector the term that is always used for single financial institutions: too big (to allow) to fail. These bailouts naturally lead to the accumulation of public debt and to a sovereign debt crisis. This happened in Europe and will be discussed below.

Financial capital, indeed, is driving its own way. It left behind its classical functions, such as providing information about investment projects, allocating capital, monitoring investments, and exerting corporate governance after providing finance. Banks used to facilitate trade, diversification, and management of risk, and did mobilize and pool savings. Instead of offering these traditional banking services, "during recent years," as Jürgen Stark concludes, "the financial sector had lost focus in playing this role and instead had become more self-referential, undertaking activities characterized by search-for-yield with inadequate risk assessment and pricing." [16]

How did this dramatic structural change happen in contemporary capitalism? From the turn of the nineteenth century until the mid-twentieth century, the industrial sector dominated the economic structure of the advanced countries. Advancement and industrialization were virtually synonyms. [17] From the 1970s–80s on, the advanced Western world experienced a spectacular *de-industrialization*. During the last third of the twentieth century, the labor force employed in manufacturing declined from 48% to 20% in Britain, from 42% to 16% in the Netherlands, from 40% to 21% in Italy, and from 45% to 18% in Sweden. [18] By 2004, industry's contribution to GDP in the euro-zone amounted to only 27%. Several polluting industries, mining, and then the highly labor-intensive industrial branches migrated to developing countries, where the looser environmental rules and cheap and unlimited labor resources offered higher profitability.

From the 1990s on, this trend became virtually all-European: post-communist Central and Eastern Europe suddenly and rapidly followed the Western trend, although its driving force was different. De-industrialization in this region was the consequence of the collapse of most of the inefficient local industries after these countries opened their economies to foreign competition. In one-and-a-half decades between 1989 and 2004, industry's contribution to GDP declined from 42% to 32% in Poland, from 40% to 28% in Hungary, and from 57% to 32% in Romania. The share of industrial employment in the labor force was 31.2% in the euro-zone, and 33.0% in the ten former communist countries in 2004. [19]

This trend was accompanied by the so-called *service revolution*. The rise of the service sector more than counterbalanced the decline of the industrial and agricultural sectors and gradually rose to a dominant role. In the 1970s, the service sector produced about half of the total value added, but at the turn of the century, it produced nearly three-quarters of it.[20] Services employed half of the labor force in the postwar years, but this share increased to nearly three-quarters around the turn of the millennium.[21] Within the service sector, financial services rose to be the most important and largest branch. Banks, insurance companies, and so-called "parallel banking" (the "shadow banking" system[22] and the "near-banks"),[23] i.e., the financial sector as a whole became the leading branch of the advanced economies. The financial sector outgrew all the others in the last third of the twentieth century.

The spectacular rise of the financial sector started in Britain in the late nineteenth century, but the "first industrial nation," which reached economic maturity before others, was not followed soon by others. The service revolution and the financialization of the economy emerged in continental Europe after World War II, especially after the collapse of the Bretton Woods international regulatory system in August 1971. The Bretton Woods Agreement in July 1944 established an international monetary order by stabilizing currencies and regulating international commercial and financial relations.[24] When the Nixon administration left the gold standard and Bretton Woods collapsed, floating exchange rates became incompatible with capital control, thus it was eliminated and the barriers to the free movement of capital were dismantled. These changes made it important for investors to diversify their portfolios to spread their risks. At that point a changed, modern financial system emerged. It was characterized by massive capital flows, and widespread speculation with currencies and the arbitrage[25] business.

Financial panics accompanied the history of the financial system in Europe.[26] Nevertheless, the crisis that started in 2007–8 was rather different from financial panics as we knew them. All of the previous financial panics happened in the age of merchant and then industrial capitalism. This new one arrived in the era of a highly financialized capitalist economy in the advanced Western world. Financialization itself became one of the main causes of the crisis. Although the liquidity crisis and financial panic were global, recession hit the advanced, financialized Western world the most, and not the industrializing, developing world.

The so-called emerging countries virtually remained outside the crisis. Financial panic and transitory liquidity crisis did not influence their real economy, and they regained robust growth in a few months. In 2009, when Europe (and the United States) declined into recession, Asian growth continued by an average of 6.6%, the Middle East by 2.4%, and Sub-Saharan Africa by 2.1%. [27] Most of the emerging countries, however, are not only rising industrial powers, but are also highly different from the Western world in their strictly regulated and in many ways state-directed systems. Instead of the Western world's financialized, deregulated capitalism, the emerging countries have a well-organized state capitalism[28] that excluded most of the domestic prerequisites of such an economic crisis.

Financialization and globalization

The financialization of contemporary Western capitalism emerged in the framework and economic environment of *globalization*.[29] This trend especially characterized the financial systems that genuinely had strong international activities and developed to maturity within a widespread connection of networks. The financial panic and the debt crisis naturally became much more contagious in this globalized financial and economic system. The collapse of one major bank or the debt crisis of one single country might generate an avalanche and carry away several other countries' banking sectors. Globalization thus multiplied the danger and harshness of an international crisis. This impact is discussed below.

One should add to this connection that globalization and financialization have another major interrelationship. Namely, that nowadays, the Western capitalist market system is partly the outcome of a globalized capitalist market economy. The 1970s–80s—when globalization rose to new heights—were also the stage for a set of dramatic technological changes.[30] Among them was the communications revolution. A new and explosively developing information technology emerged and made possible several financial innovations and the permanent flow of an enormous amount of capital throughout the world in minutes.[31] In the post-Bretton Woods era, foreign direct investments, consequently, started to soar: they amounted to $107 billion in 1980, but increased exponentially to $1,230.4 billion by 2006. About half of the latter amount ($589.8 billion) went to Western Europe (European countries partly investing in each other), and $92.4 billion to transforming Central and Eastern Europe, including the successor states of the Soviet Union.[32]

The flow of foreign exchange transactions skyrocketed and became many times bigger than the output of the real economy and hugely surpassed the financial strength of the nation states.[33] Financial transactions, especially after their explosion in the early twenty-first century, generated an unheard-of amount of capital flow: in 2007 they surpassed the aggregate GDP of the world by 66 times.[34] Foreign exchange transactions amounted to $15 billion a day in 1973, $186 billion in 1986, $800 billion in 1991 and between $1.5 and $2.0 trillion by 2006, 50–60 times the value of world trade. From these astronomical figures, about 20% was connected with trade or investments at the beginning, but at the end only 1% was, and 80–99% was speculative business, so-called "hot money," run into and out of countries in a few hours or days. This hot money, among others, served currency speculations, borrowing, exchanging, and selling a currency, speculating on its devaluation, thus on the repayment of the borrowed money with a huge profit (discussed below). Another profitable use was the speculative arbitrage business, when financiers were simultaneously buying and selling assets exploiting the price differences on various markets.[35]

Globalization is run by tens of thousands of multinational companies that are working internationally, establishing subsidiaries throughout the globe.[36] The banking industry, genuinely multinational from its nineteenth century birth on,[37] owns and dominates the international financial markets. Nevertheless, until the 1960s, international banking did business from their home bases. Credit institutions enjoyed a natural monopoly in the country in which they were located. This practice changed from the 1970s, and by 1986, less than one-fifth of the gross international banking continued the traditional practice. Banking became thoroughly internationalized. Banking institutions are collecting deposits internationally and also lending the money throughout the world. The European banking system became totally "Europeanized." Cross-border, cross-currency claims in Europe that amounted to $20 billion in 1964 increased to $3,117 billion in somewhat more than two decades. International lending in Europe and the euro-zone became entirely pan-European.[38] Today, we can speak about a global financial system.

In a controversial way, however, the world and especially the European economy remained in the traditional framework of nation states. Although the states lost a great part of their real independence, international governance did not emerge. Joseph Stiglitz speaks about three main institutions that "*govern* globalization," the International Monetary Fund (IMF), the World Bank, and the World Trade Organization (WTO). True, these institutions have an important role in the globalized system. However, one can hardly speak about their role as "governing" globalization. One of the most experienced international hedge fund speculators, George Soros, has a totally different view: "We are sadly lacking in the appropriate financial authorities in the international arena . . . additional institutions may be necessary. . . . We also have to establish some kind of international supervision over the national supervisory authorities. . . . No individual state can resist the power of global financial markets and there are practically no institutions for rule making on an international scale. Collective decision-making mechanisms for the global economy simply do not exist."[39]

Financialized and globalized market capitalism does not tolerate the strait-jacket of the strict regulations that were introduced after the Great Depression and partly internationalized after World War II. This system has a tendency to liberate itself from state control that limited its movement. The new international financial system, indeed, became deregulated. Governments and international agreements mostly eliminated binding regulations. The freedom of the financial markets belongs to globalized capitalism. "Liberalization," concludes John Eatwell, "has created a seamless financial world."[40]

The deregulated market system

From the 1970s on, hand-in-hand with the financialization and globalization of the market system, deregulation gained ground and created—or better, re-established[41]—the laissez-faire, self-regulating market. In this system, the "economy is directed by market prices and nothing but market prices . . . without outside help or interference." [42] "In the 1980s, the attitude toward international capital transactions shifted gradually but significantly in favour of deregulation and liberalization. . . . [The Maastricht Treaty codified it:] All restrictions on the movement of capital between member states and between member states and third countries shall be prohibited."[43] The self-regulated system ruled market capitalism for a third of a century before the 2008 crisis.

Deregulation "liberated" the financial system, banks, and shadow banking from safety regulations. The significantly lowered barriers to leverage, the ratio between borrowed money and owned assets, thus eliminated the buffer or reserves required to defend the banking sector against sudden losses and shocks. Financial institutions became able to sell their loans by packaging them as securities (bonds), which undermined the need for careful evaluation of the borrowers' creditworthiness. Banking institutions—since they were "sharing the risks" through securitization—became much more risk-taking. Deregulation made financial business more hazardous, offering huge profits, but also creating dangerous vulnerabilities and a much bigger chance of a crash. This is the topic of this sub-chapter.

This regime is built upon the abstract idea that the market is perfect and balanced if not disturbed from outside (by the state). According to the "Say Law" of classical economics, supply automatically creates its demand. In reality, however, the cyclical trend of economic development proves especially clearly that there is no ideal harmony in the market system, and the lack of demand often leads to recessions.[44] Most times in history, as Karl Polanyi maintains, markets were regulated and the economy subordinated to the society. In a self-regulating market regime, society is subordinated to the interests of the economy.[45] Economic growth and globalized banking became the new Golden Calf. If business is growing, the idea was, profit will trickle down and the entire population will get a share of it. This new ideological economics-regime was part of the change of the Zeitgeist after the dual political and economic crises that took place in Europe from the end of the 1960s and during the 1970s.

The 1968 mini-revolution in Paris, and the Left and Right terrorism against the state and business establishments in Germany and Italy during the 1970s, together with rising globalization and the transforming world order, generated a major about-face in the cultural-ideological environment of the Western world.[46] Doubts emerged about the unintended negative side effects of postwar policies and institutions. Several liberal, left-wing intellectuals became deeply disappointed and turned against their former ideas. Genuinely traditional conservatives, pushed aside after the war, reemerged and became influential again. They opposed the "unaffordable" state interventionism and the redistributive welfare policy. The welfare state, they declared, undermines the basic values of capitalism.[47] In the globalized world, when employment became uncertain, jobs outsourced, and investments shifted to low-wage countries, huge groups of workers perceived their enemies in immigrant workers who occupied their jobs. Many of them have turned toward the anti-immigration Right.

The entire concept of enlightened rationalism, which dominated social thinking and actions since the eighteenth century, was vehemently questioned. Belief in historical progress and the power of human actions to influence it was replaced by skepticism about the possibility of understanding the world and truth. Disappointment generated relativism and nihilism. Left-leaning parties—communists, socialists, and left-liberals—lost their self-confidence and the belief in a politics they had regarded as successful before. Their identity crisis undermined their organizations. Communist parties virtually disappeared; social democracy turned to a "Third Way," a "higher synthesis" of left and right, and shifted to the center.[48] The Left became fragmented, disorganized, and their mass parties lost the masses.

This environment became the hotbed of a rising new political culture and ideology. From the 1970s on, neo-liberalism emerged, triumphantly rejecting Keynes and negating state interventions and regulations. Because the externally, politically generated oil crises[49] ignited high inflation, the additional Keynesian demand-creating measures did not work. The financial side of demand creation is inflationary financing of job creation. When Keynesian economics had no answer to the crisis, neo-liberalism gained ground. Naomi Klein, in journalistic language, called this emerging regime "disaster capitalism."[50] The various disasters, economic, human, and even natural,[51] were used to eliminate regulations and re-introduce the self-regulating market economy. It merged with the rising neo-conservatism or the new Right, and a whole set of post-modern ideologies. Neo-liberal economics became the most powerful new ideological trend. The return to a simplified classical liberal school in an extreme way not only dethroned Keynesian economics, but also offered a new comprehensive ideological-political base, which was later often called market fundamentalism.

The prophets of this new Zeitgeist were Ludwig von Mises and Friedrich Hayek of the Vienna School of Economics, and several members of the neo-liberal Chicago School of Economics, from Milton Friedman to Robert Lucas Jr. Hayek and Friedman launched an ideological war advocating deregulation, privatization, and unrestricted free markets as the only solutions in a free society in the grips of cut-throat global competition. Both Hayek and Friedman connected laissez-faire policy with social and political principles. Undisturbed self-regulating markets, they claim, guarantee social and individual freedom and prosperity. State intervention, on the other hand, is *The Road to Serfdom,* as the title of one of Hayek's books proclaims.

For Milton Friedman, state intervention was the real cause of economic trouble because it disturbed market automatism. A self-regulated market is able to correct itself. Welfare institutions represent brutal intrusions upon personal freedom. He advocated radical privatization, radical tax cuts, and the introduction of a uniform flat tax rate of around 16% for everybody. Government expenditures have to be drastically reduced by privatizing nearly everything, including pension schemes, the health service, and schooling, as well as making families and individuals responsible for their own schooling, healthcare, and pension schemes. Friedman also advocated "a high natural rate of unemployment" as a prerequisite of a dynamic and progressive economy.[52]

According to neo-liberal ideas, undisturbed and unregulated markets may solve all of society's economic *and* social problems. Its believers are convinced that undisturbed free market mechanism and the profit motive may well regulate the social sphere as well. An advisor to Margaret Thatcher wrote in *The Guardian* in February 1985: "Ideas from Hayek and Friedman . . . were assimilated precisely because experience had already created a place for them by convincing people that neo-Keynesian economics, trade-union hegemony and the permissive society had failed."[53] Francis Fukuyama expressed the Zeitgeist of the triumph of neo-liberal democracy in the most characteristic way. He declared the "end of history," maintaining that liberal, free-market democracy conquered the world, defeated all its rival ideologies, and became the "end point of mankind's ideological evolution" and ended in the "final form of human government."[54]

The financial markets, which wanted to get rid of binding regulations to gain more freedom, more flexibility, and more lucrative business opportunities, were able to realize their goals in this new political-ideological environment. Nothing can be more typical than a spring 2006 speech by Panagiatos Thomopoulos, the deputy governor of the Bank of Greece. He triumphantly informed his European colleagues of the "radical transformation" of the Greek banking system, "evolving from the highly regulated sector it was 15 years ago, when the Bank of Greece set over 150 different levels of interest rates to become a free competitive and dynamic sector and a key pillar in Greece's successful economic performance."[55] Three years later, as discussed in Chapter 1, the entire Greek economy collapsed.

How did it happen that the strictly regulated market system, with fixed exchange rates, restricted international movement of capital, and bank activities that were strictly controlled and directed by rules and laws to guarantee safe operations and counterbalance risks, was so easily eliminated? How did it happen that the lessons of the devastating Great Depression were so rapidly forgotten? How did it happen that a system, which "subordinated the economy to the society" and built up the welfare state, was so radically deregulated, and replaced by self-regulating markets?

The neo-liberal economics and ideology were at hand already for a while. The economic crisis of the 1970s, the conservative political and ideological turn of the 1980s, the collapse of a Keynesian solution all prepared the political soil, and globalization gave a strong incentive to act. Globalization virtually ignited the deregulation drive under the banner of sharp worldwide competition. Each country had to adjust to the new situation and be competitive, able to race with the most flexible countries, which had the best advantages. Banks put aside the traditional compulsory strict credit standard and the intensive monitoring of their credits to be able to lend and invest more.[56] Systematic deregulation began in the 1980s and ran amok until 2004. Consecutive American governments—Republican and Democratic—have rushed to clear the way for financial institutions. In 1980, the first major deregulatory reform since the Great Depression, the Depository Institutions Deregulation and Monetary Control Act, was signed by President Jimmy Carter. Among other things, it lowered the mandatory reserve requirement for banks and founded a five-member Deregulation Committee.

President Ronald Reagan and Prime Minister Margaret Thatcher became the main political representatives of the neo-liberal, deregulatory ideals and realized them in the United States and Britain. "The most dramatic change," noted Joseph Stiglitz, "occurred in the 1980s, the era when Ronald Reagan and Margaret Thatcher preached free market ideology . . . ."[57] The policy, however, continued under their successors, George H.W. Bush, Bill Clinton, and George W. Bush, as well as under Tony Blair's Labour government.

During the Reagan administration, the pioneer and initiator of the world-wide deregulation policy, major changes followed each other. In 1982, savings and loan institutions were allowed to engage in commercial, corporate business, and investment activities. In 1988, the Glass-Steagall Act of 1933—the most important banking regulation of the Roosevelt administration—was repealed and made investment business possible for commercial banks and other financial institutions. Pooling and selling mortgage loans became possible. Between 1989 and 1993, swaps and derivatives were exempt from all regulations. The amount of exchange of securities business (swaps)—interest rates and currency swaps—totaled $426.7 trillion by 2009. In 1998, a major merge of Citibank, Travelers, Salomon, and Smith Barney created a giant financial institution that united commercial banking, investment banking, and insurance businesses. In 1999, the Gramm-Leach-Bliley Financial Services Modernization Act opened the floodgates for subprime mortgages.[58] In 2004, the law allowed for investment banks to determine their own net capital. With a series of deregulations, government control was reduced and eliminated to increase competitiveness.

As Willem Molle argues regarding the European Union: "progressive abolition of regulations was stimulated by the experience in many countries." Unregulated "offshore markets" created huge competition. Britain and the Netherlands unilaterally deregulated, and in 1992, the entire European Union also decided to follow.[59]

Banks pooled and sold mortgage loans as bonds. Private rating companies with government recognition rated bad mortgage loans as AAA-rated bonds in a corrupt system, where the rating companies legally received fees from banks for the rating.

The United States, a traditional laissez-faire oriented country, pioneered deregulations, and the new type of self-regulated market spread over Europe and other parts of the world. The main institution for spreading these reforms was the so-called G-10 group of the richest countries, such as the United States, Canada, Japan, and the leading European countries such as Britain, Belgium, France, Germany, and Italy. The representatives of the G-10 countries—central banks and regulatory authorities—decided to promote uniform capital requirements to guarantee competitiveness. They established the Basel Committee in 1988 to standardize bank regulations. The recommendation of the Committee, the so-called Basel Accord, was not binding, but it still became law in the G-10 countries by 1992. This accord was updated and amended in 1990, 1991, 1993, 1995, and 1996 and created a kind of uniform system.

Europe thus followed suit in the deregulation mania. As the European Central Bank's experts summed up: "Following a process of de-regulation and innovation in credit markets over the two decades prior to the credit crisis . . . European banking markets became increasingly integrated and more competitive. . . . It forced banks to operate closer to the best practice."[60] European banking institutions thus adopted the American-initiated financial practice and system.[61]

Beside the G-10 group, as Joseph Stiglitz noted, "The IMF and the World Bank became the new missionary institutions, through which these ideas were pushed on . . . countries that often badly needed their loans and grants."[62] When the crisis undermined the Latin American countries, and then the Soviet Bloc collapsed in 1989–91, neo-liberal policy became virtually mandatory in the developing Latin American and the so-called "transforming countries" of Central and Eastern Europe via the IMF's "conditionalities" for loans. Deregulation, in advanced Western Europe and the transforming countries of Eastern Europe, also became part of globalization.

Globalized deregulation, especially of the financial markets, undoubtedly created a more flexible system, and consequently cheap and abundant credit. Liberal trade and capital flow strategies gave the incentive for export-led growth strategy as well. Risky bank actions and the birth of "shadow banking" systems, including venture capitalists and hedge funds with their ever-increasing investment activities, as well as the transformation of the bank and insurance businesses into investment banking with their successful credit creation, all helped to cope with the difficult crisis situation of the 1970s–80s. With the help of an unlimited and cheap credit flow, prosperity was reinstated and became dominant during the 1990s and early 2000s. As an OpEd page article in the *Wall Street Journal* triumphantly declared, "Never in history of the world has the human race enjoyed such material prosperity." The article was published in August 2007.[63] The deregulating legislation and other measures, as the deputy governor of the Bank of Greece proudly declared in 2006, "Would allow the European financial service sector to gradually realize its full potential. . . . [Because] major changes have taken and are still taking place in the regulation landscape."[64]

The over-financialized and deregulated market system introduced a new type of capitalism with important new features. What are its main characteristics? Bank safety regulations such as keeping a sufficient capital cushion behind lending and separating commercial and investment banking were all revised and decreased to make a more aggressive lending policy possible. "Shadow banking" became widespread: even credit unions and insurance companies became investment banks, and most of all, the newly emerged hedge funds became investment banks without any regulations.

Hedge funds have been the most extreme players of the deregulated financial system. They not only operated as investment banks without any restrictions, but—unlike banks—they did not have their own capital; they used only their clients' money. Hedge funds' profit was the fee the clients paid if the investment was successful. In this case, the hedge fund's fee amounted to 20%, and sometimes an even higher percentage of the gain. If the investment failed, and the money of the client was lost, it was the loss of the client and not that of the hedge fund. This means that hedge fund managers were motivated to take the highest possible risk to run for the highest possible gain. Risk counted little because of the lack of any possibility of real loss. The genuine gambling character of the hedge funds is well expressed by the fact that the typical leverage ratio of a hedge fund is $30 of debts for $1 of actual capital. And half the credits created in recent years were created by unregulated hedge funds and similar institutions.

An even more gambling-like type of hedge fund activity is trading currencies, betting on the rise or decline of the value of certain currencies. Hedge funds attack some currency to make a huge profit. Currency speculation ruined several national currencies, among them even the British pound and several Asian currencies. George Soros' Quantum Fund launched a deadly attack against the British pound in the summer of 1990. They borrowed quietly, from various sources, about $15 billion worth of British pounds and exchanged it for US dollars. The noisy attack started by short-selling pounds. George Soros gave a series of interviews about the unavoidable devaluation of the British currency. This generated a run on the pound by other worried investors, and, at the end, the John Major British government—after failed defensive actions—devalued the pound by 15%. Using the dollars he exchanged when the pound had a higher value, Soros could now buy cheaper pounds after the devaluation and repay the pounds he'd borrowed. "Soros not only made roughly a billion dollars in quick capital gains but also established himself as perhaps the most famous speculator of all time."[65] This was not the only case. In his 1988 book, Soros himself confessed: "it must be admitted that hedge funds like mine did play a role in the Asian currency turmoil."[66] Hedge funds became major players on the financial markets.

Deregulated banks played a similar speculative role. As we have seen in the example of Icelandic banks in Chapter 1, they used borrowed money, and were ready to pay higher interest to get huge assets to invest in risky projects that promised high profits. Short-term credits were often invested in long-term projects. "Overbanking," or investing heavily in long-term, illiquid securities issued by various corporations based on deposits of investors, increased volatility and risk.[67] The second Basel Accord, for example, allowed the large banks to make their own risk management system. This step of deregulation itself had huge consequences. Some analysts flatly blame this change for the crisis.[68] Actually, these self-calculations also served the rating agencies that evaluated creditworthiness. In other words, the entire rating system became a kind of self-service by the banking institutions. "By relying on the risk calculations of the market participants, the regulators pulled up the anchor and unleashed a period of uncontrolled credit expansion."[69]

One of the most important financial innovations allowed by deregulation was the *securitization* of credits, which entirely transformed commercial lending. Creditors (who offered mortgage loans, credit card loans, personal loans, student loans, corporate loans, car loans, etc.) performed this transaction by pooling their loans and packaging them as issued securities—called collateralized debt obligations—and then selling their existing loans to investors in this form. Selling these assets became legal in the 1970s in the United States, first in the mortgage business, but they were also used from 1985-6 in non-mortgage businesses, such as car loans and credit card loans. From 1990, it spread to the insurance business as well.

Securitization became one of the most flourishing financial activities. Britain followed soon after, and during the Reagan-Thatcher 1980s, this became part of the Anglo-Saxon deregulated financial system. Banks, hedge funds, pension funds and other institutions were ready to buy the securitized loans to diversify their assets and get higher interest rates. The borrowers mostly do not even know about these actions, but their payments went to the new investors, gradually paying the fully amortized securities back in the specified term. This new method, one of the "innovations" of the financial markets, totally eliminated the traditional lending standards.

Again, it is a commonly shared view that this shift in banking generated the explosive growth of crediting. Bank credit became—to use the financial jargon—an "originate-to-distribute" action. The bank "originated" the credit, and then sold or "distributed" it to other investors. This model made it possible to neglect the existing regulations on lending limits that were designed to prevent excess risk-taking. The sold loans were off-loaded from the bank records and providing new loans became possible. This innovation also made possible aggressive and excess lending. A part of this business was the so-called "credit default swap," another jargon term for a pledge by the seller to the buyer to compensate him in case of a loan default. The buyer, in this case, is compensated for the entire amount, and the seller gets back the loan and tries to recover it. This credit default market skyrocketed in the decade between 1997 and 2007 from $94 billion to $45.5 trillion in the United States. This innovation spread to Europe as well.

Securitizing credits increased money circulation; the company that issued the loan did not have to wait until the borrowers fully repaid it, sometimes in three to 30 years, but sold it after a few years during the period they collected only interest from the buyer, received immediate cash, increased its liquidity, and could issue new credits and gain new profits. Besides, they could report the transaction as new earnings that attracted investors and steeply increased CEOs' bonuses. Deregulation opened the door for easier access to credit, including the less- and least-creditworthy consumers. The lending companies transferred the risk to other companies. Between 1995 and 2005, these transactions increased in the United States by 19% per year. By 2005, the amount of securitized credits amounted to $8.06 trillion. About one-third of it was mortgage credits, 40% were corporate credits, and one-fifth credit card loans. American household debt, which accounted for 80% of the disposable income of the borrowers in 1986, reached 140% by 2007. However, the indebtedness of British households was even greater. Deregulated financial markets offered the advantage of more flexible and risky financial activities, which mostly earned higher profits and resulted in cheap credit for the economy.

The other main financial innovation that followed deregulation was the *derivatives* business. This was first introduced by an IBM–World Bank transaction in 1981. Traders—first of all commercial and investment banks and insurance companies—bought and sold future contracts of future commodity trading, most of all oil. They made deals on future options on shares, bonds, currencies, and interest rates. Firms in different countries have different comparative advantages on interest rates; if they change securities it may be mutually advantageous. The derivatives business, however, is one of the most popular forms of business gambling, speculation on price, interest, and exchange rate changes. In Germany, the leading banks established a Derivative Forum in 2004 to provide risk ratings. An International Swap and Derivative Association was also founded.

Banks ended their traditional practice of assessing the creditworthiness of their clients because of this trading practice. These transactions aimed to avoid risk by selling or buying at an assumed (forecasted) price to eliminate future changes in exchange or interest rates or commodity prices. The derivatives business thus served risk management, but it was itself at the same time a major risk, involving speculation about future prices, exchange rates, and interest rate movements. In other words, this business became gambling, based on assumed future price movements. That offered huge profits as well as huge losses, based on real price and rate formations. According to the Bank for International Settlements, the world's derivatives trade, which stood at $75 trillion in 1997, rose to $600 trillion by 2007. To evaluate these astronomical figures, it pays to note that the 1997 figure was already two-and-half times the world's global GDP, but in the early twenty-first century it amounted to about nine times global GDP. It thus became impossible for any single company, or even a single nation, to handle the potentially huge losses. In the title of its 1994 article, *Fortune Magazine* offered a good starting point for understanding the attitude of financial institutions toward the new business methods: "Learning to live with derivatives. They're here, and they're not going away. Yes, these beasties bite, but companies that tame them have a competitive edge."[70]

Deregulation led to excessive lending and borrowing. Cheap credit flooded the European countries. Signaling a ballooning bubble in the early 2000s before the credit crisis, bank credits had excessively increased by more than 10% per year. The stock markets, the real estate business, and private consumption flourished. The huge expansion of private debt before 2008 became one of the causes of the debt crisis in the euro-zone[71] as will be discussed in Chapter 4.

Indeed, many experts agree that deregulation was one of the main causes of the 2008 crisis. "Financial deregulation in the United States," states Joseph Stiglitz, "was a prime cause of the global crisis that erupted in 2008, and financial and capital market liberalization elsewhere helped spread . . . [the] trauma around the world." "Even the IMF now admits," he added "that total deregulation of financial markets was a mistake."[72] Jürgen Stark, a former representative of the European Central Bank agrees: "The current financial crisis is largely the result of excessive risk taking and faulty risk management . . . deficiencies in fiscal regulation and supervision in some advanced countries."[73]

Deregulation, while it definitely increased competitiveness and resulted in abundant cheap credit, tremendously increased the risk of finances.[74] The risk of business actions in the longer run became incomparably higher and the entire market system became much more fragile. Assets bubbles, easy credit and excessive consumer spending became regular phenomena in the deregulated financial markets.[75]

The new international financial order that helped to cope with the crisis of the late 1970s and 1980s, and generated high prosperity in the Western world during the 1990s and in the early 2000s, made the entire system highly volatile. This became manifest in the late 1990s, when an Asian financial crisis erupted and spread to Russia and certain parts of Latin America. "In recent years the volatility and contagion associated with the new international financial order have produced major financial crises," noted an analyst in 2000.[76] Indeed, the facts are really shocking. Between 1622 and the 1990s, more than three-and-half centuries, 39 major financial crises hit Europe. The increased volatility, however, made currency, banking, and financial crises a household phenomenon in today's capitalism: between 1970 and 1995, the IMF counted 158 currency crises and 54 banking crises, and 130 countries had at least one financial crisis.[77]

The mere size of the overgrown deregulated and globalized financial sector thus became a danger for smooth functioning of the market system. If one adds the changed activities and function of the sector, Jürgen Stark's harsh judgment is well-founded: "the current financial crisis is largely the result of excessive risk taking and faulty risk management practices in financial markets."[78] Three economists made pioneering calculations about the role of the financial sector in the economy and concluded that, if credits to the private sector exceed 110% of the GDP, then it has a negative impact on growth.[79] Unfortunately, that was the case throughout Europe in the 2000s. The oversized financial sector, with its highly speculative, gambling-type business activities—in contrast to the central and positive role of traditional banking and credit creation—plays a negative role in the economy, partly by misallocating the financial resources from areas where they would be used better to create real value and jobs. Meanwhile gambling activities are also undermining the solidity of finances and increasing the fragility of the entire economy. As Douglas Dowd phrased it: "As the economy has come to be dominated by finances, finance has come to be dominated by speculation, which, as such, contributes nothing to the economy except the means for a self-chosen few to make money."[80]

Excessive speculation is closely connected with declining credit culture and business morals. In traditional banking, as Joseph Schumpeter summarized, "the banker should know, and be able to judge, what his credit is used for. . . . This is not only a highly skilled work . . . but also work which requires intellectual and moral qualities."[81] In the over-financialized and deregulated economic world, the banks lost most of these qualities. Given the securitization of loans and the sale of them as bonds to other investors, the old business morals lost their importance. Banks even stopped evaluating borrowers' creditworthiness. In their excessive crediting practice, lending officers of banks and other financial institutions did not carefully measure the possibility of risks and losses. As mentioned before, hedge funds were interested only in huge gains and were not endangered by losses. Besides, in several countries, especially in the peripheral regions, the business world and the governments were still carrying the burden of traditional crony capitalism. They have been ignoring efficient reforms of the financial system, neglecting solid corporate governance and accurate accounting. Personal connections, networking and corruption are the basis of running a business. In this environment, it was easy to overlook irregular and reckless practice and even falsified books, manipulated rates and reports.

In the "wild West" practice of financial irresponsibility, the driving force was the highest possible gain, which was easier to achieve by gambling through currency speculations, securitization, derivatives, and the arbitrage business than with solid crediting, investment, trade, and industry. As John Maynard Keynes prophesied in 1936: "Speculation may do no harm as bubbles on a steady stream of enterprise. But the situation is serious when enterprise becomes the bubble on a whirlpool of speculation. When the capital development of a country becomes the by-product of the activities of a casino."[82] That actually happened in contemporary financialized and deregulated capitalism that contributes to the relatively frequent possibilities of major economic meltdowns.[83]

The German Minister of Finance, Peer Steinbrueck, harshly blamed the "reckless Anglo-Saxon financial engineering," the "laissez-faire ideology [that] was as simplistic as it was dangerous," for generating a gambling morality in the financial sector. In his speech at the Bundestag on September 25, 2008, he blamed the "blind drive for double digit profits . . . the irresponsible exaggeration of the principle of a free, unrestrained market."[84] A few months later, Nicolas Sarkozy, the French President, spoke about the need to return to solid capitalism: "We need to literally rebuild the international financial system. We want to lay the foundations of entrepreneurial capitalism, not speculative capitalism."[85]

Indeed, contemporary capitalism with its excessive financial manipulations is near to so-called Ponzi schemes[86] (or Madoff schemes). Fraudulent Ponzi funds offer huge interest rates that are many times higher than official bank or bond rates, and so attract money that they do not even invest. They do not earn profit, but they pay the interest—for a while—from new clients' money. Investors are attracted to invest for the huge promised interest, and for a while they really receive it. Money flows in—until the business collapses and the investors' money disappears. Contemporary Western, including European, financialized capitalism is strongly characterized by the speculative hedge fund activities, speculative securitization, and derivatives business that do not create real value, but only huge profits. Tremendous amounts of money are misallocated in this way, withheld from value- and job-creating investments. In the case of failure, the astronomical amount of speculative business transactions may cause tragic losses. Their scale nowadays is much higher than is absorbable by a whole country or even a group of countries.

The structural tribulations of the European Union and the euro-zone

Global capitalism transformed the European market system. However, integrated Europe has its own special features. Among the causes of the 2008 crisis, especially of the process when the financial panic became a sovereign debt crisis and a crisis of the common European currency, one can find special structural factors in the European monetary unification. The structural weaknesses of the financial integration of Europe have an outstanding role and responsibility in the sovereign debt crisis of the euro-zone. How did it happen?

During the decades from the 1970s to 2008, when the Western market system transformed into financialized-deregulated-globalized capitalism, Europe itself entered into a new stage of its historical integration process that culminated in the introduction of the common currency, the euro. That seemed to be the greatest progress in the integration process, a milestone toward the dreamed-of federal unification of Europe,[87] but it soon turned out to endanger the entire existence of the integration process and to threaten the disintegration or collapse of the Union. Understanding it requires a brief account of the state of the European integration process around the turn of the millennium.

The visionary new President of the European Commission, Jacques Delors, who took office in 1984, initiated a historic response to the international changes of globalization and the erosion and collapse of communism in Eastern Europe. The European Economic Community, after a decades-long stagnation, entered its most dynamic phase of development by both 'deepening' and 'broadening' the integration. In the new world economy, Delors stressed in a speech in Bruges in 1989, *deeper integration* is unavoidable. "Nations cannot act alone." The reality in the new world system, he argued, is the "growing interdependence of our economies, the internationalization of the financial world . . . [which makes] full national sovereignty" a fiction. Europe has to consider "worldwide geopolitical and economic trends. . . . [It is] losing its place as the economic and political center of the world. . . . European market and common policies have supported national efforts to adapt to the new world economic order. Europe is once again a force to be reckoned with."[88]

Delors and the Commission set the agenda to complete the common market, i.e., the elimination of still existing obstacles to free trade and the free movement of labor, capital, and services, and thereby to reach the level of an economic union without internal frontiers. The Single European Act, the first major revision of the Treaty of Rome, was signed in Luxembourg in February 1987. This set a deadline to realize the goals by 1992. Since the member countries signed the Single Market Act, trade among them has already increased by an amazing 23 times and increased the aggregate GDP of the six countries by 5%. To eliminate all existing barriers, the European Union started to accomplish the "four freedoms," i.e. the undisturbed flow of goods, labor, capital, and services. This has been partially realized in a decade, but it required further harmonization of education, taxation, monetary and fiscal policies to level national differences.

Part of this ambitious agenda were two agreements in 1985 and 1990 that led to the acceptance of the Schengen Treaty, signed by all the continental member countries of the Community, to eliminate all frontier control of the movement of people. Borders were shifted from their national borders to the external borders of the Union.

The 1980s also became the beginning of a breakthrough in monetary unification and the introduction of the common currency.[89] In 1979, nine member countries established the European Monetary System that provided fixed but adjustable exchange rates of the member countries. The heads of states of the Community made the decision on the common currency at their Paris summit in 1988, and the Delors Report of 1989 presented an exact, three-stage plan and timetable for the introduction of the euro that happened in 1999–2001.

The other main parallel trend in Europe's integration was the significant *broadening of the Union*. The founding six countries, all of a sudden, started accepting more and more new candidates. A massive enlargement process began in 1973 when Britain, Ireland, and Denmark were accepted. During the 1980s, after the collapse of South European dictatorships in Greece, Spain, and Portugal, these three countries joined the Union in 1981 and 1986. In 1995, Sweden, Finland, and Austria's applications were accepted.

In his Bruges speech in 1989, Delors put further enlargement toward Eastern Europe on the agenda by stating that the Union "did not want Europe to be cut in two at Yalta . . . [and do not] close the door to other European countries."[90] Indeed, in the early 1990s, several former Soviet Bloc countries applied for membership and became official candidates. In 2004, eight former communist countries—Poland, the Czech Republic, Slovakia, Hungary, Slovenia, Estonia, Latvia, and Lithuania—and two others, Cyprus and Malta, were accepted by the Union. In 2007, Romania and Bulgaria became members of the European Union of 27. With this step, another 100 million consumers enlarged the single European market, and also provided a backyard for advanced Western Europe with a well-trained, very cheap labor force in proximity.

From the 1970s to the early 2000s, at the same time as market capitalism was financialized, deregulated, and globalized, the old European continent itself has been transformed into a deeply integrated and significantly broadened European Union. With its more than 500 million inhabitants and an aggregate GDP bigger than the United States', the European Union became an economic superpower with significantly strengthened competitiveness in the global economy, using a common currency. The common currency and a single European Central Bank became the most important supranational institution of the otherwise mostly intergovernmental organization of the Union. The common currency offered significant financial advantage, the elimination of conversion costs and exchange rate fluctuations. It also played a role in price equalization, the unification of the financial markets, and efficient control of inflation.

The common currency was an instant success. Its value, originally in 1:1 parity with the US dollar—after a short and transitory decline—reached the 50% higher rate of €1=$1.5. The European common currency became a second world reserve currency—beside the declining dollar. In a few years, one-quarter of financial transactions in the world used the euro instead of the dollar. No new currency has ever had such a success in such a short period of time.

While the introduction of the euro was enthusiastically welcomed by most of the member countries of the European Union, it was not well received by a few. In January 1999, 11 European Union member countries—Austria, Belgium, Finland, France (with its overseas territories), Germany, Ireland, Italy, Luxembourg, the Netherlands, Portugal, and Spain—qualified to join the euro-zone. Many more were working hard to meet the prerequisites of joining and were accepted when it happened: Greece (2001), Slovenia (2007), Cyprus and Malta (2008), Slovakia (2009), and Estonia (2011). Six non-European Union member mini-countries[91] also officially adopted the euro as their national currency. Some major European Union members such as Britain, Sweden, and Denmark, however, decided to keep monetary independence and remain outside the zone.[92] Other Union members have not qualified yet to join. In 2010–11, when the currency declined into a dangerous crisis, 17 countries of the European Union from the 27 member countries used the common currency.

The introduction of the successful common currency, the euro, however, was an extremely controversial achievement. From the very beginning, it was pregnant with the danger of a major crisis. Two crucial mistakes made the euro fragile: it was the currency of a group of integrated, but independent, countries of extreme economic diversity; and it was based on monetary unification without fiscal unification, a construction that had never existed in history. Let's further peel the onion by analyzing these factors.

The gradual development toward a federal Europe, the progress toward an "ever closer union," the dream of the founding fathers of postwar unification, was not unrealistic since the six founding countries were more or less on a similar level of economic development. When the Treaty of Rome was signed in 1957, their respective per capita GDPs were nearly equal at $6,000 or $7,000.[93] The West European half of the continent, and especially the North-Western core, was culturally also closely connected. Their social structure and behavioral patterns exhibited basic similarities.

The enlargement process that started in 1973, and led in three decades to an increase in the number of member countries from six to 27, radically changed the situation. Most of the newly accepted members are located on the peripheries of Europe and represent a much lower level of economic maturity. While the core was industrialized during the nineteenth century, most of the peripheries remained agricultural until the mid-twentieth century. The highly urbanized core differed greatly from the mostly rural peripheries. Quantifying the difference between the core and the peripheries of the European Community one may use the per capita GDP level as the most general comparative index.

While the founding core reached, as an average, more than $12,000 in per capita income in 1973, when Ireland was accepted into the Union, it reached only roughly 58% of the core level. When Greece was accepted in 1981, its income level amounted to 63% of the core's. In 1986 when Spain and Portugal joined the Union, their income level amounted to only 66% and 58%, respectively, of the six core countries' average. In 2004 and 2007, ten former Soviet Bloc countries joined, and some of their per capita income levels were at a historical distance from the core: the five Central European countries' level totaled 56%, the three Baltic countries' level 21%, and the two Balkan countries had less than 10% of the core's economic maturity. The enlargement process thus included 14 peripheral countries with a significantly lower economic level. [94] The enlargement, consequently, created a hugely divided and polarized European Union with countries of significantly diverse economic level. Two different groups may be distinguished, the North-Western core countries (Britain, the Netherlands, Belgium, the Scandinavian countries, Finland, France, Germany, and Austria), and the peripheral countries (Greece and the Mediterranean countries, Ireland, and the Central and Eastern European countries). This division characterized the euro-zone as well. The common currency, nevertheless, generated a one-size-fits-all monetary policy. As interest rates converged, economic performance diverged. Low interest rates fueled a housing boom, reallocated capital, and decreased competitiveness. This situation was naturally pregnant with the possibility of crisis that emerged, indeed, on the peripheries of Europe.

The past of the peripheries is still alive in many ways and forms in the present of those countries. Several of them had a successful catching up development in the last three–four decades and, on per capita income level, several of them, such as Greece and Spain, almost reached the average level of the traditionally advanced West European core, and some, such as Ireland, even surpassed it. If that happened, how can one say that the peripheral past is still around? Two major elements of the survival of the peripheral past are the most visible. One is a kind of dual economy character of some of those countries. While foreign investments and multinational companies created the most vigorous, dynamic, and modern sectors of the economy, the domestic sectors remained somewhat traditional and less developed. More importantly, the social-behavioral pattern hammered out for centuries, are pretty long lasting and very slowly changing. Even at an advanced economic level, clientalism, networking, corruption, a different work ethic and lifestyle, the traditional attraction of the noble spending lifestyle, looking down on thrifty living, and other features are deeply embedded in those societies.

These differences are clearly embodied in the huge contrast of labor productivity, a crucially important index that, besides the technological level, also expresses organizational and managerial skills, work ethic, educational standards, and behavioral patterns of the population. In 1950, when the entire European transformation began, a West European worker produced $5.82 of value in one hour. A worker in the Mediterranean peripheral countries produced only half of that, $2.89, and a Central and East European worker hardly more than 40% of it, $2.41. When the Soviet Bloc collapsed in 1989–91, and its countries started their process of transformation, one worker in this region still produced only $6.83 value in an hour, hardly more than one-quarter of a West European worker's production of $25.30 in that time.[95]

The prerequisites for acceptance by the European Union were not enforced.[96] Before 1989, the European Union was happy to accept countries because of the Cold War division of the continent. Each new member strengthened the Western alliance.[97] After 1989, new countries were easily accepted because they had cheap and well-trained labor in proximity and strengthened the competitiveness in the cut-throat world competition. The rush to enlarge was probably most visibly controversial when Romania and Bulgaria were accepted in 2007. Not only because these countries had only about 10% of the income level of the European Union average, by far the lowest among new members, but also because of the deeply rooted corruption embedded in the history of the Balkans that represented a markedly different cultural environment.[98]

The "original sin" of the euro's construction

Including a big part of the European peripheries in the euro-zone made the monetary union fragile.[99] Deep polarization within the Union and the euro-zone became the source of a genuine economic weakness during crises that kicked back to the core countries after 2008. The most crisis-ridden countries of the European Union were generally peripheral countries. Among them, several used the euro and undermined its existence.

The other factor, as mentioned above, was the structural weakness of the monetary unification. Unified but still independent countries introduced a common currency and created the supranational common European Central Bank (ECB). They engaged in monetary unification. However, the ECB was not a fully authorized central bank because its mandate sanctioned the defense of price stability, but not the role of lender of last resort, a decisive function of central or so-called national banks in which they lend to their governments. ECB rules ban lending to governments and buying government bonds from governments on the primary markets, although it may and does buy on the secondary markets.[100]

Monetary unification had different outcomes for different groups of countries within the euro-zone. For the peripheral countries, the introduction of the euro led to much lower interest rates and, consequently, cheaper credits. All of a sudden, the government bonds of peripheral countries were more easily salable for lower interest rates, as well. This generated an inflow of cheap credit, discouraged savings, and led to over-investment in some sectors. The peripheral countries averaged higher growth rates than the core countries, but also faster price and wage increases than the core group. Budget deficits and indebtedness, unlike in most of the core countries, started accumulating in this group of countries. At the same time, as euro-zone members, these countries lost important weaponry to decrease deficit and increase competitiveness by currency depreciation. The monetary arrangements practically eliminated the elbow room for crisis-ridden countries to avoid or maneuver out of the crisis, as Argentina did less than a decade before the Great Recession. They became unable to increase their own interest rates to slow down economic growth when the economy was overheated during high prosperity years. The possibility for the central bank to be the lender of last resort had also been eliminated, which left crisis-hit countries without the usual assistance of a central bank to buy government bonds. In other words, monetary unification was planned for prosperity and left the system paralyzed during the economic crisis.

Even more importantly, the financial architecture exhibited a dangerous shortcoming that was already debated by several economists at its introduction: monetary unification was not accompanied by fiscal unification of the member countries of the euro-zone. This means that monetary policy, including issuing banknotes and deciding upon interest rates, is made jointly, but fiscal policy remained the sovereign right of each member state. They have national budgets, and they decide upon taxation and government borrowing independently. The euro-zone and the governing institutions of the European Union have nothing to do with fiscal policy and no right to make fiscal decisions. This was a rather contradictory arrangement, since throughout history monetary units have always been combined with a sovereign fiscal policy mandate because of the close connection between the two.

Here, one reservation has to be made. The Treaty on the European Union, or to use its more common name, the Maastricht Agreement of 1992, transformed the European Economic Community into the European Union, and introduced the common currency. This Treaty also introduced the "criteria of convergence" that determined certain prerequisites that had to be fulfilled before a country could join the euro-zone. Four main rules were fixed: 1. A candidate country's rate of inflation may not be higher than 1.5% above the average of the three countries with the lowest inflation rates; 2. A candidate country's budgetary deficit must not surpass 6% of its GDP, and its public debts must not surpass 60% of its GDP; 3. Candidate countries have to join the Union's exchange rate mechanism of the European Monetary System and for two consecutive years before joining may not devaluate the national currency; 4. A candidate country's long-term inflation rates may not be above more than 2% of the three countries with the lowest inflation rate.

Inflation rates and long-term interest rates thus have to converge in those countries that use the euro. In the 1990s, all those countries that wanted to enter the euro-zone made significant efforts to meet the convergence criteria. In 1997, the Stability and Growth Pact made the Maastricht "convergence criteria" a permanent rule for the euro-zone countries to keep fiscal discipline. When the fulfillment of the criteria was controlled before the introduction of the common currency in 1998, except for Greece, all the candidate countries were eligible to join.[101]

In other words, joining the common currency required a solid and stable fiscal order. To enforce these rules, a surveillance system was created under the authority of the European Commission. In case of a lack of discipline in one or more of the euro-zone countries, the Council was authorized to make policy recommendations, but in case of excessive deviation, penalties might also be imposed. The common authorities had the right to punish the country that did not fulfill the requirements with a penalty of 0.2–0.5% of the country's GDP.[102]

However, the Stability and Growth Pact's strict rules were not taken seriously. Belgium and Italy were permitted to enter the monetary union in 1998 with higher than allowed debt levels of 117% and 115% of GDP, respectively. At the same time, Spain and Portugal violated the 3% budget-ceiling rule. Actually, Germany was also unable to keep to this rule after carrying the heavy financial burden of German re-unification: its budget deficit level was above the norm between 2002 and 2005. France also violated this rule for three years. By 2009, ten out of 16 euro-zone countries surpassed the public debt ceiling regulation. In 2003, the European Council of the Ministers of Finance decided to look the other way and not to sanction the excessive German and French debt violation because they were "exceptional and temporary." As *The Economist* rightly stated, "France and Germany led a rebellion against the disciplines of the 'stability and growth pact' on the first occasion it looked about to catch them. That signaled a free-for-all."[103] In 2004, when it became known that Greece joined the euro-zone in 2001 by falsifying its statistics, the European Union swallowed this criminal violation as well and accepted the promise of the Greek government to fix the problem.

Several experts nurtured severe doubts about the common currency even at the time it was introduced. A one-size-fits-all system in a situation with diverse economic levels might easily be explosive. In an economic recession, let alone a depression, the lack of a *real* Central Bank that is lender of last resort to governments, together with a non-unified fiscal policy, means that fiscal disorder in a couple of countries may endanger the currency. This was already clearly known in the 1990s when the euro's introduction was on its way.

Why didn't the experts and the authorities of the European Union consider this structural weakness a danger? Partly because the grandiose project, the milestone step of further integration, blinded the European authorities, and they just could not think about dangers. One should not forget that this took place in the 1990s, at the time of a new prosperity. As mentioned in the Introduction, economists did not even believe in the possibility of a return of an economic crash. They had confidence in their ability to handle it. All the government advisors and expert members shared this view. Retrospectively, it was a major mistake to make plans for good years only, but that is what happened.

Another factor should also be mentioned. The years at the turn of the 1980s and 1990s were filled with optimism. The Cold War had ended, and the dangerous European polarization was finished. More than a dozen countries, including the richest, like Switzerland, Norway,[104] Sweden, Austria, and Finland, and then all of the former Soviet Bloc countries, knocked at the door of the European Union. And at that time, charismatic leaders and highly committed heads of governments—Jacques Delors, François Mitterrand, Helmut Kohl and others—wanted to grab the opportunity of the moment, and believed that further steps would follow soon.

Were they "deeply impractical romantics," as Paul Krugman believes, driven by "the dream of European unification, which the Continent's elite found so alluring that its members waved away practical objections."?[105] Or were they committed leaders, who had learned the lessons of history, especially the two world wars of the twentieth century? Yes, they had a vision of the future. Was it an empty romantic daydreaming?

Not at all.[106] One widespread interpretation of the history of the development of the European Union is that one important step forward automatically generates other steps to follow suit. The integration process has an expansive logic of "spillovers." As always happens, one integrating step requires a further step in related areas. To accomplish the original goal, further integrative steps are needed.[107] They established a common market, and it made it necessary to free labor and capital movement. If they introduced the free movement of labor, they must harmonize the qualification and education systems. If they have a closely and strongly integrated single market, they had better have a monetary union and a single currency, and if they have a common currency, they need a common fiscal policy. The monetary union thus might be considered as one of the major further steps on the road that will be followed by others, including fiscal integration. As Helmut Kohl once noted, integration is like cycling: you must continue forward, otherwise you fall.

Nevertheless, the negative impact of a unified currency for diverse economies, and the mess of conflicting monetary and fiscal policies, was still seemingly evident. The common currency that could work in prosperity had to decline in crisis in the period of major economic troubles. When the crisis emerged, the system, indeed, became faulty. P. Krugman is right to state:

"The continent's economies were too disparate to function smoothly with one-size-fits-all monetary policy, too likely to experience 'asymmetric shocks' in which some countries slumped while others boomed."[108] Troubled countries had no room for maneuver and Greece could not devalue its currency, a usual step in such a situation that can ease debt burdens and stimulate a crisis-ridden economy. Greece, Ireland, Portugal, and Spain were unable to print more money, another usual way to revitalize a paralyzed credit system and the economy. And most of all, the monetary union was unable to equally serve different countries with different economic levels and cultures, including the somewhat loose fiscal policy and spending habits in countries of the European peripheries, mostly in the South, and the serious fiscal order in others, mostly in the North-West.

History matters. Modern industrial capitalism was born in North-West Europe while the peripheries were laggards. That was not accidental. Economic development is embedded in the complex history, culture, and political environment of a country or region. The peripheries had rather different histories, cultures, and legacies than the North-Western core of Europe. Although this situation is not constant and changes over time, e.g., peripheral countries and regions may catch up and join the core, alteration is extremely gradual and takes generations. Behavioral patterns change much slower than economic growth may progress.

Although the leaders and authorities of the European Union had a rational concept behind the ignited process, as we have seen before, the entire structure became vulnerable and weak. The European Union and the euro-zone, as it is, are a historical fact to contend with. This does not mean, however, that changes are impossible. However, it does require a major restructuring of the Union and the euro-zone. At the end of 2011, the renewed European sovereign debt and currency crisis thus required a definite and strong answer, a further radical movement forward. Like Bertolt Brecht's heroine during the Thirty Years War, Mother Courage, who was so frightened that she "escaped forward" through the line of combating and murderous armies, the European Union must have the courage to escape forward to a "closer union."

Can this breakthrough happen? Having researched the half-century history of the European integration process, I risk answering, "Yes." This history was characterized with long periods of stagnation and then, when seriously challenged, major jumps forward. The European Union is too big to fail, and the euro is much more than a currency. As Angela Merkel, the Chancellor of Germany and one of the key figures in European decision making, stated in the middle of the crisis of the euro, the solution is "not less Europe but more. . . . It is now the task of our generation to complete the economic and currency union in Europe and create, step by step, a political union."[109]

If this market system with its reckless business attitude, excessive crediting, and high risk-taking, together with a controversial structural weakness of integrated Europe, are strongly responsible for the failure, it is only one side of the coin. The other side of the same coin is the similarly reckless borrowing and spending by the population, the habit in a great part of Europe of living beyond their means.

4

THE SOCIAL CAUSES: LIVING BEYOND OUR MEANS

The 2008 crisis, which became essentially an indebtedness crisis, was not only an economic, structural, and policy phenomenon, but a social one as well. When we are searching for causes we also have to analyze the population's lifestyle, spending habits, and consumer attitudes. In the previous chapters, I made a few remarks about households' indebtedness and the madness that created huge housing bubbles in several countries. In some of them, these social factors played the central role in the crisis. In some countries, such as Spain and Ireland, public finances were in order, but private spending and indebtedness were the starting point of economic troubles and collapse.

The new dream: consumption

Household spending and indebtedness were all clear signs of a new mentality: *living beyond one's means*. One may not forget, of course, that two to three European generations experienced the lean years of two world wars, a devastating and long Great Depression in between, and inflation after both wars that eliminated life-long family savings. For those generations, saving was less attractive and longing for a better life more central. Those decades were also the period of the greatest migration in Europe. Millions of people were uprooted and moved because of border changes, expulsion, and hunger, and they had to leave almost everything behind. They were hungry to reestablish life and at last be materially comfortable again. In two long periods of prosperity after World War II—during the 1950s–60s, and especially during the decades around the turn of the millennium—European lifestyle and consumer behavior changed radically. This was not without a preceding long trend of development toward the consumer society. Even lavish consumption is not a brand new phenomenon. Jan de Vries published a huge book about the "industrious revolution" in the Low Countries in the eighteenth century, when people were ready to work more for luxurious consumption. Household inventories exhibited the spread in that time of luxury items such as watches, even in lower-layer households.[1] The title of N. McKendrick and his co-authors' book is "The Birth of a Consumer Society," in eighteenth-century Britain. Thorstein Veblen's famous book on *The Theory of the Leisure Class*, published at the end of the nineteenth century, introduced the term "conspicuous consumption," the habit of the "leisure class" and *nouveaux riches* to consume and exhibit possessions to demonstrate their social status. The useful qualities of consumed goods and services lost importance in favor of a public demonstration of wealth, good taste, and status.[2] The consumption habits of the "leisure class" started spreading in parallel with luxury consumption. Fashion, as Georg Simmel called to our attention at the beginning of the twentieth century, trickled down from higher to lower layers of society.[3]

The twentieth century created more wealth than at any time before. Compared to 1900, an average European worker produced ten times more value in an hour in 2000. The amount of goods and services, food, clothing, housing, vacations and travel, health and educational services available for an average family was five times greater than a century before. The monthly consumption spending of a blue-collar Italian family, in comparable prices, was $180 in 1890 and $1,600 in 1990.[4] Swedish GDP increased by nineteen times, and per capita income by eleven times, in the twentieth century.[5]

Gilles Lipovetsky speaks about three stages in the development of consumer society. The first stage was between 1880 and World War II, when mass production and standardized goods at relatively low prices created the modern consumer in the West. In the period from World War II to the 1970s, a mass consumption society emerged. Goods were available for every social group, and consumption was democratized in the Western societies.[6] Consumption started growing during the postwar boom, when the German press first began speaking about a *Fresswelle*, eating wave, followed by the *Kleidungswelle*, clothing wave, and the *Reisewelle*, travel wave. This consumption trend still fit into the relatively lower layers of Abraham Maslow's famous pyramid, or "hierarchy of needs," that starts with the physiological needs of eating and drinking, but, if those are satisfied, climbing to safety, social needs such as love and belonging, and then the needs of esteem, achievements, and respect, and at last the limitless stage of self-actualization.[7]

From the 1970s, however, consumerism emerged onto a new, higher stage. In 1974, Daniel Bell published his milestone book about the rise of a new type of American capitalism, where the Protestant ethic is eroding and the society is strictly organized for consumption.[8] The dream ideal was already at hand in Europe: the prosperous American consumer society. This environment offered the possibility to realize these dreams in Europe as well. One may not forget the determinant political structure of the world: the Cold War competition between the West and the East. This was not only a lunatic arms-race and a contest of economic efficiency and technological progress, but also a battle over lifestyle and living standards. One of the most symbolic embodiments of this side of East–West competition was the famous "kitchen debate" between Richard Nixon and Nikita Khrushchev in Moscow's Sokolni Park at the American Exhibition in July 1959. The United States exhibited a suburban house to demonstrate that the average American could afford it. The televised debate took place in the kitchen of this model house, cut in half to be visible to viewers. The presentation and propagation of the Western lifestyle aimed to weaken and defeat the Soviet Bloc.

All these became the solid base for the third stage of emerging consumerism from the 1970s–80s. It was characterized by the "technologization of the home," and "equipping and multi-equipping the individual." This period became the age of "hyper-individualistic hyper-consumption with a cult of, and obsession with, the brand."[9] The much richer and self-oriented life that was emerging during the boom periods for the well-to-do half to two-thirds of the population, and in most cases for nearly the entire Western population, transformed old psychological patterns. The parents' generations wanted a better life for their children who grew up in affluence and became more self-centered and even spoiled. Besides, they could expect a significantly longer life, in which they would seek more pleasure, entertainment, and comfort for decades after their active working-life had ended.

A large portion of people was not ready to carry the "burden" of a family any longer. Many remained single or outside wedlock. Half of marriages ended in divorce, and the one-child family pattern became predominant. Smaller families, often with two working people and two salaries, lived much better and owned bigger homes. In many countries, 70% to 80% of the population lived in privately owned houses. Roughly three-quarters of people had white collar jobs. Long, paid vacations of five to six weeks, and shorter work weeks of 36 to 40 hours, created much more free time for entertainment and traveling. They also had state-guaranteed pensions for their older years in postwar European welfare states.

Consumer societies emerged and shopping became an entertainment for a huge portion of the population. Experts speak about "the biggest consumer boom ever known," and a "consumption race," the "Nirvana of ever greater consumption," a "runaway consumption" without "enough enoughness."[10] The "consumer passion" became an exit from everyday life.

Modern financial "innovations" and several kinds of credit arrangements, from mortgage loans via personal bank loans to credit card loans, made shopping and even uncontrolled spending much easier and more attractive. The "buy now pay later" arrangements became widespread. Consumerism consumed credits as well. A whole industry of demand creation generated demands people did not even know they had. Marketing did not "promote materialism. Quite the opposite. It promotes a narcissistic pseudo-spiritualism based on subjective pleasure, social status, romance, and lifestyle, as a product's mental associations become more important than its actual physical qualities."[11]

An unstoppable technological revolution offered ever newer goods and services to buy. Consumption, even luxury consumption may not, of course, itself be blamed, if people can afford it. Planned consumer indebtedness, up to a certain level, also belongs to modern societies. Taking on debt at a younger age, when income is lower, and paying it back at a later age when income increases, helps to get better housing and more comfort and avoids unnecessary hardship when income levels are not sufficient. Debt for buying a house and for financing children's education may also be considered a good investment. Exaggerated consumption beyond one's means, however, led to excessive indebtedness. What we are facing in contemporary capitalism is overconsumption financed by debt. The traditional savings culture changed, and debt became a way of life, and not a short-term solution for temporary problems.[12]

The condemnation of consumerism has generated a huge literature. Ralf Dahrendorf speaks about a next step after the "consumption mania," the new wave of "cheerful indebtedness" that started in the 1980s. As a consequence, "capitalism mutated from savings capitalism to consumption capitalism . . . [that] started down the fatal path to the capitalism of easy credit."[13] Credit "has to some extent assumed mythic qualities. . . . As debt grew and nothing dire happened, people started to believe that the modern economy was somehow able to function unimpaired with increasing credit and diverse forms of debt."[14]

One can read harsh laments against consumerism. Even before consumerism reached its height, some spoke about a "moral decline," and competitive "prestige buying" in the post-Cold War "relaxation of self discipline in the West."[15] Others mention a deformed affluent lifestyle, corrupted by a manipulative consumer industry, by "advertainment," where shopping and spending is the main form of "construction and reconstruction of self-identity." The created self-identity must also have social confirmation, and "a personalized self-identity can be communicated to others through the use of various symbols."[16]

A whole library could be filled with studies about "consuming the future," exploiting and deteriorating the environment through the North's over-consumption that endangers the sustainability of economic growth and life. Questions are often asked as follows: "How much, and what, do we consume? Why? Are we made happier in the process? How much is enough?"[17] Criticisms of consumerism argue about the "immorality of consumption," and sometimes recommend the return to Christian teachings "to escape the materialism that seeps into our mind via diabolically clever and incessant advertising."[18] In some places in the United States, so-called "voluntary simplicity," or "simple living" movements, emerged in the 1990s, and advocated "spiritual development over material consumption."[19]

Presenting affluent consumption and consumerism as the modern devil is thus rather widespread. Consumption, however, is not an evil, but also enriches life. Traveling builds character, for example. A family can undoubtedly live in a 70-square-meter apartment, but who can tell what size home is extreme and unnecessary? Two-hundred or five-hundred square meters? As Gilles Lipovetsky argues, one cannot equalize consumerism, with "moral decadence. . . . [This] is a myth. . . . We need to stop demonizing the world of hyperconsumption."[20] However, negative effects begin if consumption is connected with excessive spending, beyond the available income of families. Beyond a certain level, when disposable income cannot cover the expenses of the family and service debt for an extended period of time, one can, indeed, speak about over-indebtedness. These accumulating debts, if it is a mass phenomenon, endanger social and economic stability. Without these social phenomena, the 2008 crisis would have been unintelligible.

A new social setting for consumer society

After World War II, Europe experienced spectacular *demographic changes*. Life expectancy dramatically increased, by 20 to 25 years in half a century. Within this period, in the decade between 1995 and 2005, it increased by four years and reached 81 years. After a gradual catching-up process, the demographic gap between the European core and peripheries was suddenly leveled[21] after 1990, and long life became almost general throughout the continent.

The countries of the European Union, including the Mediterranean countries, exhibited a sharp decline in the birth rate, averaging only 9.7 births per 1,000 inhabitants by 2005.[22] The fertility rate, i.e., the average number of children per woman, dropped to 1.5 children in both Western and Southern Europe by that year. Only the Nordic countries represent an exception, with birth rates around the break-even level of 2.1 children, while Central and Eastern Europe had an even lower fertility rate of 1.3 children per woman.

Among the most important causes of these changes was an altering lifestyle and value system, which was associated with a highly urbanized, much more educated European society, which—at least the upper layers of it—enjoyed a much higher standard of living. Modern drugs and oral contraceptives, or "the pill," have taken over since the 1960s, and abortion in many countries has been legalized as well. European societies became highly secular, and old religious rules lost their grasp on people. In addition, women were more liberated, and a great many of them worked outside the family. By the end of the century, women's participation in the workforce nearly equaled their share of the population, reaching 40% to 50% of employed people. These changes were pretty sudden: even in 1960, only 20% to 30% of married women participated in the labor force, but by the end of the century, their levels of participation in many countries reached more than half and even three-quarters.

By the end of the century, the average marriage age increased,[23] and marriage rates declined from 6 marriages per 1,000 people at the end of the century, to 4.7 by 2005.[24] The share of one-person households increased to roughly one-quarter of all households. A great many couples do not marry, but live together. Their share in Denmark reached 35%, and in France 30%, in the early 2000s. Cohabitation is often an alternative to marriage. Divorce rates also increased steeply, and one-quarter to one-third of marriages ended in divorce during the 1980s; in Sweden, more than half of marriages did so.[25] Leaving aside the peculiarities of the Nordic countries, demographic trends, for the first time in modern history, were, in several respects, surprisingly similar in most of Europe, core and peripheral countries alike.[26]

The demographic trends, which were especially pronounced during the last quarter of the century, led to a significant *aging* of the population. The proportion of young people—those under the age of 15—gradually but permanently decreased throughout Europe from roughly 24–30% in the first half of the century, to 15–16%. On the other hand, the elderly population, those above 60, represented 21–22% of the population by 2005, instead of the 14% they represented at mid-century.[27] In other words, a mounting number, in many cases one-quarter of the population, are pensioners with decades of free time without everyday work.

For the first time in history, much of society became more individualistic, materialistic, outward- and entertainment-oriented due to a new family structure, many fewer children, many families with two incomes, much longer lives, much more free time during and after one's active working life, a lot of personal freedom, and even freedom from family bonds.

This trend was significantly strengthened by structural changes in the economy and society in late-twentieth-century Europe. Nearly three-quarters of the indigenous population of Western societies became white-collar workers. The rising trend of middle-classization, and especially the psychological impact of identity change, or the spread of middle-class self-consciousness, characterized the largest part of society.[28] By 2006, hardly more than 4% of the population in the euro-zone worked in agriculture, 29% in industry, and 67% in services. At the end of the twentieth century, roughly half of service employees worked in education, health care, public administration, finances, insurance, and real estate business, areas where service employment provided middle-class status. The change in the occupational structure, in connection with the technological, information, and communication revolution, created a *post-industrial* society with a permanently increasing white-collar layer and middle class.

Middle-class self-identification and consciousness characterizes even the lower layers of service employees, those who work in the retail trade, hotel, transportation, and communication businesses, and who believe that they are part and parcel of the middle class. Identifying themselves with the middle class was significantly eased by a kind of leveling of the home environment, consumption, and lifestyle. Car- and home ownership, traveling abroad, and dressing well were all class characteristics even in the mid-twentieth century. These consumption trends extended to the entire society and became much more uniform, eliminating strict social borderlines from the 1970s on. The consumption habits of half to two-thirds of the upper-middle layers of the population also eliminated strict class borders. The "affluent society," where white collar workers and the middle class gradually became the majority in postwar America with rapid suburbanization, was emulated and spread over to Western Europe. Family houses and well-equipped households with all the modern household conveniences became common for about two-thirds of these societies. Every family in the euro-zone countries had a color TV, and most of the people watch similar crime stories and football games in the evenings. In the first decade of the twenty-first century, every European had a mobile telephone, every second person had a car and a computer, and every second European checked the Internet for information. Winter and summer vacations, partly abroad, also became widespread customs. Shorter workweeks and days became a factor in changing lifestyles. In 1973, the average person in 12 West European countries worked 805 to 750 hours a year, but s/he only worked about 650 hours at the end of the century.[29] These changes also leveled differences in society and strengthened widespread middle-class consciousness.

Another demographic factor also contributed to the spreading middle-class self identification. Europe, historically the continent of emigration, became the continent of immigration from the last third of the twentieth century.[30] In 2005, 42 million people from the European population were born outside Europe and their number increases from year to year. In the single year of 2005, 1.8 million immigrants arrived in Europe. Spain offers a good example: in 2000, 4.6% of the country's population were immigrants, but by 2006, already 10.8% were, mostly from North Africa. In eight West European countries, the proportion of immigrants was already in the double digits by 2005, surpassing one-third of the population in the mini-state of Luxembourg, and nearing one-quarter in Switzerland.[31]

The sharply rising immigration, mostly from Asia, North Africa, and the Near East, created a new lower class and even underclass. These "others," with their foreign background, different languages and religions, often different clothing, dissimilar entertainment habits, and family structures, occupied a large part of the heavy physical and unskilled work and "dirty jobs." They formed the army of jobless reserve-workers as well. Unemployment, especially young people's unemployment, was extremely high among them. In a paradoxical way, this social and *income inequality*—which is mostly increased in spite of impressive material progress for many—and the fact that a part of the societies remained poor also influenced the psychology of the majority.[32] This *new*, mostly immigrant *underclass* minority remained basically segregated, excluded from society, and in many ways victims of double discrimination: as foreigners who are strongly "other," and as economically discriminated unskilled and unemployed people.[33] They are considered to be the enemy by a great part of the blue-collar workers who voted for anti-immigration parties. The existence of this new underclass strengthened middle-class feelings even among blue-collar workers.[34] Consequently, the genuine population, almost as a whole, felt it belonged to the middle class and sought to adjust to it in habits and, as much as possible, by consumption. To separate themselves from the lower layers, it became crucially important what kind of home you live in, what kind of car you drive, and what type of high prestige clothing and accessories you wear. Widespread middle-class self-identification influenced consumption and—together with all the other factors mentioned before—led to the rise of consumerism.

Consumerism

What we call consumerism in Europe today is a relatively new phenomenon that began in the 1970s–80s. Consumerism is a kind of *redundant consumption* that goes far beyond satisfying natural human needs. This became an obsession and entertainment itself. One can speak about a transfer and a kind of homogenization of lifestyle. The United States, the first consumer society in the world, had a tremendous demonstration effect on the European countries that also established the American model and ideal. The latecomer and poorer countries of Europe wanted to follow suit. Individual identity that was basically determined by the kind of work people performed, now became more and more determined by consumption. This gained a strong symbolic importance as the expression of identity.[35] The hyper-consumption of at least half to two-thirds of the European population in several countries is driven by the feeling of self-confidence: "we do it because we can afford it." It is also driven "by rivalry rather than genuine needs."[36] Anthony Giddens goes so far as to maintain that "the consumption of ever-novel goods becomes in some part a substitute for the genuine development of self; appearance replaces essence."[37]

Even at that relatively lower stage of the "consumption pyramid," people started spending more on entertainment and luxuries, and less on basics. The so-called Engel Law calls attention to the fact that an increasing income level shifts consumption from basics to more luxurious spending. At the beginning of the twentieth century, even in rich Switzerland, about 60% of family income was spent on basics. A century later in Western Europe, about 15% of income was spent on food and clothing. Expenditures that a few decades before were considered a luxury became ordinary and dominant in family budgets. Jan Owen Jansson's calculations of changes in Swedish consumption patterns reflect a general European trend. In 1875, 50% of available income was spent on food and drink and another 10% on clothes and shoes. Health and education consumed only 13% of expenditures. By 1995, the structure of spending turned upside down: 18.5% was spent on food and clothing, but 57% on health, education, and others. Moreover, even in the very short period between 1993 and 2006, private consumption increased by 38%. Private service expenditure increased by 60%, and expenses for durable goods increased by 122%. In hardly more than the decade before 2006, people spent 50% more on restaurants, 180% more on sports entertainment, 57% more on hairdressing and beauty care, and 51% more on package tours.[38] Consumer society reached the top of the "Maslow pyramid," the often symbolic "self-actualization." This kind of consumer attitude is sometimes compared to the mental illness of narcissism, the intense need for admiration, a strong status-seeking desire "to display wealth, status, and taste."[39]

Consumption also became a race: a competition with colleagues and friends. People want the same or, if possible, an even better brand of car, a bigger and better-located house, a vacation on a more exotic continent. Many spend more than rationally viable to elevate themselves to an admired higher layer of society. And the pyramid of needs is endlessly towering to higher and higher elevations. This is also pushed by anxiety about others' judgment, the worry that others do not find someone's consumption choice appropriate. Since in the advanced Western societies about 70% of GDP is due to private consumption, in a perverted way, consumption gained a patriotic connotation as well: your consumption is needed to help economic growth and prosperity.

Demands are also created and manipulated. In contemporary society, "every aspect of human social life across the life course has been commercialized – including . . . music, sports, childhood, education, marriage, health . . . food, the human body, and even death. Each of these aspects of human life has been . . . reconsidered for its capacity to be brought to market."[40] Today capitalism produces not only goods and services, but new desires for what to have. The new products, besides satisfying new pleasures, also have a mental association that is sometimes more important than the physical qualities.[41]

Luxury consumption, often beyond people's means, undoubtedly increased. In 2005, the Germans, British, Dutch, French, Italians, Belgians, Spanish, Austrians, Swedes, Swiss, and Norwegians combined spent $278 billion on tourism, an amazing amount that was significantly more than the entire Irish GDP, and more than the total Czech and Hungarian GDP combined.[42] Europeans, as the European Commission reported, are mostly spending their vacations in other European countries, frequently in the Mediterranean region, but also in France and Germany.

In the difficult year of 2010, 60 million overnight foreign visitors were registered in Germany. Nearly half of the Swiss population spends their vacations abroad. In 2008, 180 million European tourists spent one million nights in the most popular tourist countries within Europe. An additional 25 million went to see Russia, and nearly 60 million visited overseas countries in other continents such as the United States, Canada, Mexico, China, Turkey, Egypt, and South Africa. Although some overlapping is highly possible, such as the same tourist visiting both Sweden and Norway or England and Ireland, altogether about 300 million European tourists spent at least a part of their vacation in a country other than their home state. This number might be even higher since visits to Latin America and a great part of Asia and Africa are not included in these figures. One can safely state that about 40% of Europe's population travels regularly.[43] With connected sectors, the tourist industry generates more than 10% of European GDP and employs 12% of the labor force.[44]

Tourism became so much an integral part of the European lifestyle that, as newspapers reported in April 2010, Antonio Trajani, the European Commissioner for Enterprise and Industry, announced in Madrid that "traveling for tourism today is a human right. The way we spend our holidays is a formidable indicator of our quality of life." He even suggested subsidizing tourist trips for pensioners and young people who otherwise cannot afford it.[45]

Tourism, including skiing vacations in the winter and long summer vacations at seashores became combined with buying second homes in the mountains or on the seashore in other countries as well. From Northern countries, Dutch and British people became homeowners in Spain, Portugal, and the French Riviera. In the 2000s, two-thirds of Swedish home buyers were already home owners. This is definitely a luxury that only a small layer was able to afford. In Britain between 1996 and 2002, nearly one-third of new houses were second homes. In the mid-1990s, more than 90,000 British citizens had second or third homes abroad, but by the 2010s, it increased to nearly one-quarter of a million. More than one-third of them owned a home in Spain, and another one-quarter in France. For the first time in 2005, the regular review of the European housing markets included a chapter on the second-home boom across Europe.[46]

One of the most important signs of rising consumerism was the housing boom in several European countries. Important facts have already been discussed in Chapters 1 and 2 that describe manifestations of the crisis. Home ownership, the so-called "American Dream," became an even stronger European Dream in the late twentieth century. Living in one's own house, besides higher comfort, exhibited affluence, independence, and success. Home ownership steeply increased: in several countries of Europe with an income level only about 60% that of the American level, home ownership is about 80% , i.e., significantly higher than in the United States (67%). By 2003, every 1,000 people in the EU-25 owned 422.3 homes, i.e., two persons per home.[47] Characteristically enough, several of the countries with the highest ownership ratio, such as Ireland, Portugal, and Spain, were poor countries a few decades before. Britain, on the other hand, was a traditional class society where a large layer of the population lived in poor conditions and has the same hunger for a better life that the population of formerly poor countries has. The small, mostly three-member families are living in houses that are about 40% bigger than a few decades earlier. In Ireland, between 1991 and 2002, the population increased by 11%, but the number of independent households in family-owned homes by 25%.

Increased demand generated speculation. "The rise of real estate prices in urban centers was exacerbated by speculation, as the newly emerged middle class engaged in real estate transactions as a regular source of income."[48] Housing construction in Ireland increased by three times after 1994 compared to previous decades, and it reached one of the highest levels in Europe. No less than one-fifth of the Irish housing stock was built between 1994 and 2001. In the three decades after 1970, home ownership increased by 25% in Norway, 21% in Spain, and 18% each in Britain and the Netherlands. In other words, every fifth family moved into their own house. The construction sector became one of the prime movers of the economic boom. In Estonia, its share increased from 5.6% to 9.1% in total value added between 2000 and 2007. In Lithuania, its share increased from 5.9% to 9.8%, and in Romania from 5.5% to 9.7%.[49]

Home ownership also became a government policy preference in several countries. Sociological researchers on home ownership noted that "most European governments did not pursue home ownership as a primary housing objective until . . . around the 1970s and 1980s. Britain under Thatcher's leadership presented the most ambitious program of promoting owner-occupancy."[50] The authors also stressed that Britain was not alone. Indeed, Germany turned toward similar goals at the same time, and Italy stimulated home buying by increasing mortgage loans from 50% of the selling price in the 1980s to 80% of it in 1993. Portugal deregulated the mortgage markets in the 1970s and also introduced rent-freezing (1974) that led to the stagnation of rental markets and a booming buyers' market. In 20 years, housing stock increased by 50%. By 1991, 65% of the population lived in their own house, but in a single decade their share increased to 75%. The housing boom dramatically pushed up housing prices. The price of a small (750-square-foot), two-bedroom apartment in Dublin was €400,000 in 2006, 12.5 times the average industrial wage. In the 1990s, Irish housing prices were still affordable, but one-and-half decades later became unaffordable. The housing bubble generated an upward price-spiral in Ireland, so unrealistic that for the price of a Dublin home, nine homes could have been bought in Houston, Texas, and two in Sydney. Nevertheless, nearly one-third of the world's 61 most unaffordable local housing markets were located in Britain. There were no affordable regions in the country, not even "moderately unaffordable," and half of the local British housing market became "severely unaffordable."[51]

Privately owned homes became predominant in the former Soviet Bloc countries as well. Moreover, some of them, such as Romania, Bulgaria, Lithuania, and Hungary, have the highest ratio of privately owned homes, an unheard of 90–95%, mostly condominiums. This is, however, the consequence of a special situation. In the former communist countries, the bulk of housing stock—and almost all of it in urban settlements—had been state-owned. After the regime change, the governments sold the apartments to their renters for an extremely low price to get rid of the financial burden of maintenance. These privately owned homes are very small, e.g., about 50–60 square meters, and are mostly in a run-down state. However, in the rapidly growing new suburbia, middle-class houses were also built during the last 20–25 years, and real house ownership started increasing as well.[52]

Although buying houses was the most exclusive expression of affluent consumption, car ownership followed suit not simply as a means of transportation, but also as status symbol. "Perhaps more than any other commodity . . . cars have been linked to the emergence and development of consumer societies."[53] The hierarchy among trademarks may strengthen identity, and even build personality. Luxury watches such as Rolex reflected the status of their owners. Extremely expensive Italian sports cars, Bentleys, Rolls Royce, Mercedes, BMW, Audi, huge SUVs, and several others expressed a visible and socially well-known hierarchy. "Consumers can use patterns of consumption to define public images around which to build social interactions."[54]

The number of cars per family serves extra comfort, but also a higher status. Car ownership was rather high already by 1970 in Western Europe, and started emerging even in communist Central and Eastern Europe. The last third of the century, however, became a period of booming car sales. Between 1990 and 2004, the number of cars in Europe increased by about 40%. In previously poor countries their numbers suddenly doubled. In Russia, in the ten years after 1990, car ownership jumped from 10.1 to 20.4 million, while in Ukraine it jumped from 3.3 to 5.5 million and in Poland from 5.3 to 10.1 million. In the one and a half decades around the millennium, the number of cars in Lithuania increased by 167%, in Latvia by 142%, in Portugal by 135%, in Poland by 128%, and in Greece by 121%.

As a very characteristic phenomenon, besides rich Luxembourg, which has 659 cars per 1,000 inhabitants, Italy and Portugal lead in per capita car ownership with 581 and 572 cars per 1,000 inhabitants, respectively. Most of the former communist countries also have about 280–290 cars/1,000 inhabitants, which means virtually one car per family in 2004. On average, the EU-25 countries had 472 cars per 1,000 inhabitants, i.e., roughly every second person has his/her own car, nearly 40% more than in 1990 (335/1,000).[55]

Car ownership served the interests of greater comfort, but it was definitely excessive if one considers the excellent public transportation systems through-out Western Europe, as well as the dense metro, bus, tram, and superb train services.

Car ownership also expresses another important feature—and the other side of the coin—of today's consumerism. One can speak about the "democratization of luxury."[56] Mass consumption, although on various levels, transformed the lifestyle of almost the *entire* population of rich countries. Even the lower layers of society became integrated into the consumer society and shared in the consumer culture. In this respect, the rise of an entire "counterfeit industry" to produce cheap fake Gucci, Armani, Vuitton, and other big brands also bears consideration. Eric Hobsbawm called our attention to the fact that, today, even an average person could "live as only the very wealthy had lived in their parents' day."[57]

The list of today's "conspicuous consumption" goods is endless. One special feature of consumerism that is connected with the consumers' body is worth mentioning: cosmetic surgery. This *physically* contributes to the construction of identity and the following of social patterns and ideals. Passionate shopping became an obsession for many. Psychologists speak about the "oniomania," or shopping addiction that is most widespread among middle- and low-income women. The prestige of fashionable trademarks with reachable prices became a widespread social need. The commercial jargon for the mass consumption of prestigious product, often available in discount shops, is "masstige."

Consumer infrastructure and stimulus

Consumerism was strongly assisted in recent decades by the construction of an impressive consumer-commercial infrastructure. Retail networks, self-service supermarkets, discount shops that sell prestigious brands for low prices, a "logistic revolution" that made possible the flow of goods and a perfect distribution, and most of all the new temples of consumption, the American-invented shopping malls, all arrived in Europe in the postwar decades. The first shopping mall in Europe, the Wällingby Center, was opened in Sweden in 1954. Their real construction boom started in the 1960s and 1970s, and by 2006, Europe had 5,700 shopping malls covering 111 million square meters. Several of the malls are gigantic, such as the characteristically named Portuguese "Dolce Vita Tejo" covering 122,000 square meters. Altogether, every 1,000 people in Europe are served by 226 square meters of shopping mall.

The EU-15 countries have 90% of the total number of shopping malls in the EU-27 countries. Construction even continued after the 2008 crisis. In 2009, the deepest recession year, 115 new shopping malls were opened, 18% less than in 2008 because of the cancellation of several new construction plans. The new European Union member countries in Eastern Europe rushed to follow in the footsteps of the West. On a per capita basis, Latvia has as many shopping centers as Britain, France or Spain. Bulgaria, Latvia, and Romania had the fastest mall development in the early 2000s, including during the crisis years: the area of shopping malls increased by 66%–75% per year. Since 2000 alone, 40 million square meters of shopping malls were opened in Europe.

The shopping mall industry employs 4 million of the 19 million people in the retail trade sector. The malls attract a large percentage of shoppers: one-quarter of the shopping in Europe happens in malls. In 2006, people spent €500 billion in shopping centers, which means €1,110 per capita.[58] Retail sales in Europe amounted to €2.17 trillion in 2006, an amount equal to one-fifth of the aggregate GDP of the continent. Between 2000 and 2006, the retail sector was the fourth fastest growing sector among the ten economic sectors of Europe.

The huge literature on shopping malls calls one's attention to the symbolic function of malls as "urban islands," "safe, autonomous . . . and esthetic substitutes for the everyday life conditions." The malls are "testament to the physical domination of consumption upon the urban fabric . . . and [are] symptomatic about a society in which consumption dominates production." The malls, meanwhile, are also an institution of the democratization of consumption, and they express a kind of "classlessness."[59]

An even newer shopping infrastructure was introduced by the computer and Internet age from the 1990s on: by 2005, 21% of the French population shopped on the Internet, and 39% of those who regularly use the Internet became electronic shoppers. In Germany, out of 82 million inhabitants, 31.4 million shop via the Internet and spent €13.4 billion in 2008. [60] Reports present the shocking news about 1.6 billion "global shoppers" via the Internet, who spent $23 billion for apparel and accessories alone in 2009. "The high street transforming into the haute-street . . . 'Being online'," maintains with some exaggeration the authors of the *Licensing Journal* in 2010, "is now considered a basic lifestyle need, arguably up there with the physiological needs of food, shelter, and sex."[61] Here too, one has to add that electronic shopping makes life easier, saving time for better use and hardly deserves negative interpretations.

One of the most important inventions that massively contributed to consumerism was the creation of the modern credit system and new credit instruments. *Mortgage credit* made it possible to buy homes without the money it costs. This system conquered Europe in the mid–late twentieth century and arrived in Eastern Europe after 1989.

As part of the electronic revolution, the *credit card* was invented and offered the possibility to buy everything without existing financial resources. The habit of "buy now and pay later" spread rapidly. In the "home country" of the credit card, the United States, with its 300 million inhabitants, the population uses 1.5 billion credit cards. The card appeared in Europe mostly beginning in the 1980s, and thus had existed only half as long as in the United States.

Stimulating shopping, the big *industry of marketing research and advertisement* emerged. Some authors speak about "organized habits," and of a true ruling power which manipulates consumption. A "marketing revolution" started in America in the 1960s, and rapidly spread over to Western Europe. Consumers are bombarded with information about seasonal sales, periods of price discounts, and delayed payment possibilities. An entire industry grew up to create attraction and appeal for consumption. Advertisement penetrates homes, living rooms, and bedrooms to create demand and aspirations. In Britain, 3,000 specialized consumer magazines flood the population with information on shopping possibilities and new products to create "artificial desire."[62] Advertising penetrates life and "creates an environment of consumerism," since—according to some calculations—the average American encounters as many as 3,000 ads every day, and an average child is exposed to 360,000 ads by the age of 18.[63] These numbers are not tracked in Europe, but they are definitely much lower than in the United States. Advertisements, however, are now already everywhere and have the same function as in America. In advanced countries, marketing and advertising industries employs no less than 0.5 to 1% of the active population. Based on the American experience, John Kenneth Galbraith already called attention to the new phenomenon of a "managed-market," and some of his followers speak about a "corporate-guided market," where demand depends on corporate production and manipulation of the consumers, and the "invisible hand" plays a very limited role in today market economy.[64] Experts call attention to the "hidden power of consumers," which have a huge network to inform each other via Facebook, Twitter, and other new technologies. To increase markets, new forms of marketing became one of the most important weapons to measure consumer satisfaction and gain the support of the existing consumer body for further growth of the business.[65]

Nevertheless, more important than consumer manipulation is "*demand creation*" by technological inventions. During the last three to four decades since the personal computer appeared in the early 1970s, a relentless communication revolution, zillions of electronic gadgets, created demands which people did not have, from children's games, via smaller and lighter laptops, to mobile phones, smart phones, iPods, iPads, Kindle, the digitalization of cameras, CDs, more sophisticated TVs with hundreds of channels, and several other technological inventions. Personal technology is based on private consumption and in the last decade, for the first time in history, the population at large, and not the military, were the initiators and first consumers of new communication technology. Mass consumption of these new products was made easy by introducing new technologies, such as the much more powerful microchips that today are 40 times more powerful than ten years ago. Multi-core processors made it possible to produce super tiny chips, the lithium-ion polymer batteries made it possible to make ultra-slim devices, and the same gadget often has several functions. Phones may make photos, and already allow video calls as well.

New communication technology personalizes the new products and makes smartphone and tablet an intimate gadget. "Technology is starting to adapt to the people who use it rather than force them to adapt to it. . . . Consumer technology is becoming fashion . . . and Apple is now the world's biggest fashion company." Technological innovations also led to radical price decline. When the Kindle appeared in 2007, it cost $399, but by October 2011, the cheapest sold for $79. A gigabyte of storage to hold two hours of film was $200,000 in 1980, but nowadays a disc drive holding 1,024 gigabytes costs only $100.[66] Technology became democratized and the consumerization of technology became an unstoppable force raising people's expectations and openness to use the newest possible gadgets. Demand creation, according to certain views, is "making life better . . . in ways big and small, and helping to spur . . . social progress in countless forms."[67]

If demand was created for one layer of society in one country, it generates desire for other, even lower layers of society, and in other countries as well. Without any doubt, the pattern of postwar America established a model, an ideal to follow for Western Europe, and the rich Western countries became ideals to copy in the peripheries. First in the South, and after 1989, this demonstration effect influenced Eastern Europe as well. Consumption is indeed "more or less leading towards Western standards" throughout the continent, and the "development of sustainable consumption pattern . . . [shift] to pleasure."[68]

Several of the above-mentioned factors are connected to the logistic revolution made possible by the new information technology that emerged at the end of the twentieth century. "The basic functions of logistics . . .

enable a bridging of space and time in the flow of goods." Precise delivery, distribution, control, and monitoring services offer a decisive competitive factor for products.[69]

The peripheral countries of Europe in the South and East were not only poorer, or freshly enriched, but also carried the cultural and behavioral patterns of their past. As mentioned in Chapter 3, these countries were backward; none of them industrialized until World War II, and they had, as an average, half of the per capita income level of their North-Western neighbors. This was closely connected with a long-preserved anti-business "hidalgo," or "szlachta" attitude that was so characteristic in Spain and Poland, but also in several other peripheral countries. In those so-called noble societies where the small noble elite and the gentry's attitude formed the "national characteristic," living beyond one's means, spending more than one earns, was an old tradition that expressed elegance. Thrift was looked down upon. The core elements of Max Weber's "Protestant ethic" were missing and were mocked in that area. This lifestyle of the small minority elite influenced the vast majority in peasant societies as well. From the late twentieth century and especially around the turn of the millennium, several of the former peripheral countries all of a sudden became rich. The *nouveau riche* attitude, mocked by seventeenth- and eighteenth-century French writers, became a mass phenomenon in turn-of-the-millennium Europe. This historical feature became a dominant factor in the economic crisis of 2008. That was the phenomenon behind the accusation, often heard in recent years, that the peripheral countries of Europe generated the crisis and pushed the European Union into it.

Credit consumerism

Consumption as a way of life and source of prestige, inspired by ever newer consumer goods, aggressive advertising and manipulation, and especially the creation of an attractive consumer infrastructure and several financial innovations to offer unlimited credit, easily led to overspending. People became able, and were attracted, to spend more than they earned. When consumerism started to consume huge amounts of credit, it became economically and socially dangerous. However, in prosperous times, even the accumulation of household debts was manageable up to a certain level. If debt service did not surpass one-third of available income, families remained able to repay the debt and stay solvent. However, in cyclical downturns, financial panics, but also as a consequence of income fluctuations and life events such as divorce, illness, and other kind of troubles, the ability to repay was endangered for many. Reckless borrowing and huge household indebtedness became as risky as reckless bank lending. These two phenomena were actually two sides of the same coin. Credit consumerism was the most extreme in the United States, where 300 million inhabitants have 1.5 billion credit cards, more than all other countries combined, and new home ownership was broadly based on subprime mortgage loans. When the 2007–8 financial panic stopped the free flow of credits, millions became unable to pay their mortgage debts. Personal indebtedness was also at a historic level. In 1950, the average debt of a household in the United States amounted to 34% of after-tax income. By 1980, that had reached 69%, and by 2003, the average personal debt of $32,660 surpassed the average $28,400 per capita disposal income by 15%.[70] Europe also emerged on the same road. One of the pioneering European followers of the United States was Britain, which was next after America in credit card ownership: its 59 million credit cards represented practically one card per person. The number of credit cards is equal to the number of debit cards in that country.

This situation is in sharp contrast with Germany, where 82 million inhabitants own 93 million debit cards and 20 million credit cards. France is even more behind with 39 million debit cards, and 9 million credit cards. In Germany and France, there is still an aversion to debt. Nevertheless, Germany became the second most-indebted country in Europe, with an average of $3,483 in credit card debt, while Italy has only $1,268. Millions of credit cards are in use throughout Europe, and they make shopping and spending, not to mention overspending, much easier. According to researchers, the dramatic growth of credit card use,[71] especially among young adults and adolescents, strongly contributed to increased and unchecked spending that led to the near doubling of the number of consumer insolvencies in England and Wales between 1990 and 2004.[72] Although the interest rates on card debt are 16% and sometimes even 30%, for example in Britain, for customers who default, a great number of people spend and pay off one credit card debt using another card. An average Briton has $5,188 in credit card debt (compared to $9,000 in the United States).

Debt counseling for heavily indebted people was introduced, and one counselor spoke about his "financially illiterate" clientele. He had clients with $150,000 in debt spread out over 16 credit cards. These individuals, as he summed up his experience, were earning 18,000 pounds ($31,828) a year and had 20,000 pound ($35,364) in debt. When Christmas shoppers were asked, it turned out that every fifth person was still paying off their gifts for last year.[73] A great many people suffer from financial "myopia," a dangerous short-sightedness in spending and over-borrowing. By 2007, household liabilities exceeded 100% of disposable family income in Germany, Estonia, Spain, Portugal, Finland, Sweden, and Britain, but they reached 250% of income in Ireland and the Netherlands, and more than 300% in Denmark.[74] Household debt increased rapidly in the early twenty-first century. Between 2002 and 2009, it doubled in Spain, more than doubled in Greece, and more than quadrupled in Lithuania. In Denmark, Ireland, Portugal, Spain, and Britain, household debt increased from 76% to 84% of disposable family income in the two years after 2007. Only three countries—Belgium, Germany, and Luxembourg—exhibited a slight decrease in household debts before the crisis, while Austria, Finland, France, and some other countries remained without significant levels of debt.[75] Britain closely followed the American pattern. As newspapers reported, "The UK has adopted the American habit of credit with vigor, and consequently consumers are rapidly getting in over their heads."[76] Consequently, Britain has one-third of total European debts. The total consumer debt, including mortgage, credit cards, and other forms of credit, amounted to £1.3 trillion in 2011, three times higher than it had been in 1997.[77]

The dream of joining Europe, which guided the former Soviet Bloc countries, generated the false myth that they could adopt the Western consumption model immediately. East Europeans envied Western life. They wanted to replace their Trabants and Zhigulis with Volkswagens and BMWs. From the distance and isolation of their gray everyday Eastern realities, they did not see the hard and efficient work that made Western lifestyles possible, but only an idealized "dolce vita." When Western institutions like retail chains, shopping malls, and credit cards appeared, they hoped to catch up with the West and the Western standard of living instantly.

Household spending—encouraged by wage increases, optimism, and the euphoria of joining the European Union in January 2004—steadily increased by an annual average of 5.8% between 2001 and 2006, far beyond the yearly 4.2% increase in GDP. In the three years between 2001 and 2003, household consumption jumped by 30%. In Lithuania, during the three years before the crisis, GDP grew by 8.5% per year, but private consumption grew by 11.6% per annum. In Romania, the annual growth of GDP was 6.0%, but private consumption increased by 11.1%. In Russia, the two figures were 7.3% and 12.3%. In Latvia, in the single year of 2006, private consumption jumped more than 21%.[78]

In the Baltic countries and Hungary, people preferred to borrow in foreign currency, mostly Swiss francs. There was a rationale to it, since interest rates were lower, and possible domestic financial shocks were more easily avoided. The share of family foreign currency debts within Hungary's total debt increased from 3.8% in 2001 to 41.7% by 2005, and to an incredible 70.2% by 2008. On the other hand, however, borrowing in foreign currency is extremely risky, since a devaluation in the domestic currency will increase the repayment burden in proportion to the percentage of devaluation.

The two most important components of household indebtedness are consumer credit and mortgage. Consumer credit, as an average, totals about 10–15% of household credits in Europe. A few countries, however, such as Greece (28%), Hungary (45%), and Bulgaria (52%), had a much higher percentage of the basically new credit form. The most important debt is mortgage debt: in the EU-12 countries, while consumer debts amounted to 12% of family debt, mortgage debt represented 76% of it. In the entire European Union, 67% of household debt is mortgage debt, and in the eurozone, 72%.[79] In Slovenia, where mortgage credit is rather new, its reached 31% of GDP. In the solid Scandinavian country of Sweden, household indebtedness has doubled since 1970, and reached 70% of GDP. In Denmark, the average mortgage debt per family is more than $100,000.[80] In formerly poor Ireland, residential mortgage credits grew by 25% annually in the early twenty-first century and, as was mentioned in Chapter 1, in the four years after 2003, it jumped from 40% to 65% of GDP. Mortgage credits increased by 25% per year between 2001 and 2003, and they surpassed €651 billion by 2005. Personal credit had several other forms as well. In Germany, for example, banks are legally able to lend account holders an ongoing overdraft of three times a borrower's monthly income.

Population indebtedness reached dangerous levels: in the early 1990s, households had a debt burden that was equal to 18% of their available income, but by 2005, this share jumped to 117% of their income. Household indebtedness in Ireland rose from 60% to 160% of GDP. Family indebtedness in Spain more than doubled in the decade around the turn of the century. The share of Hungarian family debt in the country's total foreign currency debt totaled only 3.8% in 2001, but, by 2008, it amounted to more than 70% of it. The world's private consumption expenditures, a great part of it financed by credit, increased four-fold between 1960 and 2000, when it totaled $20 trillion, and 60% of it was spent by the Western world, which represents 12% of the world's population.[81]

Beside irresponsible banking and lending, a similarly irresponsible spending and borrowing became predominant in turn-of-the-millennium Europe. In several European countries, this became one of the main causes of the economic crisis of 2008. This reflects a major cultural change. Indebtedness was alien and sinful in the old European culture. Nora's husband in Ibsen's drama *A Doll's House* strictly excludes the possibility of "borrowing and debts." In the German language, "Schuld" is the term for debt and sin alike. "The twentieth century is recognized as a moment when traditional fears of debt and feelings about the value of thrift were overtaken by the appeal of a hedonistic lifestyle."[82] In contemporary capitalism, however, the punishment for financial irresponsibility by the market system—"the slap by the invisible hand," as one author called it[83]—hit only consumers. They not only had to stop their previous lifestyle, but, regardless of their preceding attitudes, had to suffer severe austerity measures and the loss of a great part of their previous welfare services. They paid the entire bill, while financial institutions were bailed out from taxpayers' money, thus socializing their losses.[84]

Will "Social Europe" be rebuilt?

The greatest historical achievements of postwar Europe were the creation of the European Union and the welfare state. The latter was the outcome of a strong solidarity feeling fueled by the war experience and the social-welfare competition with the Soviet Bloc after the war. It was also closely connected with the postwar regulated market system that put society on a pedestal and subordinated the economy to social values and requirements. Europe had a relatively egalitarian income distribution. In terms of the commonly used Gini coefficient—which measures income distribution on a scale of 0 to 1, where 0 means total equality of income, while 1 is the absolute inequality when one person get all the income of a country—Europe's index was 0.23–0.26 in the 1980s. Balanced income levels were closely connected with the welfare state. The latter's main characteristics were: free education at all levels; free healthcare; comprehensive pensions; support for disadvantaged people; compensation for unemployment; certain subsidies for particular products and activities; and minimum social benefits, based on high taxation and public spending.[85] The European Union took over national welfare projects, which became a Union program from the late 1980s on. In December 1989, a Social Charter was accepted by 11 members of the then EU-12 (Britain opted out). "Progress cannot be founded simply on the basis of the competitiveness of economies," declared the European Union's Commission in 1994, "but also on the efficiency of the European society as a whole."[86] In the 1990s, a Social Protocol was attached to the Maastricht Treaty. The 1994 "White Paper on European Social Policy" formulated its social policy agenda and expressed the goal of preserving and developing the "European social model" of the welfare state.[87]

The deregulation process of the 1980s–90s and the 2008 crisis mutilated, or at least cut a deep wound in, the welfare state. After 1980, as the self-regulating market system started subordinating society to the economy, social services consequently became the target of attacks and limitation. In 1981, the OECD published its report *The Welfare State in Crisis*.[88] In 1998, Michel Camdessus, Managing Director of the IMF, delivered a speech entitled, "Worldwide Crisis in the Welfare State: What Next in the Context of Globalization?" Camdessus stated: "Welfare systems, based on the best possible motivation of . . . improving human welfare, have come to represent an enormous drain on the resources and the efficiency of many of the so called welfare states."[89]

The pension systems—also in connection with demographic changes—were totally transformed, and significant personal contributions were introduced. Instead of full state responsibility and service, new "three pillar schemes" were introduced, and the state paid only a small amount, the minimal survival level, while a compulsory personal contribution was responsible for the largest part. A voluntary third pillar was also based on personal contribution during a person's active working years. Other benefits were also reduced. Tuition fees at the tertiary level of education and limited co-payments for doctor visits were introduced in several countries. In ten European countries, public expenditures on social security and healthcare declined between 1995 and 2006 from 22.0% to 19.8% of GDP, while Sweden increased its expenditures from 22.6 to 29.5% and France from 28.8% to 29.5%.[90] The welfare state was curbed, but still preserved.[91]

After the 2008 crisis, however, severe austerity measures were introduced throughout Europe that thoroughly damaged, and in some cases even destroyed, the main features of the welfare state in quite a few countries. While the welfare state remained nearly intact in Scandinavia, it was diminished or partly dismantled in Britain, the Baltic countries, Greece, Ireland, Spain, Portugal, Hungary, Romania, and some other countries. "It is ultimately a crisis of the welfare state which has grown too large to be supported economically."[92] This statement is especially true for several peripheral countries that cannot finance the system any longer.

The dismantling of welfare institutions goes hand-in-hand with growing income disparities. Using again the Gini coefficient, inequality in Europe increased from 0.23–0.26 to 0.31 in the last decade. [93] Sweden, Germany, Norway, Austria, and some of the new member countries, such as Slovenia, Hungary, Slovakia, and the Czech Republic, represent the best situation with a 0.25–0.26 Gini coefficient. Next after them are Finland, Belgium, Denmark, the Netherlands, and Ireland with a 0.27–0.28 coefficient. France has a 0.30 coefficient, Britain, Italy, Spain, Estonia, Greece, and Bulgaria are already in the 0.32–0.33 range, while Portugal, Romania, and Lithuania have reached the 0.35 level. The gap between the most egalitarian Slovene income distribution (Gini index of 0.23) and the least egalitarian Latvian distribution (0.38 Gini index) is significant, but the situation is still better than in America, where inequality increased from 0.41 to 0.46 in the last decade, the highest in the advanced world. Rising inequality became one of the central topics at the World Economic Forum meeting in Davos in January 2012. "In developed economies, such as those of Western Europe, North America, and Japan, the social contract that has in recent decades been taken for granted is in danger of being destroyed," the report said.[94]

The rising trend is striking indeed: the top 10% of the population of Germany, Denmark, and Sweden—traditionally, more egalitarian societies— earned five times more than the lowest 10% in the 1980s, but now the gap has increased to six times. In the 34 OECD countries, which includes all the European countries, this gap is 9:1. In the Davos debates, growing inequality has been addressed not only as a social problem, but also as a danger to economic growth. Some economic inequality is inevitable, but too much is harmful for economic growth. Countries with more equitable income distributions, as the lessons of the Scandinavian model clearly prove, grew faster in the long term.[95] A paradox of the 2008 crisis is that it was much less severe in the Nordic countries where the welfare state and relative income equality are strong.

The future of Europe offers two alternatives: a slowly growing inequality and further eroding welfare state, or the reconstruction of "Social Europe," with its relative income equality and functioning welfare institutions. Which alternative will be realized depends on social-political developments on the continent, and consequently on the renewal and transformation of contemporary capitalism.

5

WHICH WAY EUROPE? MANAGING THE ECONOMIC CRISIS AND THE WAY OUT

Crisis management: stimulus packages and bailouts

When the liquidity crisis hit Europe in 2008, several governments, together with the American administration, turned to the old Keynesian method and attempted to revitalize the ailing economy with stimulus packages. Because of the global impact of the financial crisis, government interventions have been implemented worldwide. Governments throughout the world pledged $17 trillion to support the economy by bailouts and guarantees that altogether represented one-quarter of global GDP. Real government assistance, however, was only a fragment of this amount. The emergency measures were intended to stimulate demand. Billions have been spent to bail out industrial sectors, most of all the car industry that was paralyzed, and banks that had lost liquidity and needed recapitalization to start making loans again. In some countries, household assistance, tax rebates, and job creation by investment in public works were also part of these packages.

In November 2008, the European Commission initiated a €200 billion stimulus plan, paid mostly by national governments from their own budgets, and partly from Union money and contributions by the European Investment Bank. In December of that year, the European Economic Recovery Plan was launched to provide 2% of the aggregate GDP of the Union to stimulate the European economy in 2009 and 2010. Experts agreed that this stimulus helped to curb the recession that was basically driven by declining demand. Although the revitalization of the banking system became one of the most unpopular measures, it was absolutely necessary to avoid a catastrophic depression. Lack of credit would have paralyzed trade, industry, and the entire economy. These actions, however, were against the explicit rules of the European Stability and Growth Pact that excludes bailouts. The European Union temporarily suspended this regulation.

Several European governments acted to avoid the recession or the deepening of the crisis. Germany pumped €32 billion and €50 billion—1.3% and 2.0% of GDP, respectively—into the economy in two steps in November 2008 and January 2009, partly for public works and infrastructural investments. France, in December 2008, started assisting its ailing car and construction industries, reestablishing liquidity and creating jobs through €26 billion investments in public works, 1.3% of its GDP. Britain invested £31 billion, 2.2% of its GDP, in three steps (September and November of 2008, and in January 2009). Italy and the Netherlands came out with stimulus packages of €9 billion and €8.5 billion, 0.6% and 1.4% of GDP, respectively. Some of the new Central and Eastern European member countries also introduced stimulus programs: in 2009, the Czech Republic, Latvia, and Romania spent 1.99%, 1.76%, and 1.8% of their respective GDPs to stimulate the economy. In 2010, the Czech program consumed 1.37% of GDP, and the Polish took 0.81%. Altogether, the EU-27 countries invested roughly 1% of their combined GDP in 2009 and again in 2010 to assist their economies.[1]

Managing the crisis, however, required assistance to the most troubled countries that were buried by debts and became unable to pay them back. Greece was on the brink of default; Portugal and Ireland were in critical situations. While national stimulus programs targeted domestic economies, the European Union as a collective, in cooperation with the International Monetary Fund, assisted Greece with €110 billion to avoid default. The IMF contribution was €30 billion and the euro-zone member countries paid the bulk of it in a multilateral way, coordinated by the European Commission. This was only "first aid," since Greece remained unable to repay. In March 2012, another huge amount, €14.5 billion, became due. At this point, the EU forced an agreement with the creditors to absorb at least half of the losses. The old Greek bonds would be replaced by new ones, and, as another part of this major deal, the creditors would accept a roughly 3.6%–3.8% interest rate for the new Greek bonds. The agreement was signed, and the creditors lost 70% of their investments.[2] Among them are several hedge funds that bought Greek bonds for peanuts at the nadir of the crisis, hoping that the European Union will make good on them in the end. Meanwhile, Greece had to introduce more cuts to state expenditures, dismiss tens of thousands of state employees, and further cut wages. These new austerity measures were prerequisites for the new bailout. This deal, accompanied by violent protest and vandalism in Athens, at last succeeded. The EU signed a second bailout package of €130 billion ($172 billion) on February 22, 2012. The transaction will reduce the Greek debt by €100 billion to 120–130% of GDP in the coming years. "The agreement," reports stated, "could be a new turning point in the European debt crisis."[3]

The European Central Bank, which is banned by its charter from purchasing government bonds directly from governments, instead started buying Greek, Italian, and other bonds on secondary markets to ease the pressure and counterbalance the steep increase in interest rates that happened because of the lack of buyers. By July 2010, the European Central Bank held about €60 billion worth of European government bonds. This action worked and the rates temporarily declined for Italian and Spanish bonds.

Another major action by the Bank was to pump €468 billion ($628 billion) as a three-year loan with a 1% interest rate into the European banking industry. The Central Bank aimed to inspire more than 500 European banks to use the cheap loan for buying government bonds with much higher interest rates. That would indeed offer a huge profit for the banks. Together with other bank actions, the European Central Bank's lending to the banking industry totaled €979 billion. As the Bank's President, Mario Draghi, announced, a second major infusion of money into the banks followed. In the last week of February 2012, the Bank provided a second huge, €529.5 billion ($705 billion) credit infusion to 800 European banks. As with the previous similar action in December 2011, the credit was given for three years with a 1% interest rate. The two actions altogether pumped more than $1.3 trillion into the European financial system. That represents a major contribution to the solution of the debt crisis, and, in a somewhat longer time, to the stimulation of economic growth. The European Central Bank strongly contributed in revitalizing the European banking system and assisting the market of government bonds through "two longer-term refinancing operations," in other words, through emergency financing.[4]

These actions, indeed, eased the pressure on Italian and Spanish bonds, and their interest rates significantly declined. In early February, 2012, the rate of Italian 10-year bonds dropped by 35 basis points to 5.9%, and the 5-year bonds dropped from 8% to 5%. The rate of Spanish 10-year bonds declined from 7% in November to 5.5%, and their 2-year bonds declined by 79 basis points to 2.53%. Auctions in February "will be a good gauge of appetite for the peripheral bonds."[5]

In November 2011, a surprise agreement by six central banks—the American Federal Reserve, the European Central Bank, and the central banks of Canada, Switzerland, Britain, and Japan—offered temporary US-dollar liquidity exchange arrangements until February 2013 that made dollar borrowing cheaper and contributed to the liquidity of the European financial markets.[6] In 2012, talks began with China, which has an interest in market stability, to invest in the IMF to assist and bail out debt-ridden European countries. That was a topic during Angela Merkel's visit to China in early 2012.[7]

Between 2008 and 2012, with the contribution of the IMF, six European Union member countries were bailed out, three from the euro-zone (Greece, Ireland, and Portugal), and three of the new member countries (Hungary, Latvia, and Romania). All of them had belonged to the European peripheries. Until World War II, they were, in the best case, semi-successful agricultural-industrial countries with roughly half of the income level of Western Europe. Two-thirds of a century later, they are still vulnerable.

On October 27, 2011, the heads of the European Union countries agreed to a rescue plan. Its three interconnected main parts were: 1. Push the creditor banks of Greece to accept ("voluntarily") half the debts as their loss; 2. Recapitalize the European banks with €106 billion ($146 billion); and 3. Establish a "firewall" around endangered countries to prevent the spread of the crisis.[8] Europe has an agenda and a strategy to resolve the crisis in a gradual but consistent way. The actions and the summit meetings, however, regularly generate harsh criticism accusing the European leaders of being too slow and not solving the debt crisis with one single dramatic measure.

Crisis management: austerity measures

After the first year of stimulus packages, the Union countries did not return to this policy. Because the economic crisis, as discussed before, became a sovereign debt crisis, Germany, in agreement with France and in cooperation with the Netherlands and Finland, pushed the European Union toward a budgetary deficit and debt reduction policy. Instead of stimulating demand, austerity measures were planned to reconstruct balanced fiscal order. The harshness of the austerity policies has already been illustrated in previous chapters. It caused and is causing severe pain to the population, as well as the decline of domestic demand. However, these measures, at least in one respect, were seemingly working. The most successful example is Ireland where the deficit was cut from 32% of GDP in 2010 to 10% by the end of 2011. In 2011, compared to 2010, the most indebted PIIGS countries reduced their collective deficit by 8–10%.

Nevertheless, as much as the austerity measures served the reduction of the deficit, they decreased domestic consumption and economic growth as well. The successful Irish deficit reduction slowed the country's economy to near stagnation. Ireland "will suffer a sharp slowdown in growth in this year," stated the progress report of the international lenders. For three years, the Irish economy declined, but it exhibited some signs of a surge in exports in 2011. In the last quarter of that year, however, the economy declined again and, in 2012, the best-case forecasts predicted only 0.5% growth.[9] Regarding Spain, the newly elected conservative government increased income taxes and taxed savings and property. Income tax increased by 7 points to 56%, the second-highest rate in Europe after Sweden. All the cuts, including the government spending cuts, cover only half the targeted deficit reduction. This made the increase of the sales tax quite likely as well.[10] Consequently, the 2012 growth forecast reflects a new 1.5% decline in GDP.

Seventeen countries of the EU will have modest growth, including the big EU countries of Germany (0.6%) and France (0.4%), according to a forecast for the year in early 2012. Even crisis-ridden Ireland may have some slight growth. The interim report of the European Commission, however, signaled a worsening of the situation: ten countries out of 27 will stagnate or decline. The Czech Republic will stagnate, and nine countries—Belgium, Greece, Spain, Italy, Cyprus, Hungary, the Netherlands, Portugal, and Slovenia—will decline in 2012. The forecast for Italy and Spain is for a contraction of 1.3% and 1.0%, respectively. Growth will be highest in Poland (2.5%), Lithuania (2.3%), and Latvia (2.1%) and it will be very negative in Greece (−4.4%) and in Portugal (−3.3%). In place of the November 2011 forecast of 0.5% growth, the entire euro-zone of 17 countries will experience a 0.3% decline.[11]

The "Proust index"—recalling Marcel Proust's famous novel, *À la recherche du temps perdu*, or *In Search of Lost Time*—a new calculation, offers an evaluation about the "lost years" caused by the recession pushing back the countries to the economic level of earlier years. Greece, according to these calculations, dropped back by 12 years to the 2000 level. Iceland lost almost the same number of years. Portugal and Latvia both lost a decade and declined back to the 2002 level. Ireland's decline is very near to that. Hungary, Britain, and Spain landed at the 2004 level, Italy at the 2005 level. From the European Union-27 member countries, 22 lost years.[12]

It is more than a symbolic fact that on Sofokleous Street—the Wall Street of Athens, home of the former Greek Stock Exchange—the city's main soup kitchen was opened for the poor. The conservative Cameron government introduced harsh cuts to curb the deficit in Britain. Still, four years after the crisis exploded, that country is far below its pre-crisis levels. A double-dip recession is in the making in several European countries. A one-sided austerity policy easily becomes counterproductive by generating a downward spiral. In spite of the decreased budgetary deficit, stagnation or the return of recession lead to declining tax income, and at the end of the day, it may increase, instead of decrease, the deficit and debt.

Most experts are unified in their rejection of Europe's austerity "obsession." In September 2011, *The Economist*, which definitely does not have a Keynesian orientation, maintained that the "collectively huge fiscal contraction is self-defeating. . . . And mere budget-cutting does not deal with the real cause of the mess, which is a loss of credibility. . . . [C]redible rescue should start with growth and . . . a serious restructuring of debt."[13] In its leading editorial on February 1, 2012, *The New York Times* criticized the one-sided austerity orientation of the Union and spoke about a "senseless restriction on stimulus. . . . Leaders wiser than Ms. Merkel would build a stronger European Union by helping her neighbors grow their way out of debt, not squeeze them to the breaking point."[14] Among others, three Nobel laureate economists are also rejecting a one-sided austerity policy. As Joseph Stiglitz said: "It is clear that austerity alone is a recipe for stagnation and decline."[15] Paul Krugman, in his January 2011 essay, flatly stated that "the current tough-it-out strategy won't work even in the narrow sense of avoiding default and devaluation." [16] More than a year later he repeated in an article called "Pain Without Gain" that the austerity policy is an "economic doctrine [that is] responsible for this disaster."[17]

Amartya Sen, in his article of May 22, 2012, stated that the intention of the austerity policy was good, but "the foundations of the current austerity policy, combined with the rigidities of Europe's monetary union (in the absence of fiscal union), have hardly been a model of cogency and sagacity. Second, an intention that is fine on its own can conflict with a more urgent priority – in this case, the preservation of a democratic Europe that is concerned about societal well-being. These are values for which Europe has fought, over many decades."[18]

Urging a Keynesian demand-creating policy and growth has a strong rationale. In my view, however, an austerity policy in the first years of the crisis had a double importance and necessity for several European countries. Besides decreasing the towering deficit burden that endangered several countries and pushed them to the brink, fiscal responsibility and sacrifice may help to reconstruct credibility. Moreover, in spite of its controversial outcome, the austerity policy is also helping to increase competitiveness. Countries that are members of the euro-zone and consequently unable to devaluate their currency, may do it by a so-called "domestic devaluation," i.e., by cutting the cost of production by wage and benefit cuts. Unfortunately, this policy hits innocent people and even ones with low incomes. The pain is huge, but hardly avoidable.

Most of all, austerity measures have a crucially important *educational* role. It has to lead back to more responsible lifestyle and spending practices in several European countries. Governments and people that based their spending and lifestyle on borrowed money, and lived beyond their means for years, have to learn and practice responsible new spending habits, even if they are painful. After decades of an irresponsible spending spree, a few years of austerity, as controversial and even counterproductive as it might be, is unavoidable, especially at the peripheries. (Let me add my small, but expressive personal experience for a better understanding. Together with the German, French, and Greek consul generals I participated in a panel discussion on the European crisis. The German and French consuls arrived at the debate in cars they had driven themselves. The Greek consul's car was driven by a chauffeur. To get rid of this attitude requires a long learning process.)

However, the European Union, after the years of forced austerity policy, has to take steps now to end stagnation and decrease unemployment and to generate growth. Successful crisis management requires both austerity and some kind of stimulus measures in a masterful combination. At the January 2012 summit meeting, the European leaders at least made some progress in understanding the need to stimulate growth and to avoid a vicious deflationary circle. It has certainly been more than just rhetoric. "Over the last several weeks, European politicians have begun to insist quite publicly that austerity can no longer be the sole answer," reported the media. "Budget consolidation is one of the legs Europe's future must be built on," declared Angela Merkel. "But of course, we need a second leg [which is] economic growth, jobs and employment."[19] Olli Rehn, the EU Commissioner for Economic and Monetary Affairs, stated in February 2012: "Prospects have worsened and risks remain, but there are signs of stabilization especially in the recent period. . . . Decisions will be taken once we have a full picture."[20]

Europe is considering various kinds of stimuli to spur economic growth. At the EU summit meeting on March 1, 2012, for the first time since 2008, "European leaders . . . sought to show they could confront the social cost of fighting the sovereign debt crisis." The summit decided on the need for "determined actions to boost growth and jobs." Chancellor Angela Merkel stated: "this is the first step toward a stability union, toward a political union. Further steps will follow."[21] On the same day, the Italian Senate approved several measures aimed at fostering economic growth. The "Grow Italy" bill wants to increase competitiveness.

Real actions are yet to come. In the spring of 2012, especially after the elections in Greece and France, the pressure to go far beyond rhetoric became very strong. The requirement for growth policy, in spite of one-sided austerity measures, became more outstanding, and seemingly got a strong leader in the newly elected French President, François Holland. He was elected, among other reasons, because he opposed his predecessor's policy to assist the German austerity strategy. Together with the Italian, Spanish, and other leaders, and the President of the European Central Bank, Mario Draghi, a strong pressure group emerged for combining an austerity policy with growth stimulus.

Future historians, however, will probably discover a hidden strategy behind the seemingly hesitant and inconsistent German and European politics. Its first element was not to allow countries to collapse, but without a long-lasting solution. Meanwhile, long-term structural changes were forced to progress toward further integration, especially in the fiscal area. Although almost all of the steps of this policy have often been criticized, if it changes in time and also turns toward growth stimulation, this strategy works and may lead to positive long-term outcomes.

The return to a regulated market system

The most urgent measures to manage the crisis and avoid devastating defaults were crucial but naturally did not offer a real solution. Europe had to dig deep into the roots of the crisis and eliminate them. This task is extremely difficult. In a globalized world where the financial markets are closely integrated, a single country or even the European Union as a whole cannot introduce regulations alone. Such actions must be agreed upon by the advanced countries together, otherwise financial firms will migrate from regulated areas to regions and countries with fewer regulations. Regulations must be integrated and harmonized as well. The United States and, within the Union, Britain and the entire euro-zone had to act together. However, the respective interests and situations of these countries are not the same. They have several special features, unique interests that work against close co-operation. The United States is a traditional laissez-faire country that differs strongly from most in Europe. Britain has its own special interests. For instance, "The City," the British banking sector, is the real strength behind the country's economy, and it runs roughly two-thirds of Europe's financial services. Prime Minister David Cameron announced his intent to save it from strict regulations. The government and the representatives of "British interests" consider the plans and measures of the European Union as attacks against them and, moreover, as a French conspiracy to undermine Britain through EU regulations. "The French have a coordinated strategy for using the European Union regulations to level London down and to get Paris to replace it," goes a typical charge.[22] European Commissioner Michel Barnier, in a speech at Guildhall, London in January 2012 considered it important to declare: "Contrary to what I often read, there is no plot. No plot to undermine the City. No plot to boost Paris or Frankfurt at the expense of the City."[23]

Common actions and regulations require tremendous amounts of work, a great deal of compromise, and lots of time. Nevertheless, a major pre-requisite for coordinated regulations was fulfilled through quick action by the American government. President Barack Obama, just having taken office, asked Congress in February 2009 to "put in place tough, new common-sense rules of the road so that our financial market rewards drive and innovation, and punishes short-cuts and abuse." On November 3, the Financial Stability Improvement Act was accepted. On January 5, 2010, the Dodd-Frank Wall Street Reform and Consumer Protection Act was enacted by the 111th Congress of the United States. It changed the rules of the game in the most significant way since the New Deal of the Great Depression by reestablishing a regulated system. "The failure that led to this crisis," argued the authors of the law, "requires bold action. We must restore responsibility and account-ability in our financial system."[24]

An amendment of the Dodd-Frank Act, the so-called Volcker Rule,[25] was also enacted and banned banks from engaging in "proprietary trading of securities, derivatives and certain other financial instruments for the entity's own account." "Proprietary trading" is not a genuine banking business. It does not use clients' money but the banks' own assets mostly for arbitrage trading of stocks, bonds, assets and their derivatives. It is a high risk business. Banks usually established hedge funds within the banks for these activities. The restriction of speculative investments by commercial banks, the separa-tion of commercial and investment banking, the institutional separation of proprietary and private equities trading were the decisions made to eliminate hazardous activities in the financial markets. This regulation was so popular that five former American Secretaries of the Treasury endorsed the Volcker Rule in an open letter to the *Wall Street Journal*.[26]

The Dodd-Frank Act, including the Volcker Rule, was the achieve-ment of a Democratic President, and of a Democratic Congress and Senate. It soon became the target of conservative attacks after the midterm elections of November 2010, which led to a conservative victory and takeover of Congress. By September 2011, as a consequence, "only a small part of the law has taken hold. Of the up to 400 regulations called for in the act, only about a quarter had even been written, much less approved." Moreover, two dozen bills in Congress seek to dismantle parts of the Dodd–Frank Act.[27]

Although the strict regulatory regime has been endangered in the United States, the initial legal actions and regulations opened the road for international agreements on regulations. The need for cooperative international actions was evident to all countries. Following the initiative of the Canadian Minister of Finance and, later Prime Minister, Paul Martin, the G-20 organization[28] of advanced economic powers was founded and had its first meeting in Washington, D.C., in 2008. From September 2009, it officially replaced the previous G-8 organization as the main economic council of the advanced world. In their bi-annual meetings, the finance ministers, and then the heads of states or governments took the initiative in introducing global regulations.

At the various G-20 meetings, a whole set of major regulatory questions was on the agenda. Concerning the scope of the discussions and agreements on regulations, the following short list may be illustrative. At the Pittsburg meeting of the G-20 leaders in September 2009, they discussed major regulatory issues and adopted important elements from the Dodd–Frank Act into international agreements. In November 2010, in South Korea, the G-20 countries discussed the introduction of an additional supranational supervisory system for internationally important financial institutions, as well as requiring a higher loss-absorption capacity on the part of banks. This concept was realized by the Basel III principles on new global capital standards to create a much larger buffer to absorb sudden bank losses.

Reuters reported on January 6, 2010: "Global financial regulations changed little since the 2008 banking crisis, but that won't be the case much longer." The authorities of the United States and the European Union were to create a new regulatory order in 2010 that would "fundamentally change how world banks and markets operate." Strict limits on leverage and capital (the ratio of borrowed money to the bank's own funds) were introduced and slimmer bank profits were encouraged. Previously unregulated types of business, such as the hazardous so-called "off-exchange" derivatives market, had to conform to new procedures. Off-exchange, or over-the counter trading, is an important form of risky deregulated bank business. These operations were outside the standardized bank operations that use official, specialized trading facilities, including stock exchanges. This type of financial business is a bilateral agreement between a bank and a client, made by phone or computer without a standardized, safe, and transparent form. This is a highly risky enterprise because of its bilateral character and the possibility of the collapse of the partner before payment. Hedge fund regulations and the limits of securitization are also on the agenda and will be introduced. It is "becoming a complete redesigning of financial trading in Europe."[29]

In spite of the busy agenda and already-achieved agreements, several central issues such as "harmonizing national legal systems have been sidelined for future date." The same happened to the regulation of shadow banking. "Regulators are finding it difficult to design rules, agree on parameters and coordinate activities." The Cannes session of the G-20 leaders in 2011 clearly demonstrated "the inadequacy of the current international economic and regulatory governance architecture." As Jim Flaherty, the Canadian Minister of Finance, concluded: the G-20 countries are "nowhere near a consensus on a range of fundamental issues." Regulations in several areas "are at an early stage of policy development and will take years to implement."[30]

Coordinating rules between countries with differing interests is painfully difficult. A measure in one country is often not adequate in another. The Volcker Rule, mentioned above, is an evident example. This regulation, while banning the most hazardous elements of the banking business, such as making risky bets with their own money, is tailored to American banking, where commercial and investment bank activities were originally separated. The merger of their activities during the deregulatory regime made the banking system more volatile. The same rule, however, is not good for Europe. Since the mid-nineteenth century commercial and investment banking were traditionally combined in the French Credit Mobilier- and German mixed universal-type of banks. Furthermore, the Volcker Rule restricted American banks in trading foreign government bonds. This regulation would increase the interest rates that European governments have to pay for their bonds because of more limited buyers.

Nevertheless, the European Union, together with the United States, has a "shared common agenda" of regulations. The G-20 organization took the guidance for significant progress in some areas and for cooperation in regulations. Most of the rules of the Dodd-Frank Act were adopted. The excessive asset growth in the financial sector, as agreed, had to be reduced to limit the risk of asset price bubbles. Capital buffers and a secure leverage ratio and shadow-banking regulations are currently in preparation for 2012. Control of credit rating agencies was also introduced, and the idea was launched to establish a European rating institution.[31] A regulatory process initiated the integration of the European insurance market and the creation of a single European mortgage system regulated by the same rules Europe-wide. Based on the model suggested by the IMF, a so-called macro-prudential supervision system aims at more efficient control. This system would replace the regime that supervises financial institutions separately in isolation (micro-prudential). The macro-regime supervises the banking system in its interrelated connections as a whole and thus becomes more efficient at controlling excessive credit growth, regulating reallocation of capital to break the cycle of booms and busts.[32]

The central institutions of the European Union also had a busy agenda to work out principles and initiate new regulations. The European Parliament and its Economic and Monetary Affairs Committee created an agenda of the main regulatory targets and put several elements of a new regulatory system on that agenda. A few examples may illustrate the effort. In October 2011, three major issues were accepted by huge majority of the Parliament, including recommendations to separate domestic retail banking from investment banking, and the introduction of a financial transaction tax.

Already in December 2009, the EU urged the IMF to introduce a global financial transaction tax and the initiative gained some support from the OECD as well. This was not a new idea. Economists such as John Maynard Keynes had already nurtured this scheme in the 1930s. The idea was resurrected in 1972, when James Tobin suggested throwing "grains of sand in the wheels of the market" to slow down international foreign exchange transactions.[33] In the 1980s, Sweden introduced this kind of tax, which also exists in Ireland, Switzerland, and Greece. In September 2011, because of the lack of international action, the European Commission officially initiated this measure for the euro-zone region. If international agreement is reached—partly against Britain's strong opposition—this measure would displace 90% of the derivative trading in Europe. Reducing the run of hot money, and in the meantime generating income from the action, would be mutually advantageous. This tax, also called a Robin Hood tax, would also redistribute a small part of the huge profits from this kind of transaction into a fund to assist economically disadvantaged countries.[34]

A pan-European model of a regulatory system is thus in the making. Its final form is still uncertain and will be ready only after years of difficult deals and compromises. Europe, however, is turning back to the regulated market model. As an institutional backbone for it, the European System of Financial Supervisions became operational in January 2011. Its central task is coordination between the Union's agencies and national regulators, and the consistent realization of European laws and rules. This institutional change "represents a fundamental shift in the approach to financial regulation in the EU, with authority transferring from national regulators to EU authorities."[35] In this new supervisory framework, important institutions have been created. The European Systemic Risk Board is based in Frankfurt and is responsible for the macro-prudential oversight of the European financial system. Its task is to guarantee early warnings when system-wide risks are developing. Furthermore, three new European Supervisory Authorities were established: the European Banking Authority (in London), the European Insurance and Occupational Pensions Authority (in Frankfurt), and the European Securities and Markets Authority (in Paris).

This network of new institutions produces new rules across the Union for national regulatory systems. They draft guidelines and rules for the national institutions to follow since the day-to-day supervisory work of financial institutions will be done by national authorities. The supranational system supersedes national regulators in the case of cross-border financial operations. The specific legislative measures are not open to interpretation, and thus the establishment of these institutions represents the first step toward pan-European regulatory governance. Besides the monetary union or euro-system and the European Central Bank, this represents a new breakthrough toward more and deeper supranational integration, and even federalization.[36]

Regulation and supervision belong together, although the creation of a new institutional framework already signals further institutional and structural changes in the integration system.

Structural-institutional changes in the European Union

To cope with the existing debt crisis and to hinder the development of new ones, the Union created wide temporary and permanent safety nets for the member countries.

On May 9, 2010, the European Financial Stability Facility was established in Luxembourg City for a three-year period to assist crisis-ridden member states. Funding of €440 billion was provided by member states. The main contributors were Germany (27.13%), France (20.38%), Italy (17.91%), Spain (11.90%), and the Netherlands (5.71%). On July 21, 2011, the fund enlarged its capital guarantee to €780 billion. This institution acts as a European version of the IMF. The Financial Stability Facility targeted several troubled member countries, similarly to the already existing European Balance of Payment Facility (€50 billion), which provided loans for non-euro-zone countries (such as Hungary, Latvia, and Romania).

On May 11, 2010, the European Council decided to establish a permanent institution, the European Financial Stabilization Mechanism. Its funding comes from issuing bonds, of which it issued €5 billion worth for the first time in January 2011. Behind the bonds, the European Union's budget serves as collateral. The amount of the European Stability Mechanism, originally scheduled to be €500 billion (or about $700 billion), but later increased. The G-20 summit meeting in February 2012 urged the EU to increase that amount to $1 trillion. The EU leaders accepted this idea and made the required decision. Stronger financial protection might have a dual effect. Besides providing stability for indebted countries, it also helps to rebuild confidence and trust that are themselves an economic stimulus to the crisis-ridden continent.

Loans from the Stabilization Mechanism have strict conditions, including the presentation of an adjustment program. In its cooperation agreement with the European Union, the IMF guaranteed an additional half of the EU loan contribution—via the European Financial Stabilization Mechanism—up to €250 billion.[37] The Stabilization Mechanism's loans thus serve as seed money and are doubled by the IMF. This permanent institution, the Stabilization Mechanism, is a top priority agenda item for the Union, and it was already in process in the first half of 2012. All of the details have been worked out with all of the countries involved, and the Mechanism is in place and operational as planned in July 2012.

The most important step forward, however, is accomplishing monetary unification that includes the fiscal unification that has so far been lacking. The "birth defect," or structural mistake, of monetary without fiscal unification had severe consequences in 2008–10, and the Union learned its lesson. The European Union resisted solving the indebtedness problems of its members with one single financial action. The citizens of the advanced member countries did not want to spend their own tax euros on irresponsible countries. As Angela Merkel phrased it, the European Union is not a "transfer union." Loans and bailouts occurred always at the last minute, when a country's government bonds matured and billions were due in repayment. Although this practice was highly criticized by experts and the media, the Sword of Damocles hanging above the virtually bankrupt countries helped the acceptance of the German-French plan to introduce long-term, institutionalized fiscal discipline in the euro-zone.

The movement toward gradual fiscal unification cautiously progresses. In June 2010, the Council of Europe made a provisional agreement to introduce regular controls on members' budgetary issues. According to this plan, a budgetary surveillance system would be introduced. The countries have to present their budget for peer review to the European Commission. In case of excessive indebtedness, serious punishment would regulate the indebted countries, including suspended voting rights. This change is intended to fix the "birth defect" of the euro, and add a version of the required quasi-financial unification to the existing monetary union.

On December 8–9, 2011, the European Council returned to the long-term fiscal integration project. This is a very delicate issue, since it requires giving up a huge part of the national sovereignty of the member countries. Furthermore, any step forward in this direction deepens the gap between the members of the euro-zone, and those who are members of the European Union, but not of the euro-zone. The highly debated theoretical question of the so-called two-tier European Union now becomes a practical one. At a dramatic meeting of the heads of government—at which Britain's conservative Prime Minister, David Cameron, voted with a "no"—the concept of taking a major step forward to quasi-fiscal integration was accepted.

The official statement of the euro-area heads of state and government stressed that they agreed to move toward "a stronger economic union," and "a fiscally stable union." They agreed that a country's annual structural deficit may not exceed 0.5% of its nominal GDP, and, as already required by earlier agreement, its budget deficit cannot exceed a 3% ceiling of GDP. The countries' indebtedness ceilings may not surpass 60% of their respective GDPs. These rules, as a new arrangement, must be incorporated into the national legal system at the constitutional level. The Court of Justice will verify the transposition of the rules. The annual budgets will be monitored by the European Commission and Council. Deviation will set off "automatic correction mechanisms." If member states are recognized to be in breach of the ceilings, automatic consequences will be imposed (except if the majority of the member states oppose it).[38] The euro-zone countries also agreed that they will hold regular summit meetings twice a year.

In the spring of 2012, some members of the euro-zone already voted about the new rules. Although further considerations, steps, and decisions have to be made, these new rules will certainly be introduced and even incorporated into the constitutions of the member countries and the European treaties. The leading bodies of the Union are to prepare a report on deepening fiscal integration further, and also about the relationship between the euro-zone and the European Union.

Further structural changes are also needed. When the European Union was established, overwhelming financial power remained with the various individual countries. The national parliaments control about 50% of their respective GDPs (via the public sector and the budget). In sharp contrast, the European Union's budget was decided to control from approximately 1% to 1.2% of the aggregate GDP of the Union. From this minimal budget, the Union, among others, supports the income of the rural population and backward regions, and also assists the development of candidate countries. For a more closely integrated Union with more supranational institutions and funds, such a limited budget is definitely not enough. According to certain calculations, at least 5% of aggregate GDP should be concentrated into the Union's budget, which would be 10% of national budgets.[39]

If verified by the member states, these changes, especially the quasi-fiscal union agreement, virtually establish a two-tier Union with a more integrated core. The door is opened to further widening the distance between the two groups, including—theoretically—a final possible federal reorganization of the core group. The British rejection of the agreement marginalized Britain's participation in the Union, especially because David Cameron remained alone in his rejection. However, a few more countries expressed certain concerns and the need to consult with their parliaments. The Czech government joined Britain a month later. In other words, the March 2012 deadline may broaden the group of member countries that are not willing to further deepen economic integration.

Because of the lack of an immediate solution to the euro crisis, several economists and the media, as well as the financial markets, had a negative reaction. They stated that the EU has been focusing on long-term goals without solving the short-term problems. *The Economist* reported on the agreement under the sarcastic title, "A comedy of euros: Britain had a bad summit, but the euro zone had a worse one." The evaluation of the agreement went as far as to state: "Once again Europe's leaders have failed to solve the euro crisis. The new treaty could easily be killed by the markets or by its rejection in one or more euro-zone country. . . . Sooner or later, the euro will be beyond saving."[40]

A clear sign of this danger appeared in mid-January 2012: Standard & Poor's downgraded the creditworthiness of nine euro-zone countries. Among them, France and Austria lost their AAA ratings, and the ratings of Slovenia, Slovakia, Spain, Malta, Italy, Cyprus, and Portugal also sank. Only four of the 17 countries preserved their AAA ratings: Finland, Germany, Luxembourg, and the Netherlands.[41] Downgrading makes government loans more expensive. The effort to break out from the "vicious cycle of debt"[42] is getting more and more difficult. Greece, as well as Portugal, Italy, Spain, and Hungary—and in some ways, the European Union as such—is becoming more and more similar to the mythological Greek king Sisyphus, who had ceaselessly to roll a huge rock uphill, which then only rolled back downhill.

Each year and each month presents a new test for European solidarity and integration. Is the Union ready to save its (irresponsible) members from default? Will they keep providing the required money at the last minute to make Greek and Portuguese repayments possible? Last-minute assistance to save member countries and the common currency from default continues to be very probable. Contrary to extremely gloomy forecasts, I want to argue, however, that the euro and the heavily indebted countries of the euro-zone will certainly survive. The structural changes and regulations, bailouts, and the creation of the emergency funds will work in the longer run. These are the most important steps to take. Beginning in the spring and summer of 2012, these steps may bring some space to cure recession and stimulate growth. As the European Commissioner Michel Barnier stated in his speech in London on January 23, 2012, "Let's try to make 2012 the year when we finally get the debt crisis under control and put Europe back on the path to recovery."[43]

The European Union, in contrast to the often hysterical statements of the media, does have a strategy to save countries from collapse, and, using the "policy of fear," push them toward further and closer integration. This policy is, undoubtedly, focused on long-term solutions, further integration, and establishing several new supranational institutions that may pave the way for a virtual fiscal unification. Several member countries of the Union would otherwise be rather reluctant to go further on the road to deeper integration that cuts deeply into their national sovereignty. As Josef Joffe maintained, the German policy concerned more than, "We will save the euro. . . . We have the biggest resources and the biggest interest. But we will hearken fiscal probity." Jacob Funk Kirkegaard of the Petersen Institute in Washington D.C., went even further: "The Germans had a strategic insight or advantage to let the crisis get to the threshold within the European Union necessary for France to be willing to hand over the kind of sovereignty the country has always resisted. . . . You could say that the crisis has either been the wake-up call or the tool that Germany has used to beat them into submission."[44] Nevertheless, the road is rather bumpy and the near future hides various other possibilities as well.

Future alternatives for the European Union and the euro-zone

During the crisis years, several experts and the media stepped in the ancient footsteps of the mythological Cassandra who gained the ability to foresee the future. Wild and gloomy forecasts were made about the possible failure of the common currency, the replacement of solidarity by selfish actions, and even the disintegration of the European Union. Just as Cassandra was later cursed by Apollo not to be believed, the modern Cassandras may also lose their trustworthiness. The collapse of the euro or of the entire European Union is not absolutely impossible, and mistaken policy might lead to that result. A return to a mere trade community is also not totally out of the question. However, these outcomes of the crisis are the least realistic of the forecasts. The economic and political interests of all of the European countries are much more strongly geared toward keeping the integration alive, and sometimes go further toward an even closer union. One of the very probable possibilities is the further and tighter integration of the euro-zone countries with a quasi-fiscal union, based upon the December 2011 Brussels agreement. The group will have a separate summit meeting twice a year and a more coordinated economic policy. This step represents a major step toward the realization of a two-tier Union and, moreover, in the long run, toward federalization. The French President, Nicolas Sarkozy, triumphantly noted after the December 2011 Brussels summit: "A new Europe is being born. . . . [It splits into two camps,] one that wants more solidarity and regulation among its members; the other that follows only the logic of the single market."[45]

The idea of a two-tier Union has already been present for a long time. As Jürgen Habermas, the German philosopher-sociologist, stated, the "European Union is a convoy in which the slowest vehicle sets the pace for all." It has happened a few times that a single country's "No" vote stopped the implementation of a major measure, even if that country represented only 4–5 million people from the 500 million citizens of the European Union. Habermas suggested a Union-wide referendum on the introduction of new institutions, recommended by the draft of the failed EU constitution—about an elected president of the Union, a Union commissioner (minister) of foreign affairs, and the Union's own financial basis. In other words, he argued for a more federalist constitutional-institutional arrangement, based on national referenda. The outcome of the referenda would be binding for those member states in which the majority voted in one way or another. The positively voting countries would establish a fast-progressing core.[46] The fast-track core would not be an exclusive club, but open for all other members to join if they want to and accept the rules. This idea has popped up several times, and has always been rejected, but the December 2011 Brussels European Council meeting, and the British government's vote to distance itself from further integration, put this agenda item in the forefront once again.

As the project of a two-tier Europe resurfaced, the possibility of dropping out from the euro-zone and the Union itself also emerged for the first time in the half-century history of the Union. Since the exposure of the Greek crisis, some political circles—and popular sentiment in some of the member countries, especially in Germany—turned against the idea of using their tax money to finance others, and angrily advocated a policy change so as to stay away and leave Greece to default. Meanwhile, demonstrations in Athens, Madrid, London, Rome, Bucharest, and also in some other countries, openly revolted against the austerity straitjacket the European Union forced onto the country. An anti-European Union feeling, often dressed as anti-German, brings to mind the terrible experience of World War II. Some spoke about Chancellor Merkel's *Gauleiters* who dictate policy to others. Some extreme Greek newspapers presented Chancellor Angela Merkel in Nazi uniform. These accusations became part of the political discourse. In Italy, the bad memory of the 1970s was revitalized because of the violent protest in Rome in October 2011, and because of the eight terrorist bomb acts against Equitalia, the tax collecting agency, including one letter bomb that wounded the agency's director-general.

Prime Minister Mario Monti has already called attention to the gloomy possibility that one-sided austerity measures push "Italy—which has always been a pro-European country—. . . into the hands of anti-EU populists."[47] The right-wing populist Viktor Orbán government of Hungary is gradually shifting toward a Russian type of authoritarian regime, and used burning rhetoric against the IMF and Brussels in defense of "Hungarian sovereignty." Orbán's far-right opposition, the Jobbik Party, with a 17% representation in Parliament, went even further and urged leaving the Union. Nevertheless, in the end, because of the economic-financial troubles, it had to adjust to the EU's requirements and agree with the IMF.

Dangerous signals are appearing throughout Europe. The Greek political establishment practically collapsed and all the leading parties lost credibility in the eyes of the population. The Austrian Freedom Party, the Finnish True Finns Party, Marine Le Pen's Front National and several other right-wing nationalist parties are gaining strength. The economist Paul Krugman warned about the danger: "Nobody familiar with Europe's history can look at this resurgence of hostility without feeling a shiver. . . . Right-wing populists are on the rise." His main example was Hungary's "authoritarian slide."[48] George Soros, in a similar way, also warns about a "dangerous political dynamic. Instead of bringing the member countries closer together it will drive them to mutual recriminations. There is a real danger that the euro will undermine the political cohesion of the European Union. . . . What is happening today in Hungary . . . is a precursor of what is in store."[49] Indeed, Romania followed in the summer of 2012.

True, old "eurosceptics" such as Britain are distancing themselves further from the Union. It may lead some countries to lose interest in remaining within the European Union. A possible default of one or several countries, and their return to their old national currencies, is also among the possibilities.

In such a case, those countries may return to the old type of national weaponry—currency devaluation, printing more money, etc.—which may help them to cope more easily with the crisis. Nevertheless, such a development may also revitalize economic nationalism. This trend may even strengthen the possibility of disintegration if the Union used sanctions against some of its undisciplined members, suspending their voting rights if they did not uphold the Union's new laws and rules. Revolts against the "Brussels diktat" may open up the possibility that some countries would drop out from the Union.

In other words, for the first time in history, leaving the Union is becoming a real consideration and alternative for some crisis-ridden peripheral countries. Such a process, as shocking as it is, would, however, also offer advantages for the remaining strong core countries: they would get rid of some highly troubled and/or reluctant member countries of the Union. Official argumentation and government and Union statements do not mention this possibility yet. Nevertheless, one cannot exclude the probable default of some of the practically bankrupt countries, and/or an open revolt against the "outside" intervention of Brussels into the domestic affairs of sovereign countries, such as Greece, Portugal, and Hungary.

"Charlie Bean, deputy governor of the Bank of England," as the *Sunday Telegraph* reported in May 2011, "spoke this week of the 'messy consequence' for Britain if the Greek situation is allowed to descend into chaos. In truth there can be no benefit to us from a European cataclysm, beyond the opportunity it offers to . . . say 'I told you so'. . . . *What about the opportunity to leave the EU altogether? Huge benefit.*"[50]

Would the departure of one or a few countries debilitate or weaken the European Union? Irregular and disorganized defaults certainly might cause a new continent-wide wave of recession. However, the departure of some irresponsible or peripheral countries flooded by right-wing nationalism would, in the long run, not weaken but strengthen the integration of the remaining members. First of all, it would contribute to the decrease of economic diversity and assist the gradual process of homogenizing the member countries. The European Union is definitely over-enlarged and overly diverse; a "slimming cure" would thus certainly assist efforts at better governance and progress toward a closer union. Those countries may leave the Union and that would trigger severe economic shocks, but it would also eliminate certain obstacles to further integration. The same is true regarding traditionally reluctant EU member countries.

Urgent short-term interventions, however, are also unavoidable. After a seemingly rapid and promising recovery from the 2009 recession, the unsolved problems certainly generated a second recession in 2012. The one-sided austerity cure for the indebtedness crisis decreased consumption and demand. The uncertainty of government default made the credit market overly cautious, and, in spite of the reestablished liquidity of the banks, some countries are struggling with a lack of buyers for their bonds.[51] Bank credits became also restricted. "Banks tightened their lending standards for business as well as for individuals. . . . Banks are more reluctant to provide mortgage loans. And they said they expected credit to become more scarce in months to come." Even lending to well-performing Poland, the only European country that did not suffer from crisis, fell by $12 billion, as the Bank for International Settlements reported. "It suggests that hard-pressed West European banks have started withholding resources from their subsidiaries in Eastern Europe."[52]

To recreate trust in government bonds, to increase demand, and to reestablish bank credit remained an immediately central task for the European Union. Austerity measures thus had to be *combined* with actions to stimulate consumption and create jobs by public infrastructural investments. The uncertainty of government payments, caused by lack of trust, also requires radical action to rebuild trust. One possibility would be for the Union itself to guarantee member countries' repayments, and, instead of country bonds, to issue and sell euro-bonds. The modification of the European Central Bank's charter to make it able to act as a bank of last resort to buy government bonds directly also would change the situation and build up trust in financial markets. Until now, these kinds of measures were opposed, most of all by Germany.

However, several new recommendations and plans emerged in the renewed crisis situation in the late spring of 2012. Among others, the idea of shared responsibility for bank bailouts gained ground, as did the formation of a kind of banking union and establishing funds to deal with failing banks. Equally important is a new plan to combine the bad European debts into a single fund and pay it back in 25 years. Nevertheless, even the Eurobond would not be rejected in the longer run if further integration is accepted and realized by the member countries. According to the German concept, the Eurobond is one of the last steps in the process of handling the crisis that may follow the steps of deeper integration and centralization of fiscal policy. The EU summit on June 28–29, 2012 made important steps toward the solution by accepting the banking union and a Union-wide bank supervisor as well as the new mechanism that bail-out funds can directly be transferred to banks. Even the skeptical *Economist* concluded: "the summit gave reasons for guarded optimism."[53] The new agreement proved the statement of the Commission's

President: "[the euro-zone] will do whatever is necessary to assure the stability of our currency."[54]

If some totally bankrupt countries drop out of the Union and/or the euro-zone, these measures would be even easier and more acceptable for the remaining stronger fast-track countries. Would the governments and the citizens of the European Union accept such radical measures? Is there the will to further integrate at least the core of the Union? These are the central questions.

The answer depends on the countries' various interests. The foundation of the Union was the consequence of the lessons learned by a postwar generation of leading politicians and a huge part of the population at large, the lessons of two devastating wars in which Europeans killed millions of Europeans. This recognition was further underlined by the Cold War and American efforts to strengthen its West European allies. The logic of the Cold War also led to a bold broadening project: increasing the number of member countries in the Western alliance from six to twelve in hardly more than a decade. When the Cold War ended in the late 1980s, and the shocking experience of World War II gradually evaporated, mostly by generational change, the new challenge of globalization gave a new incentive not only to keep, but even to deepen, the integration provided by the Union, as well as to further enlarge it.

Globalization, of course, remains a permanent incentive to the formation of a more and not less unified Europe. To strengthen the European Union as an economic superpower is a common interest of all the member countries. The smaller countries definitely experience the limits of their sovereignty and dependence in an integrated Europe. The Danes, Dutch, Belgians, and several other small nations, find security within the framework of the Union. The bigger countries also have had the best experience from an integrated Europe, providing them with a backyard of cheap labor and large markets.

The main question, in this respect, is globalization itself. This process was the consequence of two main development trends: the objective process of technological revolution, with cheap transportation possibilities and revolutionized communication systems, and the deliberate policy to replace colonialism. Globalization, however, has winners and losers, and that generates anti-globalization movements throughout the world.

In the first decades, opponents of globalization developed the idea that advanced countries are the winners, while developing countries are mostly losers.[55] The anti-globalization movements were unable to influence policy until the main economic interests of the leading winner countries were well-served by globalization.

After a few decades, however, it became evident that globalization is not a one-way street, but a two-way road, and both core and peripheral countries may win or lose. The advanced countries lost too many jobs to the developing world, and the latter's growth far surpassed that of the advanced world. The rules of the game may thus change, and some of the advanced countries may decide to defend themselves against the competition from the developing world. China's rise is often considered a danger by some advanced world powers, and the lawmakers of those countries often urge restrictions against its increasing potential.

Larry Neal, in his study in a huge edited volume on the financial history of centuries, concludes: "The possibility of reversal [back from globalization] is always present, usually due to the response of governments trying to protect their perceived constituencies from dealing with foreign, impersonal markets that are unleashed by innovations in financial capitalism. . . . [The] same political dynamic could again thwart the new globalization of the twenty-first century,"[56] as happened after World War I with the "first globalization" of the nineteenth century.

A reversal of globalization, it should be added and underlined, may not change the objective technological-economic base of globalization that requires and serves an internationalized economic system with more supranational institutions. In this respect, globalization is not reversible in the long run. This, however, does not mean that a temporary reversal, as it happened between the two world wars, could not come. Policy changes might halt and temporarily reverse the process of globalization and would, of course, again strengthen the nation-state and its defensive regulatory policy against rivals. If it happened, the old muddle of economic nationalism, hostility, and even wars may reemerge again. From a historical point of view, however, it cannot stop the global transformation forever, but it may be strong enough to stop it for a few decades.

However, Europe is hopefully too strongly integrated to allow such a default, which would have a disastrous impact on the entire continent, strong core and weaker peripheries alike. Even a transitory victory of disintegration and a counter-globalization trend is less than probable. Europe's stake in staying together and hammering out a common solution and a new prosperity will certainly win out.

This work has focused on the economic crisis of the European Union, its causes, and the measures that would be needed to reestablish a new prosperity. Responsibility for the future of Europe requires a real understanding and the elimination of all the main causes of the crisis. Contemporary deregulated, financialized, and globalized capitalism, as discussed before, was responsible for the 2008 economic crisis. If they learn the lessons of the failures, that may help make a better and stronger European Union.

However, the European Union is much more than an integrated economic area, and the euro is much more than a currency. The founding philosophy of the Union from the 1950s on, as the preamble to the Treaty of Rome phrased it, was an "ever closer union," a gradual but steady road toward the federalization of Europe. Economic integration has always been considered a road toward political union. Not all countries shared this view when they joined the European Economic Community. Some merely wanted to enjoy the advantages of a huge common market. However, most of the countries, big and small, members and candidates, found security and prosperity within the further integration of the Union. That was the goal for those who joined and want to join the common currency system. A strong and deeply integrated Europe is the safeguard of peace on this continent that has been war-ridden for centuries. Within the framework of the European Union, the French-German reconciliation can finally be turned into peace after three major wars in less than one century. The Union can resolve the explosive and perpetually recurring border conflicts, the still-burning ambitions of relatively small national communities for national independence, and extinguish the danger posed by the Balkan powder-keg that has so often exploded.

Further economic integration, a stable single market with monetary and fiscal unification, and strong supranational institutions are the guarantees of a prosperous Europe that can respond to the challenges of the globalized world system. A unified Europe is a competitive economic superpower. In this time of transformation in the world economic system, this position is extremely important. The so-called emerging economies, China, India, Brazil, and others, with their strong state-capitalist economic systems, huge and very cheap labor force and high intellectual background, already form an economic power triangle with the United States and Europe. Their competition is extremely strong and requires high preparedness from Europe. Eliminating the causes of the economic crisis and further integration and unification are the keys to creating a peaceful, stronger, and prosperous Europe that is able to defend its position in the world economy. Meanwhile, integration offers the chance to shrink and then eliminate economic diversities and backwardness, and to create a more equal Europe with its colorful cultural diversity. These cohesive features are the real driving forces of Europe.

Although Europe is in the fourth year of economic crisis, and difficult years are still to come, there is an opportunity to take control of a good part of the crisis in the coming years. The highly troubled member countries will certainly be saved and new rules will be introduced to avoid a repetition of 2008. It is possible that the Union will be somewhat "slimmer." Some countries, most of all Greece, still may fail and drop out of the euro-zone, and probably leave the Union itself. Traditional "euro-skeptics," such as Britain, will probably further isolate themselves and may even decide to leave the Union, as certain British political forces already demand. Countries where right-wing nationalists took over and reject the "dictatorship of Brussels," such as Hungary at this time, may decide to separate themselves from the Union. This step would be severely counterproductive for any country, and it is therefore not very probable. A smaller Union would not weaken the deepening of the integration process; on the contrary, it would strengthen it.

Although pessimistic statements repeat that "every turn on the crisis tears Europe further apart,"[57] nothing proves European solidarity better than that every troubled member country was saved during the five years of crisis. A *New York Times* columnist compared the European assistance to Greece to the historic postwar Marshall Aid. In four years, Germany received an amount equal to 2% of its GDP. If we apply this to Greece, it would—in current value—be $5 billion assistance. In reality, in all different forms, Greece received $575 billion aid, i.e. 115 Marshall Plans of which 29 from Germany alone.[58]

The postwar history of Europe clearly demonstrates that its countries and governments learned from the tragic mistakes and terrible sins of their own previous history. Europe's last two-thirds of a century clearly verified that the leading nineteenth-century philosopher of history, Georg Wilhelm Friedrich Hegel, was wrong when he stated: "What experience and history teach is . . . that people and governments have never learned anything from history."[59]

NOTES

Introduction

1 Ivan T. Berend, *Europe Since 1980*, Cambridge: Cambridge University Press, 2010, 160–161.
2 Michael R. Krätke, "The First World Financial Crisis," (www.cedeplar.ufmg.br/ .../2008/crise_financeiratt_2009_2008.ppt).
3 R.A. Gordon, "Is the Business Cycle Obsolete?" National Affairs, (www.national affairs.com/public../how-obsolete-is-the-business-cycle); Martin Bronfenbrenner (ed.), *Is the Business Cycle Obsolete?* New York: John Wiley & Sons, 1969.
4 Robert E. Lucas, Jr. "Macroeconomic Priorities." Presidential Address at the annual meeting of the American Economic Association, January 10, 2003 (italics added) (citeseerx.ist.psu.edu/ viewdoc/download?doi=10.1.1.85...rep...).
5 John Cassidy, *How Markets Fail: The Logic of Economic Calamities,* New York: Farrar, Straus & Giroux, 2009, 97.
6 Ibid., 102.
7 Ben Bernanke, "The Great Moderation." Speech at the Board of the Federal Reserve, February 20, 2004 (www.federalreserve.gov/boarddocs/speeches/ 2004/.../default.htm).
8 OECD, *The Growth of Output 1960–80: Retrospect, Prospect and Problems for Policy,* Paris: OECD, 1974, 166.
9 David Colander, Hans Föllmer, Armin Haas, Michael Goldberg, Katerina Juselius, Alan Kirman, Thomas Lux and Brigitte Sloth, "The Financial Crisis and the Systemic Failure of Academic Economics," Kiel Institute for the World Economy. Kiel Working Papers #1489, 2009 (ideas.repec.org/kie/kieliw/1489.html).
10 House Committee on Oversight and Government Reform, October 23, 2008 (http://oversight.house.gov/documents/20081024163819.pdf).
11 Paul Krugman, "How did Economists get it so Wrong?" *The New York Times,* September 2, 2009. See also his *The Return of Depression Economics and the Crisis of 2008,* New York: W.W. Norton & Company, [1999] 2009.

12 John Cassidy, op. cit., 2009, 98.

13 Ibid., 126.

14 European Commission, Economic and Financial Affairs. "Economic Crisis in Europe: Causes, Consequences and Responses," *European Economy*, 7/2009. Luxembourg: Office for Official Publications of the European Communities, 2009, 16, 20.

15 Joseph Schumpeter, *Business Cycles: A Theoretical, Historical, and Statistical Analysis of the Capitalist Process*, Vol. 1, New York: McGraw-Hill, 1939, 110.

16 George Soros, *The New Paradigm for Financial Markets: The Credit Crisis of 2008 and What it Means*, New York: Public Affairs, 2008, xiii, xiv, xxiii.

17 Lehman Brothers, an investment bank strongly involved in subprime mortgage loans with $600 billion, largely housing-related assets already closed its subprime lender, BNC Mortgage, in August 2007 and suffered losses in two consecutive years, 2007 and 2008. In the first half of 2008, the bank lost 73% of its stocks value. In early September, its stocks further declined by 45%. The executives rushed to pay themselves huge bonuses. Richard Fuld received $480 million. On September 15, the company filed America's largest bankruptcy case.

1 Variations on a theme: Iceland, Greece, and Ireland's road toward the crisis

1 Spiegel Online (www.spiegel.de/international/business/0,1518,590028,00. html).

2 Joseph Schumpeter, *Business Cycles: A Theoretical, Historical and Statistical Analysis of the Capitalist Process*, New York: McGraw-Hill, 1939, 34.

3 *OECD Factbook 2007: Economic, Environmental and Social Statistics*, Paris: OECD, 2007, 49, 111.

4 The Human Development Index was introduced from 1990 on. This measures a country's development level by the per capita national income combined with life expectancy and educational attainment in one single composite index using geometric means. This index replaced the measurement of development based on simply the per capita income level, including quality of life factors, the health and educational situation of a country.

5 The Parliament's Special Investigation Commission was established in December 2008, and presented its Report on the crisis on April 12, 2010.

6 Report, "Conclusion," 19, 22.

7 Ibid., 2.

8 Ibid., 3.

9 Ibid., Chapter 21, 1–2.

10 Ibid., 5.

11 Ibid., 20.

12 Ibid.

13 Ibid., 15.

14 Ibid., 10.

15 Ibid., 3–4.

16 Peter Gumbel, "Iceland: The Country that became a Hedge Fund," *CNN Money*, December 4, 2008, (money.cnn.com/2008/12/01/.../fortune/iceland_gumbel.fortune/).

17 The Parliamentary Report stated: The Minister of Finance had the opinion "that

the presumed damage to the economy would be an acceptable cost of keeping the ruling parties in power. . . . [That was] the most significant mistake in economic policy in the run up to the collapse of the banks." (Report, op. cit., Chapter 21, 25).

18 (http://danskeresearch.danskebank.com/link/FocusAndreIceland21032006/$file).

19 Parliamentary Report, op. cit., Chapter 21, 22.

20 "Icelandic Anger Brings Debt Forgiveness in Best Recovery Story," *Bloomberg Business Week*, February 24, 2012, (www.businessweek.com/.../icelandic-anger-brings-debt-forgiveness-i...).

21 Simon Nixon, "Will Greece be an Olympic Winner? October 31, 2005, (www.moneyweek.com/.../will-greece-be-an-olympic... – United Kingdom).

22 Ibid.

23 *The Guardian*, June 1, 2001.

24 John Kenneth Galbraith, *The Essential Galbraith*, New York: Houghton Mifflin, 2001, 111–112.

25 European Commission, *Statistical Annex of European Economy*, Luxembourg: Official Publications of the EC, 2004.

26 Gro Hagermann (ed.), *Reciprocity and Redistribution: Work and Welfare Reconsidered*, Pisa: Edizioni Plus, 2007, 51–52.

27 John Nic Ifantopoulos, *The Welfare State in Greece* (video. .minpress.gr/.../aboutgreece/aboutgreece_welfare_state.pdf).

28 Ivan T. Berend, *Europe Since 1980*, Cambridge: Cambridge University Press, 2010, 256.

29 Manos Matsaganis, "The Welfare State and the Crisis, the Case of Greece" (www.espanet2010.net/.../Manos%20Matsaganis_...).

30 Stergios Babanassis, *Apo tēn krisē stē viosimē anaptyxē*, Athens: Papazisis, 2011.

31 BBC News, January 1, 2001 (news.bbc.co.uk/business/1095783.stm)

32 *The Guardian*, June 21, 2011.

33 How did that happen? Probably the big leading countries of the European Union did not want to handle this issue since they themselves violated the Maastricht rules. Even the most disciplined, Germany, was unable to keep the deficit and public debts under the required level because of the extremely heavy burden of German unification. Six Central and Eastern European countries, as an average, received $30 per capita capital inflow from the West in the early 1990s, while the former East Germany received $5,900 per capita capital inflow from the western part of Germany. See: Ivan T. Berend, *From the Soviet Bloc to the European Union: The Economic and Social Transformation of Central and Eastern Europe since 1973*, Cambridge: Cambridge University Press, 2009, 109.

34 Joseph Schumpeter, op. cit., 1939, 150 (italics added).

35 *New York Times*, October 24, 2011.

36 *The Economist*, November 21–27, 2009, 53, 89.

37 Babanassis, op. cit., 2011.

38 Ibid.

39 *The Economist*, May 8–14, 2010, 51–52.

40 Michael G. Arghyrou, "Public Expenditure and National Income," 13–14 (bura.brunel.ac.uk/bitstream/2438/879/1/00_05.pdf).

41 *The Economist*, October 29–November 4, 2011, 13.

42 "Awaiting a Greek Payout," *The New York Times*, January 11, 2012.

43 "Doubting Greeks' Resolve, Euro Zone May Hold Back Full Bailout," *The New York Times*, February 16, 2012.

44 Based on Angus Maddison, *Monitoring the World Economy, 1820–1992*, Paris: OECD, 1995, and *The Economist Pocket World in Figures*, 2008 Edition, London: Profile Books, 2007.

45 According to the American economist John B. Taylor (1993), the ideal rate of interest in the case of inflationary pressure is more than 1% raise of the nominal interest rate in case of each 1% of inflation. In other words, the Central Bank has to introduce higher interest rates if the inflation is above the targeted level to reduce it. In the opposite situation, when inflation is low and output is below full employment to stimulate output, interest rates have to be lower than the inflation rate.

46 William Seyfried, "Monetary Policy and Housing Bubbles: A Multinational Perspective," *Research in Business and Economics Journal*, 2010 (www.aabri.com/manuscripts/09351.pdf); Alan Blinder, "Six Errors on the Path to the Financial Crisis," *The New York Times*, January 24, 2009.

47 One of the first known economic bubbles, the Dutch "tulip mania" in 1633–37, at the zenith of the Dutch Golden Age when the country was the richest in the world, the newly arrived Asian flower, the tulip, became the object of speculation. At the culmination of the tulip boom, a rare bulb was sold for 10,000 guilders, an amount enough for a family to live on for three to four decades. Speculators could gain 90,000 guilders in one to two weeks. At a certain moment, and it happened at the Haarlem tulip bulb auction, all of a sudden, no one was able to bid, and a bulb, auctioned for 5,000 guilders, was sold for 50.

48 "The Fall of Ireland's Mighty Quinn," *The New York Times*, January 8, 2012.

49 Liz Alderman, "After Bust in Ireland, Ordinary People Make Do with Less," *The New York Times*, May 6, 2011.

50 *Markets at a Glance*, July 2011 (www.sprott.com/.../07_11_The%20Real%20Banking%20crisis.pdf).

2 The fall—of 2008: from the financial crisis to the crisis of the euro

1 Paolo Savona and Chiara Oldani, "Crisis, Response, and Innovation in Europe," in Paolo Savona, John J. Kirton and Chiara Oldani (eds), *Global Financial Crisis: Global Impact and Solution*, Surrey: Ashgate, 2011.

2 Based on *OECD Factbook 2007: Economic, Environmental and Social Statistics*, Paris: OECD, 2007 and *The Economist*, August 20, 2011, 54.

3 Jeremy Atack, "Financial Innovations and Crisis: The View Backward from Northern Rock," in Jeremy Atack and Larry Neal (eds), *The Origins and Development of Financial Markets and Institutions: From the Seventeenth Century to the Present*, Cambridge: Cambridge University Press, 2009, 1.

4 While Italy and Greece were nearly on the same level as the EU-15 average (92% and 97%, respectively), Ireland surpassed that average level (128%), and Spain and most of Portugal were somewhat behind it (90% and 65%, respectively). *OECD Factbook 2007*, op. cit., 2007, 26.

5 Based on Angus Maddison, *Monitoring the World Economy, 1820–1992*, Paris: OECD, 1995; Angus Maddison, *The World Economy: A Millennial Perspective*, Paris: OECD, 2001; *OECD Factbook 2007*, op. cit., 2007. (Western Europe in

1913 is the average of 27 West European countries; in 1950, 1973, and 1998, it is the average of 12 Western countries; in 2006, it is the EU-15 countries.)

6 "Greece Publishes List of 4,000 Tax Scofflaws," *The New York Times,* January 24, 2012; Beppe Severgini, "If Only . . .," *The World in 2012,* London: *The Economist,* 2012, 97.

7 Stergios Babanassis, *Apo tēn krisē stē viosimē anaptyxē,* Athens: Papazisis, 2011.

8 (http://www.npr.org/2012/02/20/147158633/portugal-plays-by-the-rules-but-economy-slumps?sc=fb&cc=fɔ).

9 (www.cbsnews.com/stories/2011/04/06/.../main20051428.shtml).

10 *Los Angeles Times,* June 2, 2010.

11 (www.nytimes.com/.../portugals-financial-crisis-leads-it-back-to-angol...).

12 *The New York Times,* November 3, 2011.

13 "Italy's Public Debts. The Ogre in the Attic," *The Economist,* December 11, 2008,

14 (www.infiniteunknown.net/.../europes-money-markets-freeze-as-crisis...); *The New York Times,* November 3, 2011.

15 "In Europe, Market Fear Shifts Focus to Italy," *The New York Times,* November 7, 2011.

16 "Anxiety Over Italy Feeds a Cycle of Rising Bond Rates," *The New York Times,* November 8, 2011.

17 *The Economist,* July 15, 2011.

18 "Regional Debts Add Woe in Spain. An Uphill Fight Against Autonomous Budgets," *The New York Times,* December 31, 2011.

19 Dean Baker, "Blame it on the Bubble," *The Guardian,* March 8, 2010.

20 Based on Angus Maddison, op. cit., 1995, and *The Economist Pocket World in Figures,* 2008 Edition, London: Profile Books, 2007.

21 *The Guardian,* March 8, 2010.

22 World Property Channel, September 29, 2010 (www.worldpropertychannel. com>...> ResidentialRealEstate).

23 European Commission. "European Economy Forecast, Spring 2011." *European Economy,* 1/2011, 121. (ec.european/economy_finance/publications/.../ec-2011-1_eu.pdf).

24 "European Lenders Look to I.M.F. for Assistance, Again, as Euro Crisis Linger," *The New York Times,* December 4. 2011.

25 European Bank for Reconstruction and Development, *Transition Report 2009: Transition in Crisis?* London: EBRD, 2009, 13.

26 Column 1 is based on Teodorovich et al. (eds), *The Croatian Economic Development: Transition Towards the Market Economy,* Zagreb: Institute of Economics, 2005, 326; Angus Maddison, op. cit., 1995, 228. Stephen Broadberry and Kevin O'Rourke (eds), *The Cambridge Economic History of Modern Europe,* Cambridge: Cambridge University Press, Vol. 2, 2010, 299, 302, published a somewhat different calculation. In most time periods it did not differ significantly, but the 2005 figure of 35% is wrong.

27 Matthias Person, "Household Indebtedness in Sweden and Implications for Financial Stability—The Use of Household-level Data," (www.org/publ/bppdf/bispap46n.pdf).

28 European Bank for Reconstruction and Development, op. cit., 2009, 68.

29 *Telegraph,* October 16, 2008.

30 Piroska M. Nagy, "Timeline for the First Phase and the Start of Vienna Plus," (www.ebrdblog.com/.../the-vienna-initiative-moves-into-a-new-phase-...); ec.europa.eu/economy_finance/articles/.../2012-01-17-viena_en.htm); Reuters,

January 20, 2012 (uk.reuters.com/.../euro-crisis-threatens-banking-system.html? ...all); "Officials Unite Again to Protect Eastern Europe's Banks," *The New York Times,* March 15, 2012.

31 European Bank for Reconstruction and Development, op. cit., 2009, 54.

32 "Poland Skirts Woes in the Euro Zone, for Now," *The New York Times,* December 15, 2011.

33 (www.steelguru.com/.../Recession...Poland.../232404.html-India).

34 European Bank for Reconstruction and Development, *Transition Report 2011. Crisis and Transition: The People's Perspective,* London: EBRD, 2011, 30.

35 European Bank for Reconstruction and Development, op. cit., 2009, 8.

36 Anders Åslund, *The Last Shall Be the First: The East European Financial Crisis,* Washington, D.C.: The Peterson Institute for International Economics, 2010, 14. I use this pioneering work on the economic crisis of the transition countries in this sub-chapter.

37 European Bank for Reconstruction and Development, op. cit., 2009, 48, 50.

38 Ibid., 10–11.

39 *Transition Report Update, 2005,* London: European Bank for Reconstruction and Development, 2005.

40 The EU-15 group was formed in 1995 after Sweden, Finland, and Austria joined the EU-12 (Germany, France, Italy, the three Benelux countries, Britain, Denmark, and Ireland).

41 Anders Åslund, op. cit., 2010, 16.

42 Ibid., 24.

43 IMF Survey Magazine, October 28, 2008, (www.imf.org/external/pubs/ft/ survey/so/2008/car102808b.htm).

44 "What was Orbán's Message," *Népszabadság,* January 17, 2012.

45 "Eastern Europe's Economies: Some Calm Amid Storms," *The Economist,* August 27, 2011.

46 Ibid.

47 "Moody's Reduces Credit Rating of Hungary to Junk Status," *The New York Times,* November 26, 2011.

48 (ec.europa.eu/economy_finance/.../2012-02-22-hungary_en.htm).

49 (www.bis.org/publ/bppdf/bispap46n.pdf).

50 *The Economist,* June 16, 2005.

51 *International Herald Tribune,* February 12, 2008.

52 Zsófia Árvai, Karl Drissen and Inci Ötker-Robe, "Reprisal Financial Interlinkages and Financial Contagion Within Europe," IMF Working Papers WP/09/6 (www.imf.org/external/pubs/ft/wp/2009/wp0906.pdf) August, 2010, 38.

53 "Following the failure of Lehman Brothers," argues Lorenzo Bini Smaghi, the Italian member of the Board of the European Central Bank, "panic set in that any bank, irrespective its size, could go bankrupt" (Bini Smaghi, 2008, Speech on October 20, "Some Thoughts on the International Financial Crisis, www.bis.org/review/r081023c.pdf).

54 In Britain, people answered the survey question "Would you say that most people can be trusted?" 56% yes in 1959, and only 30% by 1998. In the United States, these figures were 55 and 35% respectively. (Geoffrey Hosking, *Trust. Money, Markets and Society,* London: Seagull Books, 2010, 1–6.)

55 Spiegel Online, November 4, 2008.

56 European Commission, Economic and Financial Affairs, "Economic Crisis in Europe: Causes, Consequences and Responses," *European Economy*, 7/2009, Luxembourg: Office for Official Publications of the European Community, 2009, 14). The same estimation on the United States was $2.7 trillion.

57 UNCTAD, "Assessing the Impact of the Current Financial and Economic Crisis on Global FDI Flows," January 19, 2009, (www.unctad.org/en/docs/webdiaeia 20091_en.pdf).

58 *The Guardian,* October 2, 2008.

59 Spiegel Online International, "The Financial Crisis Reaches Germany's Economy," (www.spiegel.de/international/germany/0,1518,584374,00.html).

60 In the first days of October, Denmark gave a 100% guarantee on savings and Germany rescued the Hypo Real Estate by €50 billion. The French President, Nicolas Sarkozy, suggested a €300 billion bailout action, and the British Treasury announced a £500 billion bank rescue. They also pumped £37 billion to recapitalize the Royal Bank of Scotland and Lloyds TSB.

61 Automatic stabilizers are built into the economic system and work without direct government actions. This is the outcome of the role of taxation and transfer payments (such as social expenditures, unemployment benefits, poor help, etc.): in prosperity, tax revenues of the state increase and transfer payments decrease that somewhat limit the expansion of the economy. In time of recession or depression, tax revenues decreasing and transfer payments increasing thus somewhat limit the decline.

62 The Lander Institute, Wharton, University of Pennsylvania: "The Global Economic and Financial Crisis: A Timeline" (lander.wharton.upenn.edu/.../).

63 European Commission, Economic and Financial Affairs, op. cit., 2009, 13.

64 *The New York Times,* November 8, 2011.

65 Joseph Schumpeter, *Business Cycles: A Theoretical, Historical and Statistical Analysis of the Capitalist Process,* New York: McGraw-Hill, 1939, 223–224.

66 European Commission (europa.eu/.../interim_epc-spc_joint_report_ on_pensions_ final_en.pdf...).

67 OECD, Quarterly National Accounts. Quarterly Growth Rates of Real GDP (http://states.oecd.org/index.aspx?queryid=350). Poland had an insignificant contraction of 0.4% for one single quarter, while Slovakia's, although a more severe 7.62% decline of GDP, was also only for one quarter.

68 In the same month, the Royal Bank of Scotland had to write off £5.9 billion losses and the Bank of England provided £50 billion to the British banking industry for lending. In May, the Swiss giant, UBS, lost $37 billion linked with American mortgage debts.

69 European Commission, "European Economic Forecast, Spring 2011," *European Economy,* 1/2011 (ec.europa.eu/economy_finance/publications/.../ec-2011-1_eu.pdf).

70 Although an exact, generally accepted definition of depression does not exist, recession becomes a depression if the decline of the GDP is sharper and longer, for example it counts more than 10% decline in GDP for two or more years.

71 Eurostat (epp.eurostat.ec.europa.eu/statistics.../index.../unemployment_statistic ...).

72 "Euro Zone's Economy Shrank in Fourth Quarter," *The New York Times,* February 16, 2012.

73 Based on European Commission, op. cit., 2011.

74 Stergios Babanassis, op. cit., 2011; "Economic and Financial Indicators," *The Economist,* January 21, 2012.

75 *The Economist,* November 5–11, 2011, 112.

76 IMF, *World Economic Outlook: Recovery, Risk, and Rebalancing,* 2010/02 (www.imf.org/external/pubs/ft/weo/2010/02); IMF, *World Economic Outlook Update: Global Recovery Advance but Remains Uneven,* January 2011 (www.imf.org/external/pubs/ft/weo/2011/update/01/index.htm); "EU Interim Forecast: On the Brink of a Mild Recession" (ec.europa.eu/cvm/progress_reports_eu.htm).

77 Bank for International Settlement, IMF, OECD et al., December 2010 (www.jodh.org); European Commission, *General Government Data: General Government Revenue, Expenditure, Balance and Gross Debt,* December 2010 (ec.europa.eu/economy_finance/db_indicators/gen_gov_data/documents/2010/autumn2010_country_eu.pdf).

78 Global Finance (www.gfmag.com>Archives>Spetember2010).

79 "Time Runs Short for Europe to Find a Solution to Its Debt Crisis," *The New York Times,* November 28, 2011.

80 77% of the total GDP is produced by four large countries (Germany, France, Italy and Spain), while the five smallest, Slovakia, Slovenia, Luxembourg, Cyprus, and Malta, accounted for less than 2%.

81 Hannah J. Farkas and Daniel C. Murphy (eds), *The Eurozone: Testing the Monetary Union,* New York: Nova Science Publisher, 2011, 6–7.

82 Paola Subacchi, "Europe from One Crisis to the Other," in Paolo Savona, John J. Kirton and Chiara Oldani (eds), op. cit., 2011, 65.

83 "Austerity Reigns Over Euro Zone as Crisis Deepens," *The New York Times,* January 2, 2012.

84 "Italy's Leader Says Austerity Alone Isn't a Cure to Debts," *The New York Times,* January 12, 2012.

85 In 1937, the United States, after the New Deal state interventionist policy, wanted to return to a balanced budget. It turned out to be too early and the recession returned.

86 *The Economist,* "Rushing for the Exits," November 12, 2011.

87 *The New York Times,* November 11, 2011.

88 "UniCredit's Weak Issue a Poor Omen for Other Banks," *The New York Times,* January 10, 2012.

89 Paul Krugman, "Can Europe Be Saved?" *The New York Times Magazine,* January 16, 2011, 31.

90 Arjan M. Lejour, Jasper Lukkezen and Paul Veenendaal, "Sustainability of Government Debt in the EMU," in Wim Meeussen (ed.), *The Economic Crisis and European Integration,* Cheltenham: Edward Elgar, 2011, 37.

91 *The New York Times,* November 10, 2011.

92 "France and the Euro. Bail-outs? Bof . . ." *The Economist,* July 23, 2011. The same article quotes Madame Martine Aubry, head of the opposition Socialist Party, who stated in her article in *Libération:* "Greece must be saved in order to save Europe." In contrast to Germany, "in France there has been almost no public debate over whether to help Greece or other troubled peripheral countries."

93 "Signs of Broad Contagion in Europe as Growth Slows," *The New York Times,* November 16, 2011.

94 Bankers of far away Mauritius are convinced that some of the euro-zone countries "will dump the euro . . . to free [themselves] from the shackles of the monetary union . . . [they] will get rid of the single currency." *The African Executive*, September 1, 2010 (www.africanexecutive.com/modules/magazine/articles/php?article...).

95 David Brooks, "The Technocratic Nightmare," *The New York Times*, November 18, 2011.

96 Paola Subacchi, op. cit., in Paolo Savona, John J. Kirton and Chiara Oldani (eds), op. cit., 2011, 71. Between 2007 and 2009, more than $2 trillion was spent in Europe and the United States to support failing financial institutions.

97 "The Euro Crisis: Rearranging the Deckchairs," *The Economist*, August 6, 2011.

98 "Even as Governments Act to Stem Debts Crisis, Euro's Time Runs Short," *The New York Times*, November 13, 2011.

99 "Turning Japanese: The Absence of Leadership in the West is Frightening – and also rather familiar," *The Economist*, July 30, 2011.

100 Thomas L. Friedman, "Who's the Decider?" *The New York Times*, November 16, 2011.

101 "In Debt Crisis, a Silver Lining for Germany," *The New York Times*, November 25, 2011.

102 *The New York Times*, November 25, 2011.

3 The economic causes: contemporary European capitalism

1 Günter Grass, *Peeling the Onion*, Boston: Houghton Mifflin Harcourt, 2007.

2 Mentioning a few recent ones: Wim Meeusen (ed.), *The Economic Crisis and European Integration*, Cheltenham: Edward Elgar, 2011; Klaus Busch, Manfred Flore, Heribert Kohl and Heiko Schlattermund (eds), *Socially Unbalanced Europe: Socio-Political Proposals in Times of Crisis*, Chambers: The Merlin Press, 2011; Richard Heinberg, *The End of Growth: Adapting to Our New Economic Reality*, Gabriola Island: New Society Publisher, 2011; Pompeo Della Posta and Leila Simona Talani (eds), *Europe and the Financial Crisis*, Houndmills: Palgrave Macmillan, 2011. Several others are quoted and listed in the notes.

3 Jeffrey Friedman (ed.), *What Caused the Financial Crisis*, Philadelphia: University of Pennsylvania Press, 2011, 1–2.

4 Karl Polanyi, *The Great Transformation: The Political and Economic Origins of Our Times*, Beacon Hill: Beacon Press, 1964.

5 Joseph Stiglitz, "The Anatomy of a Murder: Who Killed the American Economy," in Jeffrey Friedman (ed.), *What Caused the Financial Crisis*, Philadelphia: University of Pennsylvania Press, 2011, 140.

6 Gary Gorton, *Slapped by the Invisible Hand: The Panic of 2007*, Oxford: Oxford University Press, 2010, 14, 16.

7 Jeremy Atack, "Financial Innovations and Crisis: The View Backwards from Northern Rock," in Jeremy Atack and Larry Neal (eds), *The Origins and Development of Financial Markets and Institutions: From the Seventeenth Century to the Present*, Cambridge: Cambridge University Press, 2009, 2.

8 Ibid.

9 "The [economic] system . . . will by its own working produce booms or crisis or depressions." (Joseph Schumpeter, *Business Cycles: A Theoretical, Historical and*

Statistical Analysis of the Capitalist Process, New York: McGraw-Hill, 1939, 34.) Profit-motivated competition between hundreds of thousands of entrepreneurs may generate over-optimistic investment decisions in boom times that lead to over-production and difficulties in selling and thus a decline in prices. Producers naturally react by decreasing output, laying off a part of the work force. This trend was already recognized clearly by the Frenchman Clément Juglar in the mid-nineteenth century. Since his description and analysis of the phenomenon, economics speaks about the Juglar cycle of 7–11 years (Clément Juglar, *Des crises commerciales et de leur retour périodique en France, en Angleterre et aux Etat-Unis*, Paris: Guillaumin, 1862). The regularity of fluctuation produces upward and downward halves of the cycle that actually regulates itself. The reaction of the market to a recession or depression by lowering prices and output soon leads to recuperation, a new balance of supply and demand, and to new prosperity. A couple of economists, however, recognized another type of cyclicality as well. They realized that beside the medium-time-span waves, the economy exhibits long waves as well. The Russian Nikolai Kondratiev described this phenomenon best in the 1920s (Nikolai Kondratiev, *The Long Wave Cycle*, New York: Richardson and Snyder, [1922] 1984). He statistically proved the existence of 50- to 60-year-long cycles with 20–30 upward years and the same period of downward movement since the time of the British Industrial Revolution. According to his hypothesis, the long waves are caused by changes in the technological paradigm. This idea was worked out by Schumpeter, who introduced the term structural crisis. In his interpretation, a "whole set of technological changes," or industrial revolutions, led to the decline of the old leading and export sectors, based on old technology, and gradually generates the rise of new "high tech" branches, built on the new technology. The decline of the old and the rise of the new, however, might cause a relatively long 10- to 20-year stagnation or slow-growth period. After a while, the new technology initiates a new long boom period. Robert Brenner speaks about the long booms of 1890–1913 and 1950–1973, and the long downturn of 1973–1996 (Robert Brenner, *The Economics of Global Turbulence*, London: Verso, 2006). Beside certain—irregular—but permanent economic pulsations, the capitalist market economy, from time to time, also produces unpredictable *speculative bubbles*. When a layer of the population is rich and the economy has excessive monetary liquidity and credit, and when the interest rates are low, investors look for lucrative investments and speculation starts pushing up the prices of certain high-demand goods or shares. When prices start steadily increasing, it looks like a highly profitable long-term investment for many. People start buying, often using borrowed money, in order to be able to sell later at higher prices. Like the usual "herd mentality," the trend becomes a mania for an increasing number of optimistic buyers and the value of the given goods, real estate, or shares are traded at a highly inflated and rapidly increasing price. This phenomenon is called a speculative bubble. It happened in the late seventeenth century in Holland—the so-called tulip mania—and in eighteenth-century England—the South Sea Bubble (when this term was first used). When the price reaches unrealistic heights, at a certain point all of a sudden there are not enough buyers who can and are ready to pay. The buyer's market suddenly became a seller's market, supply surpasses demand, and prices decline sharply. More and more people rush to sell to avoid greater losses, and this run pushes prices further down. The bubble bursts and destroys values, wealth, and sometimes even lives. It may also generate a years-long recession (Charles Kindleberger, *Manias, Panics, and Crashes: A History of Financial Crises*, New York: Basic Books, 1978).

10 Jeffrey Friedman, op. cit., 2011, 1.

11 Joseph Schumpeter, op. cit., 1939, 34.

12 Joan Robinson, "The Generalization of the General Theory," in *The Rate of Interest and Other Essays*, London: Macmillan, 1952.

13 (www.centralbanking.com/.../stark-demands-financial-sector-refocus).

14 Willem Molle, *The Economics of European Integration: Theory, Practice, Policy*, Aldershot: Ashgate, 2006, 5th edition, 131.

15 George Soros, *The Crisis of Global Capitalism*, New York: Public Affairs, 1998, xii, xx.

16 Ibid.

17 The unique rise of the financial sector started first in Britain during the last third of the nineteenth century. That was the time when British industry lost its world supremacy to the United States and Germany. A relative industrial decline, however, was counterbalanced by the rise and outstanding role of the London financial sector, the "City" (Ivan T. Berend, *An Economic History of Nineteenth Century Europe: Diversity and Industrialization,* Cambridge: Cambridge University Press, 2013 (forthcoming)).

18 Ivan T. Berend, *An Economic History of Twentieth-Century Europe. Economic Regimes from Laissez-Faire to Globalization*, Cambridge: Cambridge University Press, 2006, 287.

19 Ivan T. Berend, *From the Soviet Bloc to the European Union: The Economic and Social Transformation of Central and Eastern Europe Since 1973*, Cambridge: Cambridge University Press, 2009, 153–154. In 2004, industry employed 23% of the labor force and contributed 18.2% to GDP in the United States.

20 Based on OECD, *Science, Technology and Industry Outlook*, Paris: OECD, 2000, 63.

21 Its share reached 75% in Belgium, Denmark, France, Norway, Sweden, Britain, and Switzerland. Most of the other European countries have a share of roughly 70%. A part of the service sector belongs to traditional services from laundries, barber shops, and retail chains, etc., but other businesses have newly joined the sector. Accounting, for example, used to be a department of the administration of industrial firms, and was part of their activity. That was replaced by outside professional auditing services. Harvesting, performed by the agricultural sector, was in several cases replaced by independent companies that provide harvesting services for agricultural enterprises.

22 Shadow-banking is a broadly used term in economics for financial institutions without official bank status, such as hedge funds. Shadow banking credit intermediation more than doubled in five years from $27 trillion in 2002, to $60 trillion by 2007 in the OECD countries.

23 "Near-banks" is also a jargon term for finance companies such as specialized micro-financing firms, cooperative credit unions, and specialized mortgage companies—some of those are subsidiaries of banks.

24 The United Nations conference in Bretton Woods, with the participation of 44 Allied nations, reestablished the gold standard, and all national currencies had to be pegged to gold, or better to say to the US dollar that became the international reserve currency.

25 Arbitrage is a business activity of simultaneous buying and selling an asset to make a profit from price differences on different markets.

26 In the nineteenth century, it happened in 1819, 1873, and 1893. In the United States, nine financial panics shocked the economy from the late eighteenth century.

27 Peter Wolff, "Crisis in the Eurozone and What it Means for Developing Countries," Deutsches Institut für Entwicklungspolitik, (www.die-gdi.de/ CMS-Homepage/.../e.nsf/.../MRUR-7NCH5C?...).

28 "Special Report: State Capitalism. The Visible Hand," *The Economist*, January 21, 2012.

29 Joseph Stiglitz, the Nobel laureate economist, characterized globalization in the following way: "Fundamentally, it is the closer integration of the countries and peoples of the world which has been brought about by the enormous reduction of costs of transportation and communication, and the breaking down of artificial barriers to the flows of goods, services, capital, knowledge, and (to a lesser extent) people across the borders" (Joseph Stiglitz, *Globalization and its Discontents*, New York: W.W. Norton & Co., 2003, 9).

30 The cost of transportation steeply decreased and the barriers of free trade were mostly removed. An unheard-of increase in the flow of goods followed in the interconnected markets. In 1950, the value of the world's exports was $0.3 trillion, in 1973 $1.7 trillion, and by the end of the century $5.8 trillion, nearly a twenty-times increase. During those decades, Europe's exports also increased by nearly twenty times from $0.14 trillion to $2.73 trillion. In the early 2000s, trade expansion continued and became enormous, increased by 6–10% per annum. In 2009, among the world's ten top exporters of merchandized goods, five European countries were present. Germany occupied the third place, France the sixth, and Italy the seventh. The value of these exports, 9% of the West European GDP in 1950, jumped to 36% of it by the end of the century.

31 Masayuki Matsushuma, "The Asian Crisis Revisited," in Joseph R. Bisigano, William C. Hunter, George G. Kaufman (eds), *Global Financial Crisis: Lessons from Recent Events.* Conference Proceedings, Chicago: Federal Reserve Bank of Chicago, 1999, 50.

32 UNCTAD Investment Brief, November 1, 2007 (www.unctad.org/en/docs/ inteiiamisc20072_en.pdf).

33 See John Eatwell, "A World Financial Authority," in Joseph R. Bisignano, William C. Hunter and George G. Kaufman (eds), *Global Financial Crisis: Lessons from Recent Events,* Boston: Kluwer Academic Publishers, 2000, 374.

34 Zsolt Darvas and Jacob von Weizsäcker, "Financial Transaction Tax: Small is Beautiful," *Society and Economy in Central and Eastern Europe*, Vol. 33, No. 3, December 2011, 452.

35 Mark Rupert, *Ideologies of Globalization. Contending Visions of a New World Order*, London: Routledge, 2000, 79; Kevin Philips, *Bad Money, Reckless Finance, Failed Politics and the Global Crisis of American Capitalism*, New York: Penguin Books, 2008.

36 Industrial multinationals, with a home base in a great part in the United States and Europe, monopolize three-quarters of the trade with manufactured goods.

37 The Rothschilds, Pereiras, Erlangers, the Vienna Credit Anstalt, the big German "D-banks" and several other major banking institutions operated internationally from the early nineteenth century.

38 Mervin Lewis and Kevin T. Davis, *Domestic and International Banking*, Boston: MIT Press, 1987, 266, 269.

39 George Soros, op. cit., 1998, xvi, xvii, xxviii.

40 John Eatwell, op. cit., in Joseph R. Bisignano, William C. Hunter and George G. Kaufman (eds), op. cit., 2000, 375.

41 This system dominated for a few decades in the later part of the nineteenth century, but was soon challenged by protectionism, and provoked a backlash after World War I. Its reestablishment started after World War II under the wing of the United States, and became dominant again in the last third of the twentieth century.

42 Karl Polanyi, op. cit., 1964, 43. In Polanyi's explanation, the existence of markets and market economies goes back for centuries. "Previously to our time," Polanyi argues, "no economy has ever existed that . . . was controlled by markets. . . . Man's economy, as a rule, is submerged in his social relationship. . . . [Man] safeguard[s] his social standing, his social claims, his social assets" (ibid., 46). However, in the latter part of the nineteenth century, mostly from the 1860s and 1870s, a self-regulating market system took over. Twentieth-century history was a permanent struggle between the regulated and self-regulating systems. Around the turn of the twentieth century, and then in interwar and postwar Europe, social and national protection gradually took over. That period was characterized by a struggle against the imperfection of markets, "the weaknesses and perils inherent in a self-regulating market system" (ibid., 145). "National protection" against the self-regulated market system was the weapon of the weaker peripheral national economies that created a protective wall around their markets in the interwar and deep into the postwar decades. The European common market offered another kind of self-defense within the integrated markets by the flow of capital to less developed countries—and thus countries where labor was cheap— and by community assistance for backward regions. "Social protection" was provided by welfare institutions, and, after World War II, by "Social Europe." After the war, Germans called it the "social market" system, and then it was internationally called the "welfare state," with a whole set of institutions to counterbalance the negative effects of the market on society.

43 Willem Molle, op. cit., 2006, 123.

44 Supply-side economics suffered a devastating defeat during the Great Depression of the 1930s that led to the triumph of the Keynesian crisis management theory. According to John Maynard Keynes, to cope with the crisis, the state has to create additional demand through public works and other forms of job- and demand-creating intervention, financed by controlled, low inflationary policy. The situation of the 1930s and 1940s dramatically manifested the imperfection of markets and cried out for outside intervention, regulations, and the correction of failed markets. Keynesian economics became dominant for about four decades and served for as a guideline for the Bretton Woods Agreement at the end of the war.

45 Karl Polanyi, op. cit., 1964.

46 I discuss these changes in my 2010 book, which is the basis of the following paragraphs: Ivan T. Berend, *Europe Since 1980*, Cambridge: Cambridge University Press, 2010, 98–103.

47 Terence Ball and Richard Bellamy (eds), *The Cambridge History of Twentieth-Century Political Thought*, Cambridge: Cambridge University Press, 2003, 365.

48 Norberto Bobbio, *Left and Right: the Significance of a Political Distinction*, Chicago: University of Chicago Press, 1996, 7.

49 The first, in 1973, was the consequence of the Arab-Israeli Yom Kippur War, followed by the oil producer countries' boycott of the West, which backed Israel.

In 1979, the Iranian religious revolution generated another dramatic rise in oil and other prices.

50 Naomi Klein, *The Shock Doctrine: The Rise of Disaster Capitalism*, New York: Henry Holt, 2007.
51 Naomi Klein quotes Milton Friedman's article after Hurricane Katrina hit New Orleans and only four public schools remained in operation out of 123. In an OpEd article in *The Wall Street Journal* the 93-year-old economist stated: "Most New Orleans schools are in ruin. . . . This is a tragedy. It also an opportunity to radically reform the educational system." Friedman suggested giving vouchers to the families, which they could use in private schools instead of rebuilding the public school system. It is important, he added, that this change became a "permanent reform." Naomi Klein, op. cit., 2007, 4–5.
52 Milton Friedman, *The Program for Monetary Stability*, New York: Fordham University Press, 1959; *Inflation: Causes and Consequences,* New York: Asia Publishing House, 1963; *The Optimum Quantity of Money and Other Essays*, Chicago: Aldine Publishing Co., 1969; *The Tax Limitation, Inflation and the Role of Governments*, Dallas: Fisher Institute, 1978.
53 Alfred Sherman's article in *The Guardian*, February 11, 1985, quoted by Ruth Levitas, *The Ideology of the New Right*, Cambridge: Polity Press, 1986, 15.
54 Francis Fukuyama, "End of History," *The National Interest*, August 27, 1989.
55 Panagiatos Thomopoulos,, "Banking Regulation in Europe: A Brief Overview of Current Development," Athens, May 4, 2006 (www.bis.org/review/r06062f.pdf).
56 Franco Fiordelisi, David Marques-Ibanez and Phil Molyneux, "Efficiency and Risk in European Banking," European Central Bank, Working Paper Series, No. 1211/June 2010 (www.ecb.int/pub/pdf/scpwps/ecbwps1211.pdf).
57 Joseph Stiglitz, op. cit., 2003, 13.
58 "Subprime mortgage" means to provide a mortgage for people with a bad credit history, low income, late payments or bankruptcy. They do not qualify for loans with lower interest rates, thus the banks, because of the risk, offer loans for higher, and mostly adjustable, rates.
59 Willem Molle, op. cit., 2006, 123.
60 Franco Fiordelisi, David Marques-Ibanez and Phil Molyneux, op. cit., 2010, 5.
61 John J. Kirton's "Conclusion and Recommendation," in Paolo Savona, John J. Kirton, and Chiara Oldani (eds), op. cit., 2011, 295.
62 Joseph Stiglitz, op. cit., 2003, 13.
63 Larry Neal, "Lessons from History for the Twenty-First Century," in Jeremy Atack and Larry Neal (eds), op. cit., 2009, 450.
64 Panagiatos Thomopoulos, op. cit., 2006.
65 Paul Krugman, "How did Economists get it so wrong?" *The New York Times*, September 2, 2009, 123.
66 George Soros, *Alchemy of Finance*, New York: Simon & Schuster, 1988, 142.
67 Larry Neal, op. cit., in Jeremy Atack and Larry Neal (eds), op. cit., 2009, 455.
68 "Basel II rules . . . were in fact responsible for the European credit crunch and recession" Paolo Savona and Chiara Oldani, op. cit., in Paolo Savona, John J. Kirton and Chiara Oldani (eds), op. cit., 2011, 56.
69 George Soros, *The New Paradigm for Financial Markets: The Credit Crisis of 2008 and What it Means*, New York, Public Affairs, 2008, 117.
70 *Fortune Magazine*, July 25, 1994.

71 Paul De Grauwe, "What Kind of Governance for the Eurozone?" in Wim Meeussen (ed.), *The Economic Crisis and European Integration*, Cheltenham: Edward Elgar, 2011, 13, 16.

72 Joseph Stiglitz, "Listen to the IMF, America," May 5, 2011 (www.slate.com/ articles/business/.../listen_to_the_imf_america.html).

73 Jürgen Stark, speech at the meeting of Finance Ministers and Governors of the G-20 countries in Sao Paulo, November 9, 2009 (www.ecb.int>press>speeches and interviews>bydate>2011).

74 Franco Fiordelisi, David Marques-Ibanez and Phil Molyneux, op. cit., 2010, 5.

75 "[The] American economy . . . [became] more prone to assets bubbles, corporate scandals and financial crisis" (Steven Pearlstein, *Washington Post*, January 20, 2006). As the Executive Council of the American AFL-CIO declared in a statement on March 5, 2008 on the American situation, but with validity for Europe as well: "[The] crisis in the credit markets is the direct consequence of a 30-year experiment of trying to create a deregulated, low wage economy where high consumer spending is propped up by easy credit and asset bubble." AFL-CIO Executive Council Statement, March 5, 2008 (www.aflcio.org/aboutus/ thisistheaflcio/ecouncil/ec03052008a.cfm).

76 John Eatwell, op. cit., in Joseph R. Bisignano, William C. Hunter and George G. Kaufman (eds), op. cit., 2000, 374.

77 Joseph R. Bisignano, William C. Hunter, and George G. Kaufman (eds), op. cit., 2000, xi, 4.

78 Jürgen Stark speech at the Frankfurt conference of the Transatlantic Business conference on November 9, 2011 (www.ecb.int>Press>speeches and interviews> By date>2011).

79 Jean-Louis Arcand, Enrico Berkes and Ugo Panizza, "Has Finance Gone too Far?" (www.voxeu.org/index.php?q=node/6328).

80 Douglas Dawd, *Inequality and the Global Economic Crisis*, London: Pluto Press, 2009, 119.

81 Joseph Schumpeter, op. cit., 1939, 116–117.

82 John Maynard Keynes, *The General Theory of Employment, Interest and Money*, Cambridge: Macmillan Cambridge University Press, 1936, 159.

83 R.G. King and R. Levine, "Finance and Growth: Schumpeter might be Right," *The Quarterly Journal of Economics*, Vol. 108, No.3, 1993.

84 (www.dw-world.de/dn/article/0113669958,00.html).

85 *The Guardian*, October 4, 2008.

86 This name has been used in the United States since 1920 when Charles Ponzi's fraudulent investment fund collapsed and became infamous throughout the country.

87 The openly admitted end goal of integration from its very first step was a federal Europe. This was explicitly phrased in the French Minister of Foreign Affairs, Robert Schuman's plan for the foundation of the unified coal and steel industries. In his "declaration" of May 9, 1950, he stated: "this proposal will lead to the realization of the first concrete foundation of a European federation . . ." Behind the "Schuman Plan," its initiator, Jean Monnet, often called "the father of Europe," founded the influential Action Committee for a United States of Europe to pressurize governments into accepting the integration plan. Based on his initiative, the Preamble of the Treaty of Rome on the European Economic Community also confirmed that the signing countries are "determined to lay

down the foundation of an *ever closer union* among the people of Europe." The planners and founding fathers of integration, however, realized that the unification of independent states separated in Europe for a millennium, cannot happen all at once. The smoothest and surest way, they thought, would be a gradual economic integration. Jean Monnet clearly expressed the goal behind gradual economic integration by saying: "One had to go beyond the nation and the conception of national interest as an end of itself. . . . By a constant process of collective adaptation to new conditions, a chain reaction, a ferment [generate a course of action], where one change induces another" (J. Monnet, "A Ferment of Change," in Brent F. Nelsen and Alexander C-G. Stubb (eds), *The European Union*, Boulder: Lynne Rienner, 1998, 21). He added with absolute clarity: "Countries of continental Europe . . . are now uniting in a Common Market which is laying the foundation for political union" (ibid., 24).

88 Jacques Delors, "Address by Mr. Jacques Delors, Bruges, 17 October 1989," in Brent F. Nelsen and Alexander C-G.Stubb (eds), op. cit., 1998, 58–59, 62.

89 This attempt had a long history. The Hague Summit of the Community already announced the goal in 1969, and the Werner Report prepared the plan the next year.

90 Jacques Delors, op. cit., in Brent F. Nelsen and Alexander C-G. Stubb (eds), op. cit., 1998, 59.

91 Andorra, San Marino, Vatican City, Monaco, Montenegro, and Kosovo.

92 Britain was always a hesitant member of the Union. British self-identification is not fully European. She is still haunted by the memory of the island country's "splendid isolation" on the one hand, and the memory of the former empire and the British pound as a world reserve currency on the other. Besides, the presence of the past in their way of thinking, the very pragmatic present interest of the "City," the world famous and powerful financial center of London (and the world), as well as the Commonwealth economic network, also kept Britain on the sidelines of European integration.

Sweden and Denmark—old economic clients of Britain—also form a close and somewhat independent unit within Europe with their early and strong welfare priorities and highest environmental norms. The Scandinavian economy is traditionally solid and high performing. They had a very low inflation rate and budget deficit, and their public debts are far below the European requirements. Sweden also argued that the common currency in countries with rather different economic levels might cause major troubles.

The population of these countries voted down joining the common currency at the 2000 and 2003 referenda. Although the Maastricht Treaty made the common currency compulsory for European Union member countries, a small door remained open in the form of the Edinburgh Agreement of 1992 to opt out and remain monetarily independent.

93 Angus Maddison, *Monitoring the World Economy*, Paris: OECD, 1995. Only Italy was at a somewhat lower level of more than $5,000, thus by 17–29% behind, but in the 1950s and '60s, Italy's growth rate was one of the highest, at an average 5% per year, which promised a rapid catching-up.

94 Five rich new member countries, Britain, Denmark (both accepted in 1973), Sweden, Finland, and Austria (all accepted in 1995) were on the level of the core of the European Union.

95 Angus Maddison, op. cit., 1995, 249.

96 Two main motivations initiated the close integration. First was the lessons of two consecutive world wars that killed 50 to 60 million Europeans, decimated several countries and, in huge parts of the continent, destroyed half of the wealth accumulated by generations. Equal with this factor was the emerging Cold War, the deadly division and confrontation of the Eastern and Western halves of the continent and of the world system. A strong and united Western Europe became a must in this situation.

97 That was behind Winston Churchill's famous Zürich speech in 1946, when he suggested the foundation of a United States of Europe. Two years later the American statesman Allen Dulles repeated this idea in his book on the Marshall Plan explaining that this would be the best defense against communism.

98 This became manifest when Bulgaria stopped fighting against corruption—a requirement for joining—immediately after her acceptance.

99 The impact on the end goal of the integration process, the federalization of Europe, was even more devastating. Britain, a half-hearted Europeanist and hard-nose opponent of political integration from the beginning, always advocated further enlargement as a kind of guarantee against federal unification.

100 Buying on the secondary markets means to buy bonds from private bond owners, banks, and others if they sell their bonds.

101 Willem Molle, *The Economics of European Integration: Theory, Practice, Policy*, Aldershot: Ashgate, 5th edition, 2006, 279.

102 The penalty was first only a deposit, but if the deficit was not reduced in two years, it became a fine.

103 "Staring into the Abyss," *The Economist*, July 10, 2010; See also, Anders Åslund, *The Last Shall be First: The East European Financial Crisis*, Washington, D.C.: The Peterson Institute for International Economics, 2010, 92.

104 In Switzerland and Norway, although the governments applied for membership, national referenda voted down joining.

105 Paul Krugman, "Boring Cruel Romanics," *The New York Times*, November 21, 2011.

106 The vision of a federal, deeply integrated Europe was not unrealistic. Indeed, modern history had already produced similar developments on a smaller scale: the unification of the once 300 and then, after 1815, 39 independent German states started with the formation of the Zollverein, a customs union in 1834 that paved the way for political unification in 1871. John Pinder argued that "smaller member states harbor few illusions about the reality of national independence," and trade and capital market dependence made the nation-state somewhat obsolete. Some argued that if India "is seen as a nation" with its hundreds of languages and various cultures and religions, Europe "may well be described as an emergent nation." Pinder speaks about a "federalizing process" toward a "federal end." (John Pinder, "European Community and Nation-State: A Case for a Neo-Federalism?" in Brent F. Nelsen and Alexander C-G. Stubb (eds), op. cit., 1998, 190. Historians agree with Friedrich Meinecke, the German historian of the turn of the twentieth century, whose famous work concluded that the central factor of nation building is strong *Selbsbestimmung*, or self-determination: "A nation is a community that wishes to be a nation." (Friedrich Meinecke, *Weltbürgertum und Nationalstaat: Studien zur Genesis des deutschen Nationalstaates*, Munich: R. Oldenbourg, 1908, 9.) In the case of Europe, the wish is to form a federal state.

107 Wayne Sandholtz and John Zysman, "1992: Recasting the European Bargain," in Brent F. Nelsen and Alexander C-G. Stubb (eds), op. cit., 1998, 199.
108 Paul Krugman, "Boring Cruel Romantics," op. cit., 2011.
109 "Merkel Urges More Unified Continent to Save Euro," *The New York Times*, November 14, 2011.

4 The social causes: living beyond our means

1 N. McKendrick, J. Brewer, and J.H. Plumb, *The Birth of a Consumer Society: Commercialization of Eighteenth Century England*, London: Harper Collins, 1984; Jan de Vries, *The Industrious Revolution: Consumer Behavior and the Household Economy, 1650 to the Present*, Cambridge: Cambridge University Press, 2008.
2 Thorstein Veblen, *The Theory of Leisure Class: An Economic Study of Institutions*, London: Unwin [1899] 1970.
3 Georg Simmel, "Fashion." *International Quarterly*, Vol. 10, 1904, 130–150.
4 Ivan T. Berend, *An Economic History of Twentieth-Century Europe: Economic Regimes from Laissez-Faire to Globalization*, Cambridge: Cambridge University Press, 2006, 1.
5 Jan Owen Jansson, "Goods and Service Consumption in the Affluent Welfare State—Issues for the Future," in Karin M. Ekström and Kay Glans (eds), *Beyond the Consumption Bubble*, New York: Routledge, 2011, 54.
6 Gilles Lipovetsky, "The Hyperconsumption Society," in Karin M. Ekström and Ky Glans (eds), *Beyond the Consumption Bubble*, New York: Routledge, 2011, 25.
7 A.H. Maslow, "A Theory of Human Motivation," *Psychological Review*, Vol. 50, No.4, 1943, 370–396.
8 Daniel Bell, *The Coming of Post-Industrial Society: A Venture in Social Forecasting*, New York: Basic Books, 1974.
9 Gilles Lipovetsky, op. cit., in Karin M. Ekström and Kay Glans (eds), op. cit., 2011, 25.
10 Norman Myers and Jennifer Kent, *The New Consumers: The Influence of Affluence on the Environment*, Washington, D.C.: Island Press, 2004, 3, 122–123, 143.
11 Geoffrey Miller, *Spent: Sex, Evolution, and Consumer Behavior*, New York: Viking, 2009, 140.
12 Grigory Yavlinsky, *Realeconomik: The Hidden Cause of the Great Recession (and How to Avert the Next One)*, New Haven: Yale University Press, 2011, 61–62.
13 Ralf Dahrendorf, "After the Crisis: Back to the Protestant Ethic?" *Merkur*, No. 720, May 2009, 5.
14 Ibid., 63.
15 Grigory Yavlinsky, op. cit., 2004, 46, 73–74.
16 Brendan Sheehan, *The Economics of Abundance: Affluent Consumption and the Global Economy*, Cheltenham: Edward Elgar, 2010, 8–9, 46, 104; see also Stuart and Elisabeth Ewen, *Channels of Desire: Mass Images and the Shopping of American Conciseness*, New York: McGraw-Hill, 1982; Martin Kornberger, *Brand Society*, Cambridge: Cambridge University Press, 2010.
17 Thomas Princen, Michael Maniates and Ken Conca (eds), *Confronting Consumption*, Cambridge, Mass.: MIT Press, 2002, 1.
18 Ronald Sider, *Christians in an Age of Hunger: Moving from Affluence to Generosity*, Dallas: World Publishing, 1997, quoted by Michael Maniates, "In Search of

Consumptive Resistance: The Voluntary Simplicity Movement," in Thomas Princen, Michael Maniates and Ken Conca (eds), *Confronting Consumption,* Cambridge, Mass.: MIT Press, 2002, 208.

19 Ibid., 2002, 200.

20 Gilles Lipovetsky, op. cit., in Karin M. Ekström and Kay Glans (eds), op. cit., 2011, 35.

21 By 2005, the Mediterranean countries, which enjoyed only 70% of the core countries' life expectancy at the beginning of the twentieth century, had nearly reached Western levels: Spain, Portugal, Italy, and Greece reached an average of 79.5 years, and Central and Eastern Europe reached 74.1 years, more than 90% of the West's levels by 2005. Only Russia and several successor states of the Soviet Union still had an average life expectancy of only 66.9 years, less than 83% of the Western level.

22 After a drastic downward trend, Central and Eastern Europe and Russia reached the same level as in the West: 9.6 births per 1,000.

23 For men and women, compared to the postwar decade, the average age of marriage had increased by 1–1.2 years to 29.5 and 26.5 in the European Union countries, respectively.

24 This is a drastic decline compared to 1910, when there were 15 to 16 marriages per every 1,000 people in the West and 18 to 20 marriages in the East.

25 *Demographic Yearbook,* New York: United Nations, 1982.

26 However, some *minority populations* experienced different demographic patterns. Their mortality and fertility rates reflect an earlier, or non-European, demographic trend. Mortality rates remained high, especially infant mortality, life expectancy at birth remained low, and the fertility rate also remained at traditional levels, often 4 or 6 children per woman.

27 United Nations Economic Commission for Europe, *Aging Populations: Opportunities and Challenges for Europe and North America,* New York: United Nations, 2003; Livi Bacci, *Population and Nutrition: An Essay on European Demographic History,* New York: Cambridge University Press, 1991, 171; *The Economist Pocket World in Figures,* 2008 Edition, London: Profile Books, 242; Anthony Warnes, "Demographic Aging: Trends and Policy Responses," in Daniel Noin and Robert Woods (eds), *The Changing Population of Europe,* Oxford: Blackwell, 1993, 84–86.

28 At the end of the twentieth century, the top managerial and professional layer comprised 5%–27% of Western Europe's population, with quite large country-by-country differences. The middle-level non-manual labor population represented 20% to 25%, and the manual labor population totaled 30% to 43%, of the inhabitants of Europe (Colin Crouch, *Social Change in Western Europe,* Oxford: Oxford University Press, 1999, 138–139).

29 Angus Maddison, *The World Economy: A Millennial Perspective,* Paris: OECD, 2001, 354.

30 In 1990, 3% of the world population consisted of immigrants, and by 2007, 10%. During the first decade of the twenty-first century, migration gained tremendous new speed. Between 2000 and 2005, the number of emigrants increased by 15 million, in 2006, 9.9 million, and in 2007, 11.4 million refugees escaped from famine and/or persecution by crossing borders.

31 *OECD Factbook 2007: Economic, Environmental and Social Statistics,* Paris: OECD, 6–7. The acceleration of immigration is clearly signaled by the fact that in the decade between 1995 and 2005, the foreign-born population increased from

1.7% to 4.6% in Italy, from 6.9% to 11.0% in Ireland and from 6.9% to 9.7% in Britain. Foreign residents play an important role in the labor force, making up about one-quarter of all workers in Switzerland, 15% in Germany and Austria, 13% in Spain and Sweden, and more than 10% in the Netherlands, Ireland, France, and Britain. Moreover, they represent an increasing part of the population at large: 24% in Switzerland and around 10% in most of the West European countries.

32 The Gini index of inequality in the European countries increased from 0.25–0.30 to 0.30–0.37, which reflects a less egalitarian society; in some countries, such as Russia and some of the Baltic republics, the Gini index is above 0.40. The recession in recent years further increased inequalities and eroded welfare institutions. People who were unable to work, single-mother families, the uneducated and unskilled, and the frequently or even permanently unemployed represented about 10% to 15% of the Western societies at the end of the twentieth century. Unemployment has remained high since 1980, when it was a double-digit figure in most of the countries, though it declined to roughly 10% in the European Union-15 countries during the 1990s, and from 1997 to 2005, it gradually decreased to 8%. A part of the unemployed, however, became jobless on a long-term basis: from the early 1990s to 2005, 40% to 50% of unemployed did not work for at least one year. In 2007, 14% of the generally rich Irish society lived below the official poverty level. In spite of the generous state assistance in the Nordic and West European countries, 4% and 8% of the population, respectively, live in relative poverty, earning less than half of the national average. During the decade between the mid-1980s and 1990s, only four out of 11 European countries experienced faster income increase in the bottom decile of the society than the top one. The poorest 10% of full-time workers in Germany earned 60% more at the end of the decade, while the top 10% increased their income only by 22%. In Finland, the equivalent figures were 27% versus 19%. On the other hand, in Britain wage differences increased; the top 10% increased their income by 25%, while the bottom 10% by only 14%. The trend was similar in Italy, Austria, and France (Eurostat, *The Statistical Yearbook of the EU*, epp.eurostat.ec.europa.eu/tgm/table.do?tab=table&plugin=1...). Poor and unemployed people, however, mostly did not drop out from society because of the social safety net of the welfare states. *Der Spiegel* reported overly optimistically in the fall of 2006 that poor people do not lose their homes, that they have food to eat, and that several unemployed watch TV half the day (*Der Spiegel*, October 26, 2006).

33 Antonio Ugalde and Gilberto Cárdena (eds), *Health and Social Services among International Labor Migrants*, Austin, Texas: CMAS Books, 1997, 124, 128.

34 The non-integrated, ghettoized Roma minorities, both legal but especially illegal immigrants, were much less educated, live in slums in run-down inner cities or suburban regions, and a huge number of them do not speak the language of the host country, have a different religion and culture, different type of family life and gender relations, and most of them remain different in clothing and behavior. They are not integrated into the local society at all, and they are surrounded by suspicion and even hatred. The Roma underclass in Europe total between 4 and 12 million. According to certain calculations, half or two-thirds of them, and probably as many as 8 million, live in Central and Eastern Europe. Roma communities represent the largest minority in that region, reaching between 7% and 11% of the population in several countries. In Bulgaria, Romania, and

Hungary, respectively, countries with about 7% to 10% unemployment rates, according to a UNICEF Report of 2005, 84%, 88%, and 91% of the Roma population have been below the absolute poverty level. The situation is quite similar with the North African immigrants in France. They have a much lower chance of getting a job interview, and 40% of them are unemployed. The violent October 2005 riots that erupted in the Paris suburb of Clichy-sous-Bois, and which rapidly spread to 275 cities and led to the introduction of curfews in 31 cities, had nothing to do with Islam. It was a typical *sans culottes* uprising. The problem is strongly connected with a deep cultural divide and even the lack of any attempt to integrate.

35 Zygmunt Bauman, *Intimation of Postmodernity*, London: Routledge, 1992; Conrad Lodziak, *The Myth of Consumerism*. London: Pluto Press, 2002.

36 Jan Owen Jansson, op. cit., in Karin M. Ekström and Kay Glans (eds), op. cit., 2011, 52.

37 Anthony Giddens, *Modernity and Self-Identity: Self and Society in the Late Modern Age*, Cambridge: Polity, 1991, 198.

38 Jan Owen Jansson, op. cit., in Karin M. Ekström and Kay Glans (eds), op. cit., 2011, 54–55, 57.

39 Geoffrey Miller, *Spent: Sex, Evolution, and Consumer Behavior*, New York: Viking, 2009, 71.

40 Mark Davis, "Commercialization," in Dale Southerton (ed.), *Encyclopedia of Consumer Culture*, Los Angeles: Sage, 2011, 211.

41 Ibid., 39, 43.

42 *The Economist Pocket World in Figures*, op. cit., 2008, 77.

43 *Yearbook of Tourism Statistics: Data 2004–2008*, 2010 edition, Madrid: World Tourism Organizations, 2010.

44 European Commission, Enterprise and Industry (ec.europa.eu/enterprise/ sectors/tourism/index_eu.htm).

45 *The Sunday Times*, April 18, 2010.

46 Chris Paris, "Multiple 'Homes,' Dwellings and Hyper Mobility and Emergent Transnational Second Home Ownership," Workshop 24. Ljubljana: Urban Planning Institute, International Conference, July 25, 2006.

47 John Doling and Marja Elsinga (eds), *Homeownership: Getting in, Getting from, Getting out*, Part II, Amsterdam: Delft University Press, 2006, 35.

48 European Bank for Reconstruction and Development, *Transition Report 2009: Transition in Crisis?*, London, EBRD, 2009, 45.

49 Ibid.

50 Dalton Conley and Brian Gifford, "Home Ownership, Social Insurance, and the Welfare State," *Sociological Forum*, Vol. 21, No.1, March 2006, 56.

51 The 6th Annual Demographia International Housing Affordability Survey, 2010 (www.demographia.com/dhi-ix200593.pdf).

52 Bill Edgar and his co-authors drew a wrong conclusion about this fact stating that home ownership and the level of per capita GDP are not connected, and Romania, Bulgaria, Hungary, and Lithuania have a higher share of privately owned homes than in the European Union-15 rich countries (Bill Edgar, Maša Filipović and Iskra Dandolova, "Home Ownership and Marginalization," (eohw. horus.be/.../European%20Journal%20of%20Homelessness/.../E...).

53 Tim Dant, "Car Cultures," in Dale Southerton, op. cit., 2011, 133.

54 Brendan Sheehan, op. cit., 2010, 20.

55 Eurostat Press Office, Luxembourg (eurostat-pressoffice.ec.europa.eu).

56 Steven Miles, *Spaces for Consumption: Pleasure and Placelessness in the Post-Industrial City*, London: Sage, 2010, 113.
57 Eric Hobsbawm, *The Age of Extremes—The Short Twentieth Century, 1914–1991*, London: Abacus, 1995, 264.
58 European Shopping Centre Trust, *The Importance of Shopping Centers to the European Economy*, March 2008, (www.icsc.org/.../FINAL_Mar08); Cushman and Wakefield, September 2009 (www.cushwake.com/cwglobal/jsp/news Detail.jsp?repld...)
59 Steven Miles, op. cit., 2010, 98, 108, 110.
60 Germany: Consumer Goods and Retail Report, February 2009 (http://search.ebscohost.com/login.apx?direct=true&db=bth&AN=43516960&site=ehost-live).
61 Cirán Coyle, Angra Andal-Ancion and Louise French, "Reacting to Consumer Trends, Reacting to New Markets, and Mitigating Risk in a Tough Economic Environment," *Licensing Journal*, Vol. 30, No. 1, 2010, (1–7), 3.
62 Steven Miles, op. cit., 2010, 113.
63 Marilyn Bordwell, "Jamming Culture: Adbusters' Hip Media Campaign Against Consumerism," in Thomas Princen, Michael Maniates and Ken Conca (eds), *Confronting Consumption*, Cambridge, Mass.: MIT Press, 2002, 238–239.
64 Brendan Sheehan, op. cit., 2010, 152–154, 199–200.
65 Becky Carroll, *The Hidden Power of Your Consumers*, Hoboken, NJ: John Wiley, 2011.
66 "Special Report: Personal Technology," *The Economist*, October 8, 2011, 3–6, 10.
67 Adrian J. Slywotzky with Karl Weber, *Demand: Creating What People Love Before They Know They Want It*, New York: Crown Business, 2011, 328.
68 (populationenvironmentresearch.org/.../Lotze-Campen_Reusswig_Pap).
69 Richard Vehrenkamp, *The Logistic Revolution: The Rise of Logistics in the Mass Consumption Society*, EUL Verlag, 2012, 6, 7.
70 Global Finance (www.gfmag.com>Archives>September 2010).
71 In 2002, 61% of US credit card users carried a monthly balance, averaging $12,000 at 16% interest, with $1,900 financial charges a year, more than the average per capita income of 35 developing countries.
72 Hui-Yi Loan and Nigel Harvey, "Shopping Without Pain: Compulsive Buying and the Effect of Credit Card Availability in Europe and the Far East," *Journal of Economic Psychology*, Vol. 32, No. 1, 2011, (79–92).
73 (www.usatoday.com/money/world/2005-12-21-uk-credit-usat_x.htm).
74 Eurostat (epp.eurostat.ec.europa.eu/.../Household_financial_assets_and_liablities).
75 European Commission, Directorate-General for Internal Policies, *Household Indebtedness in the European Union*, Luxembourg: The Office of Official Publications of the European Community, April, 2010, 2–3.
76 (www.usatoday.com/money/world/2005-12-21-uk-credit-usat_x.htm).
77 *The Independent*, December 18, 2011.
78 European Bank for Reconstruction and Development, op. cit., 2009, 22.
79 European Commission, Directorate-General for Internal Policies, op. cit., 2010, 4–5.
80 Matthias Person, "Household Indebtedness in Sweden and Implications for Financial Stability—The Use of Household-Level Data," (www.org/publ/bppdf/bispap46n.pdf).
81 Worldwatch Institute, "The State of Consumption Today," December 6, 2011, (www.worldwatch.org/node/810).
82 Jacqueline Botterill, "Credit," in Dale Southerton (ed.), op. cit., 2011, 380.

83 Gary B. Gorton, *Slapped by the Invisible Hand*, Oxford: Oxford University Press, 2010.

84 As presented in Chapter 1, Iceland represents an exception. A huge part of the household debts was forgiven and a great number of bank executives were indicted.

85 Michel Camdessus, Managing Director of IMF, speech in Paris, October 18, 1998 (www.imf.org/external/np/speeches/1998/012198.htm).

86 European Commission, "European Social Policy: A Way Forward for the Union," A White Paper, Luxembourg: European Commission, 1994, 12.

87 Ibid.

88 OECD, *The Welfare State in Crisis: An Account of the Conference on Social Policies in the 1980s*, Paris: OECD, 1981.

89 Camdessus, Paris speech, 1988 (www.imf.org/external/np/speeches/1998/012 198.htm).

90 IMF, Social Security Expenditure Database, Washington, D.C.: IMF, 2009.

91 Ivan T. Berend, *Europe Since 1980*, Cambridge: Cambridge University Press, 2010, 257–274, 277–285.

92 Matthew Yglesias, "Europe and the Crisis of the Welfare State," December 8, 2011 (www.state.com/.../europe_and_the_crisis_of_the_welfare_state. html).

93 The most infamous situation characterizes the Third World countries in Africa, and Latin America. Namibia is leading the group with its 0.74, followed by Lesoto with 0.63, while Brazil, Chile, and Guatemala are in the range of 0.55–0.58.

94 "At Davos, A Big Issue Is the Have-Lots vs. the Have-Nots," *The New York Times*, January 25, 2012.

95 Ibid.

5 Which way Europe? Managing the economic crisis and the way out

1 István P. Székely, Werner Roeger, and Jan In't Weld, "Fiscal Policy in the EU in the Crisis: A Model-Based Approach with Applications to New EU Member States," in *Society and Economy in Central and Eastern Europe*, Vol. 33, No. 3, December 2011, 599.

2 The European Central Bank also bought €55 billion in Greek bonds to assist Greek survival, but the Bank does not want to lose on the bonds. This problem needs a special arrangement.

3 "Europe Agrees on New Bailout to help Greece Avoid Default," *The New York Times*, February 22, 2012.

4 "European Banks: Hose and Dry," *The Economist*, December 31, 2011. Although the amounts were substantial, the financial market lost trust in government bonds and started calculating to write off a part of their bond assets as it became unavoidable in the case of Greece. Consequently, the banks did not spend all of the cheap Central Bank loans on buying government bonds, but put a part of the loans on deposit at the European Central Bank. European bank deposits at the Central Bank increased from $425 billion to $617 billion in one single month ("Europe's Vicious Cycle of Debt," *The New York Times*, January 12, 2012; "The

European Central Bank is Unlikely Hero in Crisis," *The New York Times*, January 21, 2012).

5   (gulfnews.com/.../Italian-spanish-bonds-gain-as-interest-rates-fall-1.97...); "The European Central Bank is Unlikely Hero in Crisis," *The New York Times*, January 21, 2012.

6   Raymond J. Ahearn, James K. Jackson, Rebecca M. Nelson and Martin A. Weiss, "The Future of the Eurozone and U.S. Interests," in Hannah J. Farkas and Daniel C. Murphy (eds), *The Eurozone: Testing the Monetary Union*, New York: Nova Science Publishers, 2011, 15–18.

7   *The New York Times*, February 3, 2012.

8   "Europe Rescue Plan," and "No Big Bazooka," *The Economist*, October 29, 2011; Statement of the European Council Meeting, December 8–9, 2011 (www.european-council.europa.eu/council-meetings).

9   "Ireland Said to Face Downturn in 2nd Year of Austerity," *The New York Times*, January 20, 2012.

10 "Austerity in Spain: Happy New Year," *The Economist*, January 7, 2012.

11 "EU Interim Forecast: on the Brink of a Mild Recession," (ec.europa.eu/cvm/progress_reports_eu.htm).

12 This index uses seven indicators (household assets, output and consumption level, real wages and unemployment rate, etc.) to measure the lost years ("Lost Economic Time: The Proust Index," *The Economist*, February 25, 2012).

13 "How to Save the Euro," *The Economist*, September 17, 2011.

14 "Making It Worse in Europe," *The New York Times*, February 1, 2012.

15 "In Europe, Arguing to Apply Some Stimulus Along with the Austerity," *The New York Times*, January 23, 2012.

16 Paul Krugman, "Eurotrashed," *The New York Times Magazine*, January 16, 2011, 44.

17 Paul Krugman, "Pain Without Gain," *The New York Times*, February 20, 2012.

18 Amartya Sen, "The Crisis of European Democracy," *The New York Times*, May 22, 2012.

19 "In Europe, Arguing to Apply Some Stimulus Along With the Austerity," *The New York Times*, January 23, 2012.

20 "Europe Forecasts 'Mild Recession' for Euro Zone in 2012," *The New York Times*, February 23, 2012.

21 "European Leaders Address Effect of Austerity as Jobless Rate Swells," *The New York Times*, March 2, 2012.

22 Britain has a 60–80% market share in financial services—but the EU makes the rules, argued Anthony Brown at "The Columnist Conservative Home" (conservativehome.blogs.com/.../Anthony-brown-if-we-don't-set-the-...).

23 Michel Barnier, "Financial Regulation—A Review of 2011 and a Forward Look to 2012," City of London Event at the Guildhall London, 23rd January, 2012 (ec.europa.eu/commission_2010-2014/barnier/index.eu.htm). Michel Barnier is a member of the European Commission, responsible for Internal Markets and Services.

24 (www.sec.gov/about/laws/wallstreetreform-cpa.pdf).

25 Paul Volcker, former Chairman of the US Federal Reserve, was appointed by President Obama to chair the Economic Recovery Advisory Board in February 2009.

26 *Wall Street Journal*, February 22, 2010.

27 "Financial Regulatory Reform," *The New York Times*, January 26, 2012.

28 Its members are: the EU, Britain, France, Germany, Italy, Russia, United States, Australia, Canada, Turkey, Saudi Arabia, Indonesia, India, Brazil, Argentina, Japan, China, South Korea, Mexico, and South Africa.

29 Reuters, "Global Financial Regulation Overhaul Seen in 2010," January 6, 2010 (www.reuters.com/.../us-financial-regulation-idUSTRE6050NO20100...); J.C. Boggs, Melissa Foxman and Kathleen Nahill, "Dodd-Frank At One Year: Growing Pain," *Harvard Business Law Review*, July 28, 2011.

30 "The European Union Financial Regulation and Supervision Beyond 2005: An Agenda (www.ceps.eu/.../eu-financial-regulation-and-supervision-beyond-200...).

31 "Financial Regulatory Reform and the Economy," speech by Vitor Constâncio, Vice-President of the European Central Bank, New York, April 15, 2011.

32 Beverly Hirtle, Til Schuermann and Kevin Stiroh, "Macroprudential Supervision of Financial Institutions: Lessons from SCAP," Federal Reserve of New York, November, 2009, (newyorkfed.org/research/staff-reports/sr409.html).

33 James Tobin, *The New Economics One Decade Older*, Eliot Janeway Lectures, 1972, Princeton: Princeton University Press, 1974.

34 Zsolt Darvas and Jakob von Wezsäcker, "Financial Transaction Tax: Small is Beautiful," *Society and Economy in Central and Eastern Europe*, Vol. 33, No. 3, December, 2011, 450–451, 456–457; "German Official Backs Tax Vetoed by Britain," *The New York Times*, December 13, 2011.

35 Sean Tuffy, "Harmonizing EU Financial Regulation," May 1, 2011 (www.ftsglobalmarkets.com/ index.php?...eu-financial-regulation).

36 Ibid.; Michel Barnier, op. cit., 2012.

37 EFSF Framework Agreement, June 7, 2010 (http://www.efsf.europa.eu/ attachment/efsf_framework_agreement_en.pdf); (ec.europa.eu/ economy_finance/ eu_borrower/efsm/index_eu.htm).

38 Germany suggested, but later dropped, the idea that the European Court of Justice would initiate a case against a country that violates the rules.

39 Norbert Walter, "Germany's Hidden Weaknesses," *The New York Times*, February 9, 2012.

40 "A Comedy of Euros," *The Economist*, December 17, 2011.

41 "A Badge of Honor Tarnished," *The New York Times*, January 14, 2012.

42 "Europe's Vicious Cycle of Debt," *The New York Times*, January 12, 2012.

43 Michel Barnier, op. cit., 2012.

44 "Euro Crisis Hits Germany and U.S. in Tactical Fight," *The New York Times*, December 10, 2011.

45 "Game, Set and Mismatch," *The Economist*, December 17, 2011.

46 Jürgen Habermas, "What Europe Needs Now," (www.signandsight.com/ features/1265.html); Ivan T. Berend, *Europe Since 1980*, Cambridge: Cambridge University Press, 2010, 74.

47 "Italy's Monti Warns Debt Crisis Risks Rise of Anti-EU Populists," *Daily Telegraph*, January 16, 2012.

48 Paul Krugman, "Depression and Democracy," *The New York Times*, December 11, 2011.

49 George Soros, "How to Save the Euro," speech at the opening session of the World Economic Forum in Davos, *The New York Review of Books*, (http://www. nybooks.com/articles/archives/2012/feb/23/how-save-euro).

50 "Why Europe is on the Brink," *Sunday Telegraph*, May 15, 2011 (italics in original).

51 Some hedge funds and investment banks, of course, take the high risk and bid against the main currents. For example, when bonds hit bottom, the American Franklin-Templeton Investments bought $2.5 billion in Irish government bonds, and $3.0 billion in Hungarian ones, so as to gain a lot if they recover. Several hedge funds invested heavily in Greek bonds when they were down, believing in a Union bailout and huge profits. Now, they had to lose 70% of their investment.

52 "Survey of Banks Shows a Sharp Cut in Lending in Europe," *The New York Times*, February 2, 2012.

53 "Inching Towards Integration," *The Economist*, July 7, 2012.

54 "Germany is Open to Pooling Debt, with Conditions," *The New York Times*, June 4, 2012.

55 See for example Joseph Stiglitz, *Globalization and its Discontents*, New York: W.W. Norton, 2003.

56 Larry Neal, "Lessons from History for the Twenty-first century," in Larry Neal and Jeremy Atack (eds), *The Original Development of Financial Markets and Institutions: From the Seventeenth Century to the Present*, Cambridge: Cambridge University Press, 2009, 451, 462.

57 "Charlemagne," *The Economist*, June 30, 2012.

58 Hans-Werner Sinn, "Why Berlin is Balking on a Bailout," *The New York Times*, June 13, 2012.

59 In G.W.F. Hegel, *The Philosophy of History*, Kitchener, Ontario: Batoche Books, 2001.

INDEX